Hermann Sasse

Witness

Sermons Preached in Erlangen
and Congregational Lectures

Translated by Bror Erickson

Foreword by Matthew Harrison
Introductory Essay by John T. Pless

Then I saw another angel flying directly overhead, with an eternal gospel to proclaim to those who dwell on earth, to every nation and tribe and language and people. And he said with a loud voice, "Fear God and give him glory, because the hour of his judgment has come, and worship him who made heaven and earth, the sea and the springs of water."
The Revelation of St. John 14:6–7

Published by Magdeburg Press
8765 Ederer Road
Saginaw, MI 48609
www.magdeburgpress.com

Copyright © 2013, Bror Erickson

ISBN 978-0-9821586-5-4

This work has been translated and published with the expressed written consent of Martin-Luther-Bund. The original work is: Sasse, Hermann, *Zugnisse: Erlanger Predigten und Vorträge vor Gemeinden, 1933-1944.* Edited by Friedrich Wilhelm Hopf. Erlangen: Martin-Luther-Bund, 1979.

Table of Contents

Foreword by Matthew C. Harrison

John Kleinig tells a story of Sasse at an Australian pastors' conference. A well-meaning brother stood to urge more preaching "about the Gospel." Sasse shuffled to the microphone to respond. "In all my years as a preacher I have NEVER preached ABOUT the Gospel. I have only PREACHED the Gospel!" That fact is demonstrated in spades in this volume offered to us by Bror Erickson. Preachers and professional sermon hearers will do well to study its contents very carefully. After decades of reading and translating Sasse, I find myself evermore drawn to his work during the period of *Kirchenkampf* under Hitler. Here we find Sasse at his best. The New Testament Scriptures provide the impetus, the basis, the trajectory of each sermon. The white-hot cultural context of Nazism demands a confession, and Sasse provides it, now subtly, now forthrightly criticizing the dominant culture's *Führer*, gods, and demigods. But his sermons are never anything like a mere rant against the world. Not at all. Such *Führer*, gods, and demigods always threaten to become ours. His most penetrating attack is aimed at sin, death, and devil, which in the flesh always in this life retain a hold on the Christian and in the Church. Like Luther in the Invocavit Sermons, for instance, Sasse is not shy about pointing the damning finger of the Law at evey sinner in the pew: "You're the man!" We must learn from Sasse (and Luther whose spirit and words saturate Sasse's every address) what it means to understand our context and to speak the naked power of God's Law to the hearer, to preach the Law now bluntly, now surgically, to break down the crusted defenses of smug self-righteousness, to break down barriers to the Gospel. And these sermons and address are full of the richest consolation in the deepest times of struggle. In Sasse's capable oratory, the diamond which is the Gospel tumbles, the beams of Christ flashing and reflecting now for forgiveness, now for encouragement, now for hope, now for consolation, and finally all for faith solely in the merits of Jesus delivered by the Scriptures, in the Word preached, in Absolution, in Baptism and Supper. The Gospel is for you.

While rummaging through Sasse's *Nachlass* in Adelaide at the Lutheran Church of Australia's archives in 2000, I learned that Sasse's student Hans Siegfried Huss[1] had traveled to Adelaide shortly after Sasse's death in 1976 and retrieved his papers (or at least a significant portion of them). Huss shred some of them with Feuerhahn, but now they rest in a Bavarian archive awaiting scholarly inquiry. But if these sermons were part of that treasure, then we have more than enough for which to thank Huss for sharing them with Hopf, who saw through their publication. The great Lutheran themes, which dominated Sasse's theological thinking and writing until his death, are crystal clear in these sermons. And in our own time in the once

---

[1] Dr. Ron Feuerhahn informed me as I was annotating this book that on one of his three visits to Huss before his death, Huss informed him that he had assisted Sasse with his papers before the latter immigrated to Australia. Sasse saw that many of his documents were destroyed, not wanting issues in Germany to follow him into his new vocation. Huss reported that he tried to preserve certain papers, but Sasse insisted upon their destruction. Did this include sermon manuscripts? MH

Christian West—in many ways, I'm convinced, increasingly similar to the era of the *Kirchenkampf*—these sermons teach us how to confess, how to preach, and, above all, how to believe in Christ and his Church *cruce tectum*.

Matthew C. Harrison
Assistant Pastor, Village Lutheran, Ladue
President, The Lutheran Church—Missouri Synod
Ascension 2013

Translator's Preface

One needs no excuse or reason to translate or read Hermann Sasse, the fact that it is there is reason enough. A class assignment in Homiletics, Dr. Quill told us to go read sermons by others and summarize them. I went to the library and found a copy of Sasse's "Zeugnisse," and I haven't stopped reading them for over ten years. I translated my first sermon that night. They have been the source of much comfort and guidance since then.

A few of the sermons and some of the essays have been translated and published elsewhere by others. The majority of them haven't. I decided I would translate them all and keep them together in one volume, rather than piecemeal them out here and there. They are better together. They are a record of one man's protest against the Third Reich in Germany—the record of one man continuing the Lutheran tradition of speaking truth to power in the face of death that started with Luther himself at the Diet of Worms. No, quietism is not a Lutheran tradition, bold proclamation of Law and Gospel is our tradition. Standing on God's Word, retaining faith in him in the face of danger is our tradition. Sasse was but one Lutheran who maintained that tradition during WWII. Others who don't get nearly as much attention as Bonhoeffer would be Kai Munk of Denmark, Bishop Berggrav of Norway, and Bo Giertz of Sweden. The list would be quite long if we were to include stalwart laity.

As a historical record of a troublesome time, these sermons have immense value. As proclamation of God's

Word with application for the Lutheran Church today, they are even more valuable. Sasse mines the doctrine of the Church, the communion of saints, and brings this article of faith to life for the Church. He applies Law and Gospel as if he were firing a double barrel shotgun, and he shows the Church for what it is: sinners made holy by the work of the Holy Spirit on account of her Lord Jesus Christ, who alone is holy. Sasse reaches through time to use history as a mirror of the Law for us, then also to reflect the Gospel to our own day, to our people, and through it all with a simple trust that this is God's Church. It is his doing, and the gates of hell will not ever prevail against it. Despite all the trouble with which the Church is beset, God uses her to do his will in this world.

I want to thank Donavon Riley for his help in editing the manuscript and Wade Johnston for taking on the publication of this work, which other publishing houses oddly found not worth the time. Professor Pless also deserves thanks for pushing and prodding me to complete this project and get it published. It was an honor to have Rev. President Harrison's hand in helping to both edit and annotate this text. He did in a week what would have added years to this project if I were to attempt it myself. As always, First Lutheran Church of Tooele, Utah, has really made this work possible. It is a joy to be the pastor of such patient and forgiving saints, who don't mind their pastor pursuing such endeavors. And of course, many thanks to Laura, who on more than one occasion has had to wait patiently for me to finish reading through the manuscript and making adjustments and corrections.

Bror Erickson
Tooele, Utah
The Sixth Thursday of Eastertide

Hermann Sasse the Preacher

Whether it was preaching in congregations in and around Berlin in the early years, sermons delivered to the university and townsfolk in Erlangen around the time of World War II, or sturdy proclamation to refugees in Australia during the final years of Sasse's life, Hermann Sasse[2] (1895–1976) knew that theology must serve proclamation. For Sasse, the theological task was anything but a cloistered academic pursuit disconnected from the life of the Church. His preaching, like his theology, was confessional, that is, it engaged in the act of confessing Christ Jesus as Son of God and Savior. Hence, also like his theology, his sermons could be polemical as they unmasked the gods of this age even when they concealed themselves behind the faces of respected theologians and church leaders. That is the way it must be if preaching is the very act by which God kills and makes alive. Sasse's preaching was formed in the crucible of crisis where either unbelief or faith would prevail. His sermons are timeless precisely because they bear the marks of the troubled times in which they were given[3]. The goal of his homiletic is ever the

---

[2] For an overview of Sasse's life and theology, see John T. Pless, "Hermann Sasse," *Lutheran Quarterly* (Autumn 2011), pp. 298–325. Also see *Hermann Sasse: A Man for Our Times?* edited by John Stephenson and Thomas Winger (St. Louis: Concordia Publishing House, 1998) and Lowell C. Green, "Hermann Sasse: The Prophet" in *The Erlangen School of Theology: Its History, Teaching, and Practice* (Fort Wayne: Lutheran Legacy Press, 2010), pp. 289–98.

[3] For a description of preaching during the war years in Germany, see Hughes Oliphant Old, "Europe in Crisis" in *The Reading and Preaching of the Scriptures in the Worship of the Christian Church*, Vol. 6: The Modern Age (Grand Rapids: Eerdmans, 2007), pp. 759–

same: repentance and faith in Christ crucified and raised from the dead.

This brief essay will set key themes in Sasse's theological work in conversation sermons preached in the 1930s–40s, showing how his theology, at once both Lutheran and ecumenical, yielded evangelical proclamation in the face of a crisis that was both national and spiritual.

AC VII as the Foundation for Preaching

The whole of Sasse's theology runs through the assertion of the Augsburg Confession that it is sufficient for the unity of the Church that the Gospel is preached purely and the Sacraments administered according to this divine Word. For Sasse, Article VII of the *Augustana* is more than an ecumenical proposal; it confesses the means of grace that constitute the Church as the assembly of believers. Preaching is essential. It is not any kind of preaching but the pure proclamation of the Gospel of God's justification of the ungodly by faith alone (hence the connection with

---

872. It would be interesting but beyond the scope of this chapter to compare and contrast Sasse's preaching with that of his contemporaries Karl Barth, Dietrich Bonhoeffer, and Helmut Thielicke. Much has been written on their preaching that would also shed light on Sasse's circumstances. Here one might see Clyde Fant, *Bonhoeffer: Worldly Preaching* (Nashville: Thomas Nelson, 1975); Angela Dienhart Hancock, *Karl Barth's Emergency Homiletic 1932–1933: A Summons to Prophetic Witness at the Dawn of the Third Reich* (Grand Rapids: Eerdmans, 2013); Rudolf Hass and Martin Haug, *Helmut Thielicke: Prediger in Unserer Zeit* (Stuttgart: Quell-Verlag, 1968); John T. Pless, "Bonhoeffer the Preacher" in *Concordia Pulpit Resources* (September 17–November 26, 2006), pp. 7–10; and William Willimon, *The Early Preaching of Karl Barth: Fourteen Sermons with Commentary* (Louisville: Westminster John Knox Press, 2009).

AC IV and V). Noting the unhelpfulness of the later dogmatic division between the "invisible Church" and the "visible Church," Sasse writes in a 1961 letter, "Article VII of the Augsburg Confession in the Present Crisis of Lutheranism," that "only when we again grasp the reality of the Word of God and the sacraments will we also grasp the reality of the church as confessed in our Confessions. The church is no Platonic state, but an actuality in the world. It is 'the assembly of all believers among whom the Gospel is preached in its purity and the holy sacraments are administered according to the Gospel' (Article VII, German text). The administration of the means of grace happens in the world. They are extended to people who are quite tangible. As the Lord is active in, with, and under the dealings of men—as He baptizes, absolves, consecrates, gives His true body and His true blood, gives the Holy Spirit, faith, life, blessing—so a holy church is present in, with, and under the assembly of these concrete human beings. For the promise of God bound up with these means and remains valid under all circumstances."[4] Preaching, like the Sacraments, is concrete and tangible; it is executed through the voice of a man. For Sasse there is no dialectic between human and divine words, for the Word of God comes in human speech.[5]

---

[4] Hermann Sasse, "Article VII of the Augsburg Confession in the Present Crisis of Lutheranism" *We Confess the Church*, translated and edited by Norman Nagel (St. Louis: Concordia Publishing House, 1986), p. 51.
[5] Sasse was leery of "theories of inspiration," and a fully worked out treatment of the nature of Sacred Scripture remained elusive. Yet, Sasse

Theologia Crucis as Requirement of the Christian Sermon

Drawing on Luther's *"Unum praedica, sapientiam crucis"* ["There is one thing to preach, the wisdom of the cross"] from a 1515 sermon fragment, Sasse delineates the contours of the *theologia crucis,* noting that this theology does not reduce the Church Year into a perpetual Good Friday but rather insists that the totality of Christian doctrine is seen through the lens of the cross.[6]

The theology of the cross stands in opposition to the prevailing theologies of glory now current in Christendom. Of the theology of the cross, Sasse writes "Only of the preaching of this theology, Luther thinks, can it be said that it is the preaching of the Gospel."[7] The *theologia crucis* is not merely a preaching about the cross. On the contrary, it is the preaching of the cross in such a way that the old

leaves no doubt that the Holy Scriptures are the Word of God. Like their Lord, the Holy Scriptures take on the form of a servant, Sasse observes: "The *written Word's condition of being under the cross* comes to expression by Luther first all in that the Holy Spirit, making using of the service of human means, also puts the weakness of these means into His service"—Sasse, "Luther on the Inerrancy of the Holy Scripture" in *Letters to Lutheran Pastors I*, 1948–1951, edited and translated by Matthew C. Harrison (St. Louis: Concordia Publishing House, 2013), p. 356. Word and Spirit are together in the Scriptures, just as the two natures in Christ are never pulled apart. Hence Sasse rejects Schleiermacher's notion of the Scriptures as a mausoleum of the Spirit as well as the notion that the Bible merely contains the Word of God or signifies and represents a Word located elsewhere.

[6] "The theology of the cross obviously does not mean that for the theologian the whole church year shrinks into Good Friday. It rather means that one cannot understand Christmas, Easter, or Pentecost without Good Friday"– Sasse, *"Theologia Crucis"* in *Letters to Lutheran Pastors I*, 1948–1951, p. 387.

[7] *"Theologia Crucis,"* 388.

Adam is killed and a new man brought forth to live by faith alone. The theology of the cross deconstructs all the ways in which man seeks to secure righteousness *before* God by way of God's Law, human reason, or the exercise of a supposedly free will. The theology of the cross demonstrates that God is at work, veiled from human apprehension, in the lowliness of suffering and death to save and enliven sinners[8]. In short, the theologian of glory works by sight and preaches by way of analogy. The theologian of the cross works by faith and preaches by assertion.

God is to be found nowhere else than in the cross,

---

[8] Sasse cites Luther from *De servo arbitrio:* "When God brings to life, He does so by killing (*occidendo vivificate*); when He justifies, then He does so by accusing us; when He brings us into heaven, He does so by leading us to hell"(Aland 38; WA 18:633). Then Sasse goes on to explain: "*Occidendo vivificat* ['by killing He makes alive']–that is the adequate expression for the unreasonable way God acts. It is beneath the cross of Christ that we learn to believe that. There we see nothing but the suffering, the weakness, the torment of being forsaken by God, the shame, the defeat, the triumph of evil, the victory of death. For the believer, however, all this is the *visibilia Dei,* that which God lets us see, His strange work behind which He hides His proper work of forgiving, saving, life-giving. Deeply hidden in the events of Good Friday which were seen by human eyes is the great event of reconciliation between God and mankind, is the victory of the Redeemer of the world which can only be believed in the face of all appearance and against reason, with its doubting question: how is that possible?"—*"Theologia Crucis,"* p. 399. Luther's theology of the cross expressed in the *Heidelberg Theses* (1518) is foundational for his argument in *The Bondage of the Will* (1525). Here see Klaus Schwarzwäller, *"Theolgia Crucis," Luthers Lehre von Prädestination nach De servo arbitrio, 1525* (Munich: Kaiser, 1970) and Gerhard Forde, *The Captivation of the Will: Luther vs. Erasmus on Freedom and Bondage*, edited by Steven Paulson (Grand Rapids: Eerdmans, 2005).

which will not allow the *theologia gloriae* to take control of the Gospel. For Sasse this is critical for preaching Christ lest the work of Christ be reduced to the divine manifestation of an ancient mystery religion: "The miracles of Jesus have again and again been misunderstood this way. Certainly Jesus manifested His glory thereby as the story of the wedding at Cana testifies. But the text declares explicitly: 'And his *disciples* believed in Him' [John 2:11]. Not the people of Cana, not the five thousand whom He fed, not the sick whom He healed, not even those He raised from the dead believed in Him. For also these deeds were at the same time revelation and disguise of His divine majesty. Only in faith did His disciples see His glory. Even His resurrection was not a demonstration for the world. The empty sepulcher as such convinced no one who did not believe in Him. Like the healings (Luke 11:8), it too, could be and has been explained differently (Matt. 27:64)."[9]

Preaching is not an exercise in natural religion. The *theologia gloriae,* Sasse notes, is always a philosophy, but the *theologia crucis* is the proclamation of the Crucified One, who does not exempt either the preacher or hearer from suffering in the bearing of the cross.[10] In fact, the

---

[9] *"Theologia Crucis,"* p. 397.

[10] Here note Sasse's admonition: "A theologian of the cross cannot be without faith in the Crucified. And how can I believe in Christ if I am not prepared to take up the cross and follow Him? It is not by accident that Jesus, when He speaks to His disciples about His cross, mentions also the cross which they are to take up (cf. Matt. 16:21–24). According to Luther it is one of the marks by which the true church of Christ on earth is recognized, that she has to go through persecution and suffering. The *theologia crucis* includes the *Yes* of faith to the cross,

12

preaching of the Crucified Lord alone enables the believer to stand in the face of the uncertainties, shifts, and disappointments that adhere to this old age, which is passing away. Sasse knew that only the sturdy theology of the cross could address a world torn by war and forever disappointed in the empty promises of political progress or cultural renewal through education or programs of social betterment. This *theologia crucis* shines through Sasse's sermon "The Comforter," based on John 15:26–16:4 and preached on *Exaudi* Sunday (May 29, 1938). In this sermon, Sasse develops the biblical understanding of the Holy Spirit as the Comforter, the *Paraklete*, noting that it is the Spirit's office to console the "despairing heart in an hour of deep disappointment and bereavement."[11] Sasse illustrates this with a reference to Luther and the Reformation: "Where the word 'comforter' stands in our Bible, there it stands as a powerful, living witness of him, who as the Reformer of the church, and the church with him, had experienced in the days of the Reformation, because the Reformation was not well known as a shining triumph, but as a chain of very strenuous fights inside the church. For many at that time, it looked like the breakdown of the church. At that the church hardly saw anything else. In such times, Luther learned to confess: 'I believe in the

---

which Christ wants us to take up."–"*Theologia Crucis,*" p. 401. Sasse's preaching of sanctification is the preaching of the Christian's cross.
[11] Sermon: "The Comforter," preached on May 29, 1938. For Sasse's earlier exegetical work on the *paraklete,* see Norman Nagel, "Hermann Sasse Identifies the *Paraklete*" *Lutheran Quarterly* (Spring 1996), pp. 3–23.

Holy Ghost'—and he experienced what kind of comfort this faith could be."[12] The Spirit works *sub contraio,* under opposites to sustain and build up in the face of weakness and defeat. Sasse uses a similar approach in a Pentecost sermon based on Acts 2:1–14, "The Miracle of Pentecost," preached two years later (May 12, 1940). Here Sasse contrasts cultural celebrations of Pentecost as the festival of springtime and new life with the grim realities of war, but the Holy Spirit, the Lord and Giver of life, comes in the promise of the Gospel to call and gather a holy, Christian people for Christ through the forgiveness of sins. The miracle of Pentecost is the miracle of faith created through the preaching of the word of the cross.

Preaching like Luther Not Erasmus

Lutheran preaching as Sasse envisioned it and practiced it must move in the way of Luther's boldness not Erasmus's skepticism. In a 1968 essay, "Erasmus, Luther, and Modern Christendom," Sasse raises and then proceeds to answer the question, "Why did Luther become the Reformer and not Erasmus?"[13] Sasse finds his answer in Luther's *On the Bondage of the Will* in which he sees in Erasmus signs of things to come: "He [Luther] saw behind Erasmus's concept of an undogmatic Christianity the coming neo-paganism of the modern world."[14] Hence Luther asserts against Erasmus, "The Holy Spirit is no

---

[12] Ibid.

[13] Hermann Sasse, "Erasmus, Luther, and Modern Christendom" in *The Lonely Way*, Vol. II (1941–1976), edited and translated by Matthew C. Harrison (St. Louis: Concordia Publishing House, 2002), p. 379.

[14] Ibid., p. 381.

skeptic."[15]

For Luther, preaching is nothing less than the making of assertions based on the Holy Scriptures that have their clarity in and through Jesus Christ. Take away Christ from the Scriptures, and they are rendered dark and obscure. For Erasmus, the Scriptures are unclear without the Church Fathers and the magisterial authority of the Church. So for Erasmus, preaching becomes didactic; it is the imparting of a "philosophy of Christ"[16] drawn from and normed by ecclesial authority. For Luther, preaching depends rather on both the *sola gratia* and the *sola Scriptura*, for it's the proclamation of the gracious work of God for the sinner according to the prophetic and apostolic Word. Sasse gets to the crux of the matter that illustrates the difference Luther makes for preaching in contrast with Erasmus: "He [Erasmus] believes in God but he has not entirely lost his belief in man."[17] Preaching indebted to Erasmus seeks to enlighten and persuade. Sasse understands preaching as the apostle describes it: the divine foolishness that saves those who hear by creating faith.

For the creation of saving faith, there is only one Gospel that is efficacious: the message of Jesus Christ crucified and resurrected for the reconciliation of the world. This Gospel is immutable. It is not be trimmed to fit comfortably within the worldview of the hearers. For Sasse it will always be a disruptive Word, yet an announcement

---

[15] Ibid., p. 381.
[16] Ibid., p. 377.
[17] Ibid., p. 383.

that brings joy in the forgiveness of sins. In a stirring mission festival sermon preached on Matthew 24:14 at Gunzenhausen on July 14, 1937, Sasse proclaimed, "The Gospel is the message of Christ himself. Just as he called 'all who labor and are heavy laden' [Matt. 11:28] to himself in his earthly days, so he calls them today in the proclamation of his Church. So it is that the Church is not free to choose her message. She cannot make it like the other religions of the world, who in their glory stir up fantasies, who get at the heart with compelling myths, today with this message, tomorrow with another message, once with the myth of Edda and today with the myths of the twentieth century and later with the myths of the twenty-first century. The Church always has the same message, for all times, for all peoples, for all races, for the healthy and the sick, for the happy and the sad, for the strong and the weak, the learned and the unlearned. She has nothing more to say to a [Otto von] Bismarck [1815–1898; first chancellor of the German Empire] than she has to say to the poorest, sickest child. The world is outraged by this 'boring' message that never changes. But the Church cannot change it. Yes, because it is not her message, but Christ's message. The Christian missionary is like an envoy who travels to the prisoners of Siberia—those who are languishing in the prison, who no longer remember or know anything of freedom, and no longer hope for freedom—with orders to proclaim, 'You are free. The war is over. Come home with us!' That is the Gospel, the joyous message. It is everywhere the same, but where one

16

comprehends it there it is the greatest thing that men can hear. So the Christian mission proclaims the wonder of redemption, the miracle of all miracles, the God who becomes man. 'That is, in Christ God was reconciling the world to himself, not counting their trespasses against them, and entrusting to us the message of reconciliation. Therefore, we are ambassadors for Christ, God making his appeal through us. We implore you on behalf of Christ, be reconciled to God. For our sake he made him to be sin who knew no sin, so that in him we might become the righteousness of God' " (2 Cor. 5:19–21).

Law and Gospel as the Necessary Distinction

The clarity of the distinction between the Law and the Gospel is most sharply demonstrated in Sasse's engagement with Barth. In contrast with Lutheran theology, Barth sees God's revelation as singular, so in his system the Law is contained in the Gospel and has equal footing with the announcement of divine reconciliation in Christ.[18] Thus for him, the preaching of the Gospel is at the same time a proclamation of the Law, which demands obedience. For Sasse, this melding of the Law and the Gospel undercuts the *sola fide*, leaving the hearer in either presumption or despair.[19] Preaching the Law and the Gospel for Sasse is

---

[18] Hermann Sasse, *Here We Stand,* translated by Theodore Tappert (Adelaide, Australia: Lutheran Publishing House, 1938), 120. For Barth's position, see "Gospel and Law" in Karl Barth, *Community, State, and Church: Three Essays* (Eugene: Wipf & Stock, nd), pp. 71–100. Also see Jobst Schöne, "Law and Gospel in Hermann Sasse's *Logia* (Reformation, 1995), pp. 25–30.

[19] Here note, "The Gospel requires faith, the Law obedience. The

not a balancing act with the preacher making sure he delivers equal proportions of the same revelation. Rather the preaching of the Law and the Gospel are to be seen as the exercise of God's alien work and his proper work. It is God's alien work to express his wrath through the Law; his proper work is the forgiveness of sins through the Gospel for the sake of Christ. Thus for Sasse, the Law and the Gospel do not stand on the same level.[20] The Law[21] is preached to expose sin and destroy any refuge for the sinner in his own attitudes or actions so that God's favor in Christ might be preached for genuine consolation. Sasse writes, "The more seriously we take the immutable, eternal, divine commandments, the more we also know that the

---

congregation which grows out of the preaching of the Word, the *congregatio sanctorum,* is, according to the Lutheran view, a congregation of believers; according to the Reformed view, a congregation of believers and obeyers. Of course, the Lutheran Church also teaches that those who have received the faith, those who are justified should walk in the way of the new obedience. But their sanctity depends on their faith alone, not on their obedience"— Hermann Sasse, *Here We Stand*, pp. 137–38.

[20] "The difference lies in the fact that the Reformed believe that both Law and Gospel are parts of Christ's real work, and consequently are essential functions of the church; the Lutheran Church, on the other hand, teaches that the preaching of the Law is the 'strange,' and the preaching of the Gospel is the 'real,' work of Christ, and accordingly, although the church must also preach the Law—how else could it proclaim the Gospel?—the only thing which is essential to its nature as the church of Christ is that it is the place, the only place in all the world, in which the blessed tidings of the forgiveness of sins for Christ's sake are heard"—Hermann Sasse, *Here We Stand*, p. 129.

[21] In Sasse's own preaching, what Herman Stuempfle identifies as the preaching of "the Law as mirror of existence" seems to be most characteristic. The Law reveals the futility of a life of unbelief in the matrix of historical existence. See Herman G. Steumpfle, *Preaching Law and Gospel* (Philadelphia: Fortress Press, 1978), pp. 23–25.

preaching of the Law is not yet the final and highest thing that has been committed to us. The final and highest task of our office is this: that we lead penitent sinners to the one who is their Savior, because he has borne the sin of the world."[22] The Gospel must be explicitly articulated for a sermon to qualify as a Christian sermon: "The Gospel is this and nothing else: that in Jesus Christ there is forgiveness of sins, in him alone and nowhere else in the world, but truly in him. A sermon that did not say that, a sermon in which this real Gospel was not mentioned would not be a Christian sermon."[23] Whatever text of Holy Scripture is preached and however the richness of biblical imagery for redemption is used, the message that God was in Christ reconciling the world to himself cannot go unspoken.

This preaching will always be evangelistic in that the unbeliever cannot come to faith except through the Gospel and the believer cannot remain in faith except through the Gospel. Sermons for Christians gathered in the church do not become didactic lectures on how one now lives the obedient life or edifying discourses on spirituality. Preaching must remain the word of Absolution, which forgives sin and keeps believers with Jesus Christ in the one true faith: "For the Church lives by the Gospel. It does not live by our religion. It is not a religious society, based on certain common convictions, like the Lutheran

---

[22] Hermann Sasse, "The Lutheran Doctrine of the Office of the Holy Ministry" in *The Lonely Way*, Vol. II, p. 125.
[23] Ibid., p. 125.

Laymen's League or the Ladies Guild or the Young People's Society. And the Gospel by which the Church lives is not a doctrine, a religious philosophy, a sacred book as such. It is rather the gracious Word of Jesus Christ himself by which he forgives us all our sins and gives us life and salvation. It is not a doctrine about how and under what conditions there can be forgiveness; it is rather the forgiveness personally proclaimed to us: Thy sins are forgiven thee! We hear this Gospel in the Absolution. We hear it in the sermon if it is an evangelical sermon. We hear it in the celebration of the Sacrament, and we receive the true body and the true blood of our Savior as the pledge of the forgiveness. That is the reason why we must go to church if possible. Why it is almost impossible to keep the faith without going to church? I cannot absolve myself, as I cannot baptize myself. I cannot celebrate the Lord's Supper alone. Of course it is possible to live on the written Word of the Bible alone or even on what has been left of my former knowledge of the Word, (e.g. in a Siberian prisoners' camp). But this is a state of emergency. In order to remain a Christian, I need the means of grace. For what will become of my faith without the Holy Ghost who is given to me by the means of grace?"[24]

Preaching Word and Sacrament: Liturgical Preaching

The oft-used phrase "Word and Sacrament" was for Sasse more than a cliché, as it indicates a coordinate relationship that if pulled apart destroys preaching and

---

[24] Hermann Sasse, "The Problems of Lutheran Evangelism," p. 4. This manuscript has not been published.

reduces the Lord's Supper to human cultic activity. A renewal in preaching will also mean a liturgical revival, and a recovery of the liturgical heritage will reinvigorate preaching. For Sasse this does not mean that preaching is liturgical because it occurs in the context of a church service or because the sermon is a commentary on liturgical action. Rather liturgical preaching is the Lord at work through the proclamation of his Gospel to create and sustain faith by anchoring the hearers in the promises of Christ bestowed in Baptism, Absolution, and the Sacrament of the Altar. Sasse was not hesitant to refer to elements of the liturgy in his sermons or even use the pulpit as an opportunity for instruction and explanation of one part of the Divine Service or another, but the sermon was not reduced to a lecture on liturgical history or rubrics. Nor would Sasse preach generically on the means of grace as though they were interchangeable. Hence he writes in 1956, "As Lutheran theologians we should follow the example of the Augsburg Confession in our theological thinking as in our teaching and preaching and never start from one common doctrine of the means of grace by itself in its own particularity: Preaching the Gospel, Baptism, confession and absolution, the Sacrament of the Altar. Only then will we be able to understand the fullness of God's dealing with us, the different ways by which He comes to us, and the whole uniqueness of every single means of grace and so come to a proper use of each (consider the orders of the articles of the Augsburg Confession and the arrangement of confession between Baptism and the Lord's Supper)."[25]

According to Luther, "This sacrament is the Gospel."[26] Preaching the Lord's Supper is nothing other than an exposition of the words of institution since they "contain the whole Gospel."[27] Likewise preaching Baptism and the Absolution is to preach the Gospel: "Baptism is the Gospel, because the whole Gospel is contained in it, not only in words but also in what our Redeemer does in His mighty rescue of us from sin, death, and the devil. Absolution is the Gospel, the forgiveness of sins, the anticipation of the verdict of justification that will come in the last judgment."[28] But each must be preached in its particularity.

What is given in the Sacraments determines how they are preached for Sasse. They are not the "representation" of Christ's past work in the way of Odo Casel.[29] The death of Christ is not made present in the Sacraments. It is a unique and unrepeatable historical event. Rather in Baptism, the baptized is joined to the death of the crucified and risen Lord so that the future of this Lord is now the future of the one who in faith clings to the promise of this Christ. In the Lord's Supper, the church is engaged not in cultic reenactment but in the receiving of the benefits of Christ's

---

[25] Hermann Sasse, "Word and Sacrament: Preaching and the Lord's Supper" in *We Confess the Sacraments,* translated and edited by Norman Nagel (St. Louis: Concordia Publishing House, 1985), p. 21.
[26] Ibid., p. 23.
[27] Ibid., p. 23.
[28] Ibid., p. 25.
[29] Ibid., p. 26. For more on Sasse's critique of Odo Casel, see John T. Pless, "Hermann Sasse and the Liturgical Movement" *Logia* (Eastertide 1998), pp. 47–51.

death given now by His body and blood under bread and wine. Thus the Sacraments are preached as Gospel.

Eschatological Note in Sasse's Preaching

Eschatological awareness marks Sasse's preaching. This can especially be seen in his sermons from the end of the Church Year and in Advent where one would naturally expect it but it is there generally in his preaching. Circumstances in Germany brought the practical nature of eschatology to the fore in Sasse's theology and hence in his preaching. Reflecting back in 1952, Sasse writes, "In our day the Biblical doctrine of the Last Things has come alive for us as a gift given in the midst of what the church has had to endure. At the beginning of this century a complacent church regarded the Last Things as an element of the first Christian proclamation which more or less belonged to that first period, a form of the Gospel which was for us only of historical interest. Or alternately, it was thought of as something that might be of significance for the future, at the end of our lives, or at the end of the world, something we needed to study only in preparation for such an end. That there is for the church no more vitally relevant doctrine than that of the Last Things was brought home to Christians by all they were called upon to endure."[30] The application of this for preaching is brought forth in the same essay: "All preaching is preaching of the Last Things when it is preaching of the Gospel. And no preaching is preaching of the Last Things if it is not preaching of the

---

[30] Hermann Sasse, "Last Things: Church and Antichrist" in *We Confess the Church*, *p.* 108.

pure Gospel—even if it were an exposition of nothing else but the Revelation of St. John and other eschatological texts of Holy Scripture."[31] Sasse brings this out with utter clarity in a sermon, "Advent's Ageless Question," preached on the Third Sunday in Advent, December 17, 1933: "The historical man, Jesus of Nazareth, who was executed before the gates of Jerusalem during the reign of the great Tiberius and under the government of Pontius Pilate, is the Christ, the true Redeemer of the world, who will come again in glory to judge the living and the dead, whose kingdom will have no end."[32] Crisp, creedal language is employed by Sasse to bring the congregation to a realization that Advent is nothing less than the proclamation of Jesus Christ to the world.

In a sermon preached on the First Sunday in Advent (November 29, 1936) on Hebrews 10:19–25, Sasse asserts that "the Church has a different relationship to time than the world."[33] While the church lives in this world of hours and days, months and years, see lives in the continual presence of the One who came in the flesh and will come at the end to judge the living and the dead. His presence and His final coming enliven the church to wait with patience even in the midst of the German church which has become "like a great field of ruins"[34] Yet it is here, Sasse says that the church lives in hope which does not disappoint. Hence

---

[31] Ibid., p. 109.
[32] Sermon: "Advent's Ageless Question," preached on December 17, 1933.
[33] Sermon: First Sunday in Advent, November 29, 1936
[34] Ibid.

he concludes the sermon: "Here the Church, wherever she lives, learns about who her Lord is, about whom she waits for despite all disappointment. And she can wait for him because he is with her. That is the mystery of the expectation of the Early Church. She could wait, because she was with him, hidden under the means of grace, in the Lord's Supper. That is the mystery of the coming Christ. Come, Lord Jesus! 'Surely, I am coming soon!' "[35] A similar note is struck in another sermon, "The Mysteries of God," based on 1 Corinthians 4:1–5 from the Third Sunday in Advent (December 15, 1940) where Sasse calls the Church "a congregation of poor sinners wandering through the centuries of history, despised and abused by the world."[36] Yet it is this Church that lives by the promises of her Lord extended in Baptism and the Holy Supper, enabling her to journey with confidence and patience: "She travels through the angst and distress of this world, from his incarnation to His return. Yes, the future of our Lord Jesus Christ is the blessed future of the Church."[37]

The eschatological note is sounded in a sermon on Ephesians 6:10–17 prepared for the Twenty-first Sunday after Trinity and published in a book of sermons. Following Luther, Sasse sees this pericope as a military sermon as Paul employs the imagery of defense gear and offensive weaponry to the Spirit's equipment of believers for a life of battle with the world, flesh, and devil in God's army, the

---

[35] Ibid.
[36] Sermon: "The Mysteries of God," preached on Third Sunday in Advent, December 15, 1940.
[37] Ibid.

Church. To war-weary and beleaguered fighters, Sasse does not cajole but consoles with the sweet news of a victory already achieved. After extolling the power of the Word of God, "the sword of the Spirit" which we have been given, Sasse concludes the sermon: "Our eyes do not yet see a victory. So the Church of all times must fight. Her human eyes have seen so little of the victory, she is like the Spanish soldiers in Alcazar of Toledo, who could no longer offer a brave defense until they heard the liberating sounds of victory. As they waited for their liberator, so the Church waits for her Lord. And she knows that the victory will belong to him when he comes. That is the faith and the hope of the Church as God's fighting army in the world: Our fight follows His victory. And so we look to the glorious day of victory, 'Then comes the end, when he delivers the kingdom to God the Father after destroying every rule and every authority and power. For he must reign until he has put all his enemies under his feet' (1 Cor. 15:24–25)."[38] The strong, assuring word of a promise of a victory that is real but hidden masterfully wraps up the sermon, leaving the hearer with the confidence of Christ's triumph over every enemy.

The Crisis of Preaching

Given the fact that all Christian preaching is eschatological, it also entails crisis. Writing in 1968 in the midst of an era when it was in vogue to voice criticism of institutions and authority, including the ministry and

---

[38] Sermon: "The Army of God," Ephesians 6:10–17, Twenty-First Sunday after Trinity.

sermon[39], Sasse authors an essay titled "The Crisis of the Christian Ministry." In this essay, he addresses a double crisis of the ministry, making a distinction between "the crisis that belongs to the nature of our office" and that which is "conditioned by the church in a certain age."[40] Rehearsing various "crises" that have emerged in the history of the Church, beginning with the death of the apostles, Sasse examines how the Church has responded and survived. In the contemporary Church, Sasse argues that the crisis of the ministry is one of the truthfulness of the Gospel. If the Gospel is not true, the ministry is evacuated of any significance and ministers will seek to create other tasks to validate their professional existence. But even this contemporary crisis is not unique, for as Sasse observes, "Where there is prophecy, there is also false prophecy, and at all times the number of false prophets has been greater than that of the true prophets of God. This was already so at the time of Jeremiah and Ezekiel."[41] Yet in an age when people have grown accustomed to being lied to by politicians and the media, the truthfulness of the preacher's message is also suspect. Writing in 1934, Sasse observed, "The people want someone to tell them the truth about God, and about men and their sin, about judgment and redemption, about death and life. They want to hear the truth, whole and

---

[39] See, for example, Helmut Thielicke, *The Trouble with the Church*, translated by John W. Doberstein (New York: Harper and Row, 1965).
[40] Hermann Sasse, "The Crisis of the Christian Ministry" in *The Lonely Way*, Vol. II, p. 356.
[41] Ibid., p. 357.

unvarnished. They do not want the truth to be veiled with rich flowery rhetoric. They want their pastor to vouch with his person and life that what he says is true. They have painted very fine pictures of even us theologians, and, therefore, many have lost enthusiasm for the Church. They wonder if the one speaking really believes, or if he only believes in faith. It is astonishing with what seriousness the German people, the genuine ones, not those joining the masses of the great cities, the farmers, and the workers, judge their church and their pulpit with the question of truth. But so long as the last question arises in the hearts of the people: the question of God and his will, of his judgment and his forgiveness, of the Redeemer, who also bore the sin of the northern men and the German people on the trunk of the cross, of the communion of saints, which transcends all congregations, of the resurrection of the body with which all theories of race and materialism must end. And so long as our people do not want to hear beautiful, uplifting clichés on this question, but the truth, then one will not tell us the people have no interest in dogmatic questions or that they don't understand theological matters. Neither should they need to understand them. They have no interest in arguments, but they have an interest in the truth. And they will not betray or give up the Church or the truth she proclaims."[42]

Sasse notes that the crisis that belongs to the nature of the office is only resolved by God himself. "The deepest nature of this crisis lies in the fact that God always

---

[42] Cited by F. W. Hopf in "Preface" to *Witness*.

demands from his servants something which is, humanly speaking, impossible."[43] This demand was laid upon Moses, Jeremiah, and Paul, making for them the ministry of preaching a burden: "No one can understand the ministry of the Word, who has not understood why the OT prophets called the 'word' a 'burden.' No one can understand it unless he knows what Jeremiah and Paul have understood: 'Necessity is laid upon me. Woe to me if I do not preach the gospel' (1 Cor. 9:16)."[44] The crisis of the ministry is rooted in the fact that God uses sinners as his servants. "This contradiction disappears and the crisis is solved only where it is understood that the *missio peccatorum,* the sending of sinners, and the *remissio paccatirum,* the forgiveness of sins, are two aspects of the one grace of God."[45] God's solution to the crisis of the ministry is found in the promise of Isaiah 55:11 that his Word accomplishes its divinely given purpose; it does not return to him empty. According to Sasse this alone is the preacher's confidence in the humanly speaking impossible task of preaching.

Conclusion

In Sasse, we see the truth embodied in the title of Gerhard Forde's book *Theology Is for Proclamation.* Sasse's theology is not merely a theology about preaching or a prolegomena for preaching; his theology could be preached and it was preached in the sermons he delivered. His sermons bear lasting testimony to the truth that

---

[43] Sasse, "The Crisis of the Christian Ministry," p. 356.
[44] Ibid., p. 357.
[45] Ibid., p. 357.

preachers of the Gospel are never given over to despair, for the Word of life, hidden under cross, suffering, and defeat, is not bound but continues to triumph over all that is death and dying. Authentic preaching that delivers the Lord's gifts is never in vain, for Jesus is raised from the dead, giving preachers and preaching his own future.

John T. Pless
Assistant Professor of Pastoral Ministry &
Missions/Director of Field Education
Concordia Theological Seminary
Fort Wayne, Indiana

Preface

"The thought of a judgment day to which every man and every people approaches has been extinguished in the souls of men. This is perhaps the deepest revolution the Christian West, and with it, the German people of the last two centuries, have undergone." This unusual and exciting sentence is found in one of the weighty sermons of the great Lutheran theologian Hermann Sasse, gathered in this volume (The Mystery of the Last Things, Matt. 25:1–13). Here speaks a deeply grounded interpreter of the Holy Scriptures, who together with this gift is given the ability to speak the words of Scripture in the immediate present. For him it was the present of the '30s and '40s. Yet despite the distance in time—this sermon was delivered in the year 1938—do they not hit close to home for us? The deep moving revolution, of which Sasse spoke, has truly worked itself out in our day. The extensive dimming of the eschatological horizon destroyed the inner tension of the Christian faith.

In an Advent sermon from the year 1933, the year the National Socialist Party took over power[46] (Advent's Ageless Question, Matt. 11:2–11), he writes, "The Church lives on this message alone. She does not know of any German Advent or of an American Advent or Chinese

---

[46] The Nazi Party, as a result of the 1932 elections, achieved the largest representation in the Weimar Republic's parliament. Hitler became Chancellor on January 30, 1933. After the Reichstag Fire in February, parliament gave Hitler dictatorial powers on March 23. See Lowell Green's, *Lutherans Against Hitler: The Untold Story* (St. Louis: Concordia Publishing House [CPH], 2007), pp. 53ff. MH

Advent. She only knows the Advent of Jesus Christ.. . . . With this message, she went to the great cultures of the East and the people of Africa." Such a sentence can be spoken and heard the same even today when the conversations with the cultures and religions of Asia and Africa are largely determined by the ecumenical discussion.

Herman Sasses died in 1976 [August 9] in Adelaide, Australia. He had immigrated to there from Germany in 1949.[47] Yet from this great distance he critically observed the events of the Church in his old home while working in the theological seminary of the Lutheran Church of Australia. To the very end, he cared about how all of Christendom and the Lutheran Church in particular moved. The sermons and essays presented in this volume stem out of the great period of work before his time in Australia.[48] From 1933 to 1949, Sasse was professor of Church history, dogmatic history, and symbolics in Erlangen. However, he was also involved in New Testament studies, and took a stand on the frontlines in the Church battles of that time. The now available "Witness" (*Zeugnisse*[49]), the collection

---

[47] Sasse left Germany because his own church, the state church of Bavaria, joined the EKiD, a union of Lutheran, Reformed, and united churches. The great moment, Sasse believed, for Lutheranism to assert again the doctrinal necessity of a Lutheran church governed by leadership beholden to the Lutheran Confessions, was lost. See *Letters to Lutheran Pastors I* (St. Louis: CPH, 2012), pp. lxv.ff. MH

[48] It is somewhat a conundrum that we do not possess more sermons by Sasse. Of thirty-six listed by Ron Feuerhahn, most are contained in this volume. *Hermann Sasse: A Bibliography* (Lanham, Md. & London: The Scarecrow Press, 1995), pp. 242–43. MH

[49] *Hermann Sasse, Zeugnisse. Erlanger Predigten und Vorträge vor Gemeinden 1933–1944. Mit einem Geleitwort von Hermann*

and delivery of which many friends of Sasse and readers are thankful for, shows this professor for what he originally was, a parish pastor. In particular, a great many Lutheran pastors thank him still today for his essential insights into the Gospel and Church history, which are so helpful in testing the spirits of their respective times.

It is uncalled for to reproach Sasse, the preacher and theologian, for being at times time-bound. This is compensated for by the powerful unmasking of the idols of that time. Behind this stands the German people's encounter with Christ's all-encompassing view and the tormented worry for the possible apostasy of our people from the Gospel. Sasse's preaching is certainly very different from that of today: not very psychological, not very individualistic, and without much moral appeal. This is because the kingdom of God, the Church of Jesus Christ, and the Gospel are central to them. Because of this, one often hears these sermons simply and often enough one forgets they are separated by the distance of half a century.

There remains for me to show one fascinating peculiarity in the following. Throughout these sermons we encounter what people today call the ecumenical dimension in the distinctively Lutheran Sasse, and this in the midst of the Third Reich, when Germany was shut off from the rest of the world. And this ecumenical reality was as vertical through the centuries as it was horizontal throughout the whole world: It is found in the Christians and churches in

Dietzfelbinger. Herausgegeben von Friedrich Wilhelm Hopf. Martin Luther-Verlag Erlangen 1979. Feuerhahn bibliography pp. 190ff. MH

America and Australia, in the mission congregations in Japan and China like early Christianity, in the ancient Church of the Eastern lands, in the Middle Ages and the Reformation, in Rome and the *Anfechtung* of Christendom through the Enlightenment and in more recent times. One sees this most in the sermons from the Pentecost season in the Church Year. But in all the sermons, the ecumenical Sasse does not deny the standpoint of a Lutheran theologian bound to the Scriptures. Yet, he is thoroughly ecumenical. The glorious freedom discovered by the Reformation, the "eternal gospel" (Rev. 14:6ff.), illuminates the time and peoples there.

It is our desire that this book gain new students and old friends of Sasse.

D. Hermann Dietzfelbinger[50]
Munich, the 8th of February 1979

---

[50] Dietzfelbinger (1908–84) followed Hans Meiser as bishop of the Lutheran Church of Bavaria and served 1955–1975. MH

Who Was Hermann Sasse?

In the spring of the Revolutionary year, 1933, Sasse was a professor at the University in Erlangen, whose theological faculty at that time was still stamped with a magnificently recognizable Lutheran character. Sasse's teaching commission encompassed both Church and dogmatic history as well as the wide area of confessions. In August of 1949, he immigrated with his family to Australia, where the United Evangelical Lutheran Church had called him to teach at the Theological Seminary in North Adelaide. Behind his farewell to Erlangen stood Sasse's protest against the connection of the Evangelical Lutheran Church in Bavaria with the Evangelical Church in Germany [EKiD] (1948), which he rejected as unionist. From Australia, he took part in the ecclesiastical events of Germany through his "Letters to Lutheran Pastors" and through extensive correspondence until he passed away on August 9, 1976.

His birth on July 17, 1895, in Sonnewalde (Kreis Luckau /Niederlausitz) to a drugstore owner brought with it rich proceeds that were seen already during the decision-filled years of his teaching office in Erlangen. In the University of Berlin, he was recognized as a highly gifted student and renowned scholar, and also through a promotion (1923) that was to follow his post-doctoral studies in the field of the New Testament.[52] His studies

---

[52] See Matthew C. Harrison, "Hermann Sasse's Quest for a Christocentric Doctrina de Scriptura Sacra," unpub. S.T.M. Thesis (Ft. Wayne: Concordia Theological Seminary, 1991) for Sasse's own

were interrupted however when he was placed on the Western Front in the First World War. During this vital experience, as he stressed often, he attained the foundational knowledge of Martin Luther's "that man is not in control. He learns to deny himself and to hope in Christ." He also grasped "Karl Barth's powerful call from subjective religion to the objective Word of God." When he returned home after the war, he went to his spiritual office with the question: What should I preach?[53]

"With the Word of God the Confessions of the Church

---

description of his lecturers at the University of Berlin, including Harnack, Holl, and Deissmann. MH

[53] Sasse provides personal recollections in "The Impact of Bultmannism on American Lutheranism, with Special Reference to His Demythologization of the New Testament" in *Lutheran Synod Quarterly* [Mankato, Minn.], 5.4 (June 1965) pp. 2–12. "More than any other theologian Karl Barth represents the great change that has taken place in continental theology. He himself doubts, and his friend and co-worker Thurneysen rejects, the idea that the new theology stems from the great disillusionment following World War I. It cannot be denied, however, that the collapse of optimism concerning man and the world paved the way for new attention to the Word of God. It is significant that the new theology did not issue from some university but rather from the manse and the pulpit. Instead of the homiletician's query "*How* shall I preach to modern man?" Barth and his friends once again posed the preacher's primary question: "*What* shall I cry?" Once again they say that the preacher's task in not to teach religion, nor to arouse religious sentiments, nor to proclaim human wisdom, but rather faithfully to deliver the message entrusted to him by God, to preach the Word, the whole Word and nothing but the Word, that Word of the Cross which is foolishness to the world. Here was the crucial shift from subject to object, from the thoughts, sentiments, desires, and needs of pious man, to the Word which God has given us in the Bible." Hermann Sasse, "European Theology in the Twentieth Century", in *Christian Faith and Modern Theology*, ed. by C. F. H. Henry (New York: Channel Press, 1964), p. 13. Feuerhahn no. 504. Sasse's comments on Barth are really autobiographical. MH

come alive, and the people will be re-awakened, like in the awakenings of the nineteenth century when men returned to Scripture and the Confessions under the leadership of great men in the Church at that time, men like *August Vilmar* [1800–1868][54] and *Wilhelm Loehe*" [1808–1872].[55]

Sasse's spiritual development proceeded with continual and evermore intensive academic studies and research while in living contact with his environment in the Church and the world. For instance, he set to work earnestly as a parish pastor, first in Templin then in Oranienburg in 1921, and in 1928 went to Berlin and was pastor of the *St. Marien Kirche* (Church of St. Mary). A year of study in the United States (1925/26) gave him a deep insight into American church life.[56] He participated in the first world conference for Faith and Order (Lausanne 1927) as a member of the German delegation. He interpreted French and English for their negotiations. He remained on the committee as the

---

[54] Sasse published and wrote a preface for Vilmar's *Dogmatik. Vilmar, August F. C. Dogmatik: 1. 2. Gütersloh: Bertelsmann, 1937.* Feuerhahn 164. He also wote a preface to Vilmar's *Die Theologie der Tatsachen*, 1938; Feuerhahn no. 191. MH

[55] Sasse recounts his indebtedness to Loehe's *Three Books on the Church* in the preface of *Here We Stand: Nature and Character of the Lutheran Faith*, translated by Tappert (New York & London: Harper & Bros., 1938). MH

[56] See Sasse's "American Christianity and the Church" in *The Lonely Way I* (St. Louis: CPH), pp. 23–60 "Personally I must confess that it was in America that I first learned fully to appreciate what it means to be loyal to the Lutheran Confessions; but for what I learned from the Lutheran theologians and church bodies in the United States, I probably could never have written this book." *Here We Stand: Nature and Character of the Lutheran Faith* (Harper, 1938), pp. x–xi. MH

official German reporter.[57] He continued the strong stream of international connections and responsible ecumenical cooperation for many years.[58]

As a social pastor (a pastor charged with social work) in Berlin, he was also a sharp observer of the spiritual, political, and social powers of the time.[59] The least of his publications in the volumes of *Church Year Book for the Evangelical Church of Germany* (1931–1934), "Contemporary Issues of the Church,"[60] shows his proficiency to depict and discern even in view of the political powers of the time.[61]

Professor Sasse came to Erlangen as an alert Lutheran after serving the Church of the Old Prussian Union. His conversion through a genuine confessional renewal burned ever stronger and became his greatest matter of concern. Sasse grew evermore sharply critical of the state of the

---

[57] Sasse edited the official report of Lausanne in which he provided what has been recognized as the earliest significant history of the ecumenical movement. *Die Weltkonferenz für Glauben und Kirchenverfassung. Deutscher Amtlicher Bericht über die Weltkirchenkonferenz zu Lausanne 1927. Berlin Furche-Verlag, 1929.* Feuerhahn no. 019. MH

[58] Ron Feuerhahn asserts in his unpublished Ph.D. dissertation that Sasse was the most active German theologian in the ecumenical movement prior to WWII. Ronald R Feuerhahn, *Hermann Sasse as an Ecumenical Churchman* (1991), p. 42 MH

[59] See Sasse's "The Social Doctrine of the Augsburg Confession and Its Significance for the Present" (1930) in *The Lonely Way I*, pp. 89ff. Feuerhahn no. 053. MH

[60] "*Kirchliche Zeitlage*" in *Kirchliches Jahrbuch*; Feuerhahn nos. 071, 091. MH

[61] Sasse was editor of the yearbook for the entire Protestant church in Germany for several years. *Kirchliches Jahrbuch für die evangelischen Landeskirchen Deutschlands 1931, Gütersloh: Bertelsmann, 1931.* Feuerhahn nos. 069, 089, 110, 119. MH

Church that would embrace differing confessions as contrasting "directions" and political Church parties, and became evermore determined to fight this. At the same time, he was always ready to enter a genuine "thoughtful parochial confederation of confessions that have developed from the history of the Reformation, on the condition that these not cease to be confessions and confessional churches."

As in Germany, so he also had one rule for involvement in the ecumenical movement in general, that the "confederation assemble on the basis of strict truthfulness."[62] Everything about him centered on this great matter of concern. It guided his academic work, even as he grounded his multiple-faceted fights in deep pastoral concern. His whole life's work attested to the sanctifying Gospel and the Holy Sacraments in unadulterated biblical purity.

Looking back on the theological and ecclesiastical life work of this man, one recognizes three concrete points jutting out from the immense fullness of his research, and the nearly limitless extent of his knowledge. The first point to be noticed in Sasse is the great circle around the meaning of *the Seventh Article of the Augsburg Confession* concerning the true unity of the one Holy Christian Church. This was a highly comforting article of faith for him personally.[63] Here he found the biblically grounded trail

---

[62] See Ronald Feuerhahn, *Hermann Sasse as an Ecumenical Churchman,* Unpub. Dissertation (1991), pp. 4ff.
[63] See *Letters to Lutheran Pastors* 53 (1962), "The Seventh Article of the

map to the concrete conclusions and demands so complete in all his confessional discussion. This became the basis for many contributions to the ecumenical movement, especially with the Roman Catholic Church, where his particular interest laid.[64]

Because Sasse was devoted to the witness of the unity of the Church, the circle around her true unity, and the fight against false unity, the Sacrament of the Altar was the second demanding and concrete point of his piety.[65] His New Testament research and his study of the Church and dogmatic history hung together and expanded on manifold assessments of the liturgy of the Divine Service. He applied this to actual questions concerning church and altar fellowship and in defense against dubious new attempts at concord.

The third concrete point was at the forefront of all Sasse's theological work for the last decade of his life. This was his unfortunately incomplete remaining study on the *Doctrine of Holy Scripture*. By this Sasse meant the divine mystery of inspiration through the Holy Spirit; as he employed his spiritual character in the words of men, the eternal Word of God enters into this external limit, just as we find and hold the true Son of God only within the limits

---

Augustana in the Present Crisis of Lutheranism." Feuerhahn no. 377. MH

[64] See *Letters to Lutheran Pastors* nos. 49, 50, 54, 57, 58, 59 on the Second Vatican Council. MH

[65] Sasse's *This Is My Body: Luther's Contention for the Real Presence in the Sacrament of the Altar, Augsburg 1959,* is still the greatest book in English on Luther's teaching on the Lord's Supper. MH

of his true humanity.[66]

The general picture of the Lutheran theologian and churchman Herman Sasse would lack a characteristic feature if it did not observe how sharply he observed and criticized political events throughout the world. He constantly recognized the great questions of life for the Church in history and behind different contemporary movements and challenges in the life of the people, particularly in the expressions of revolutionary circles. His famous critique of National Socialism is the most well-known example (the church yearbook of 1932!).[67] Article 24 of the party's program, made according to Sasse's sharp judgment "any discussion with a church impossible," because thereby the morality and the moral feeling of the Germanic race would become the standard for the toleration of the Church in the Third Reich, and secondly because the doctrine of the Church, in particular the evangelical teaching of original sin, is a permanent insult to this morality and moral feeling.[68] One has to keep in mind

---

[66] See *Sacra scriptura : Studien zur Lehre von der Heiligen Schrift, Friedrich Wilhem Hopf, Verlag der Ev.-Luth. Mission, Erlangen, 1981*; Feuerhahn no. 1981; and *Scripture and the Church: Selected Essays of Hermann Sasse*, ed. J. Kloha and Ronald Feuerhahn (St. Louis: Concordia Seminary, 1995). See also the extensive treatment of this issue in *Letters to Lutheran Pastors I* (St. Louis: CPH, 2012), lxxxiiiff.. MH

[67] *Kirchliches Jahrbuch . . . 1932. Gütersloh: C. Bertelsmann, 1932.* Feuerhahn no. 089. MH

[68] For an English translation of Sasse's rejection of the Nazi party platform (the earliest published) see Peter Matheson, *The Third Reich and the Christian Churches* (Grand Rapids: W. B. Eerdmanns, 1981), pp. 1–2. The text is also found in *Letters to Lutheran Pastors I*, p. lxii. See Lowell Green, *Lutherans Against Hitler: The Untold Story* (St.

this confrontation of the biblical Lutheran teaching with the revolutionary worldview that triumphed in 1933 when reading this volume, "Witness," the sermons of which begin in that year. However time-bound these sermons may be, one can still recognize a groundbreaking spirit in them. Here stands the ecumenical Lutheran, Sasse, embracing the people of his own culture with pastoral care while experiencing and suffering the revolutionary change of seasons. For Sasse the preacher, the frightening matter of God's verdict over the German people stood behind every irritating occurrence of day-to-day political history, and the deep shocks in the Confessing Church's fight of those years. Already in the spring of 1933 he wrote:

> The peoples are called by God. His call calls peoples who have no history into history. It makes a cultureless people into a culture. He called the Philistines and the Aramians, the Assyrians and the Babylonians, the Egyptians and the Persians onto the stage of world history. He called the people of the ancient world to the beginning of human history, and he will call the people of the end times to the last, most terrible history our earth will experience. He called Israel, his own people, to a particular history, for salvation and to be a warning for all people of the earth. He called each people to its own particular mission, which he alone

---

Louis: CPH, 2007), for a complete treatment of Sasse's activities during the Third Reich. For the history of Lutheran opposition (including Sasse!) to the Nazis see Green's *Lutherans Against Hitler*, ch. 6, "Opposition to the Aryan Paragraph and Oppression of Jewish People," pp. 129ff. MH

knows. And just as his call to this mission is the beginning of a people's history, so his judgment of rejection means the end of their history. If this judgment of a people is spoken, then neither the height of its culture nor the purity of its race can stop it from going under. There is an end to every culture's history just as there is death at the end of every man's life. That is, according to the Christian faith, the mystery of the peoples, their becoming and their passing."

And later he writes:

"It is ever the greatest event in the history of a people when they for the first time have the Gospel preached to them. This not only means that they will have a new religion with which they can bind the people of this culture together in a new union. The call to repentance of the Gospel can and must work itself out also the dissolution of the spirits. Yes, it can ultimately lead to the destruction of a culture's unity in extreme cases, as the history of many emigrations for the sake of the Gospel testify. It means, rather, that the call of God is repeated. It means that God remembered to call this people who forgot their "call" and that he also calls these people to be true, eternal people of God. It means that he gathered them from all peoples of the earth, and that they are a genuine, real people in a much higher sense than any historical people, because the essential law of the true people is fulfilled in them: you will be my people, and I will be your God.

"From here on it is clear what the presence of the Church means for a culture. It doesn't mean that there is an institution like other useful cultural institutions adopted for the care of the spiritual life and the resurrection of the deep spiritual power of this national tradition. She is not concerned about increasing and internalizing a people's culture, but about the existence of a people as a people. Then when the existence of a people is based on the call of God, then the existence or nonexistence, the life and death, of a people depends on the renewal and hearing of this call. This happens in the Church. And it is literally a question of life and death for any people, that once the Gospel has been heard in its midst the Church of Christ, the people of God, exist hidden before the eyes of the world, and yet recognizable in the proclamation of the pure Gospel" (*Jahrbuch "Auslanddeutschtum* and Evangelical Churches" 1933, printed as issue 20 of the series "Confessing Church," 1934).[69]

That the deceased's unpublished manuscripts of his Erlangen sermons after 1933 were unexpectedly discovered and are all now complete and available, is most of all, thanks to the endeavors of the true disciple of the *Sasse School of Pastors,* Hans-Sigfried Huss.[70] Sorrowfully, there are also no known sermons from the years 1945–1948 in existence. Our collection is complemented by two previously published sermons and one of a series of essays

---

[69] Sasse himself was co-editor of the Confessing Church's series of publications during the Third Reich. MH

[70] We suppose Huss had been a student of Sasse at Erlangen. When Sasse died in 1976, Huss traveled to Australia and collected many of Sasse's papers and returned with them to Germany. The sermons of this volume were presumably in that collection. MH

for congregations. As publisher I would like to thank the Martin Luther Verlag for their willingness to give the missing voice of Sasse the preacher a fresh hearing for many. A particular thanks to them, for without their support this book would remain unpublished. A special thanks also to the [Bavarian] territorial bishop, D. Hermann Dietzfelbinger, for his preface that renews an expression of deep understanding for the individual confessors of the Lutheran Church.

We hope for readers among preachers and hearers of the divine Word that for the proclamation of every standard will apply what Hermann Sasse published forty-five years ago (in the *Kirchliches Jahrbuch* 1934, S, 15[71]). He wrote, "The people want someone to tell them the truth about God, and about men and their sin, about judgment and redemption, about death and life. They want to hear the truth, whole and unvarnished. They do not want the truth to be veiled with rich flowery rhetoric. They want their pastor to vouch with his person and life that what he says is true. They have painted very fine pictures of even us theologians, and, therefore, many have lost enthusiasm for the Church. They wonder if the one speaking really believes, or if he only believes in faith. It is astonishing with what seriousness the German people, the genuine ones, not those joining the masses of the great cities, the farmers, and the workers, judge their church and their pulpit with the question of truth. But so long as the last question arises in the hearts of the people: the question of

---

[71] Feuerhahn no. 119. MH

God and his will, of his judgment and his forgiveness, of the Redeemer, who also bore the sin of the northern men and the German people on the trunk of the cross, of the communion of saints, which transcends all congregations, of the resurrection of the body with which all theories of race and materialism must end. And so long as our people do not want to hear beautiful, uplifting clichés on this question, but the truth, then one will not tell us the people have no interest in dogmatic questions or that they don't understand theological matters. Neither should they need to understand them. They have no interest in arguments, but they have an interest in the truth. And they will not betray or give up the Church or the truth she proclaims."

Friedrich Wilhelm Hopf[72]

---

[72] Hopf (1910–1982) had been a student at Erlangen 1928–1932 under Procksch, Elert, and Preuss. Sasse began teaching there in 1933. He was closely associated with Sasse in the *Kirchenkampf.* Sasse repeatedly stated that after WWII his students were being driven from the preaching office and thus he himself had to go into exile. Hopf was removed from office as pastor at Mühlhausen for opposing the Bavarian Church's entrance into the EKiD in 1949. In 1950 he joined the Independent Evangelical Lutheran Church and became Missions Director at Hermansberg, where he died in July 1982. He was an early and significant opponent of Apartheid in South Africa, where the independent Lutherans carried on mission work. Through *Lutherische Blätter*, Hopf helped spread Sasse's writings to the world. For a comprehensive look at Hopf's life and work, see *Friedrich Wilhelm Hopf: Kritische Standpunkte für die Gegenwart. Ein lutherischer Theologe im Kirchenkampf des Dritten Reichs, über seinen Bekenntniskampf nach 1945 und zum Streit um seine Haltung zur Apartheid. Herausgegeben von Markus Büttner und Werner Klän. Oberurseler Hefte Ergänzungsband 11.* MH

In the New Church Year
1st Sunday in Advent
November 29, 1936[73]
Hebrews 10:19–25[74]

Therefore, brothers, since we have confidence to enter the holy places by the blood of Jesus, by the new and living way that he opened for us through the curtain, that is, through his flesh, and since we have a great priest over the house of God, let us draw near with a true heart in full assurance of faith, with our hearts sprinkled clean from an evil conscience and our bodies washed with pure water. Let us hold fast the confession of our hope without wavering, for he who promised is faithful. And let us consider how to stir up one another to love and good works, not neglecting to meet together, as is the habit of some, but encouraging one another, and all the more as you see the Day drawing near. (Hebrews 10:19–25)

It is certainly more than a coincidence when in the modern world the Church Year and the common year, which at Luther's time coincided, have drifted farther and farther apart from each other. Today, as we celebrate the beginning of a new Church Year, we see a glimpse of the fact that the Church has a different relationship to time than

---

[73] Sasse had been under a travel restriction for his rejection of the Nazi Party platform. Earlier in 1936 he traveled to England: "When I visited Archbishop Temple the last time in York—1936, it happened secretly, for I was already under prohibition of travel, but I had to finish my business as secretary of Faith and Order for the continent." Sasse to Domprobst Danell, Oct. 17, 1958. Feuerhahn, *Sasse as Ecumenical Churchman*, p. 37. MH

[74] *Predigt: 1. Sonntag im Advent (29 Nov. 1936) "Im Neuen Kirchenjahr."* Feuerhahn 159.1a. MH

the world. The Church also lives in this world where the laws of the Creator rule. The laws of the Old Testament are clothed in the great words: everything has its time [Eccles. 3:1]. Yes the Church also lives in this world where the heavenly bodies follow their orbits, where the years and the year's seasons change, where generations are born and generations die.

And yet the Church has a special relationship to time. She can wait. For nineteen centuries, she has sung in her liturgy, "Hosanna to the Son of David! Blessed is he who comes in the name of the Lord!" [Matt. 21:9]. For nineteen centuries, she has raised her heart up to he who comes to judge the living and the dead. For nineteen centuries, she has prayed: "Amen. Come, Lord Jesus!" [Rev. 22:20b]. And she has heard the answer: "Surely I am coming soon" [Rev. 22:20a]. For nineteen centuries, she has had to hear the mocking question: "Where is the promise of his coming? For ever since the fathers fell asleep, all things are continuing as they were from the beginning of creation" (2 Pet. 3:4). And through all these centuries, even to this very day, she has had no other answer than the comforting and admonishing word of the New Testament concerning the time of Christendom: "But do not overlook this one fact, beloved, that with the Lord one day is as a thousand years, and a thousand years as one day. The Lord is not slow to fulfill his promise as some count slowness, but is patient toward you, not wishing that any should perish, but that all should reach repentance" (2 Pet. 3:8–9). God has patience with us. And so the Church waits patiently. The world does not know this patience. It cannot wait. It must have everything immediately. That is true of everything in the modern world, of the people of the last century. Therefore because it is a hope that has not yet been fulfilled in these nineteen centuries, it is simply refuted. We must all be clear about this, beloved Advent Church, about just how ridiculous we make ourselves in the eyes of the world, when today in the year 1936 we gather in this house of God around our hope for the coming of the Lord to strengthen, to suffer, and to pray with the Christendom of all centuries: "Amen. Come Lord Jesus!"

If only we at least had a new hope, and not just the old that has become so disappointing. But that would not be the truth. That is what makes the Church so boring, that she lives by an old hope, and by an old faith. The world always wants to say and to hear something new like the Athenians in Acts (Acts 17:21). New research, the newest results of science, new worldviews, even brand new myths that still smell of the printer's ink from which they originate, that is what the world searches for, new truths for which the ears itch, as the New Testament so clearly says (2 Tim. 4:3). But the Church always has the old truth. We do not know what the newspapers say about Christmas, Easter, and Pentecost, but what is preached here from the chancel about Christmas, Easter, and Pentecost, we know this well. On this high festival there is nothing else to be preached than what has always been proclaimed, the greatest action of God that happened once and for all. So today on the threshold of the new Church Year in the Advent of 1936,

49

we still have no other message to hear than that which Christendom in all times and all peoples have heard and should hear in the preaching of Advent.

We hear this message from the Epistle, which is selected according to the order of our Church for this Sunday, from the Letter to the Hebrews. Here we immediately hit upon a great difficulty. Whoever these people may have been, to whom this apostolic writing was directed, they were in any case Hebrews, baptized Jews, Christians of Palestinian descent. And the picture described in this letter is a picture of the temple in Jerusalem, the Holy of Holies, and all the saints, and the curtain between them through which the high priest goes on the great day of reconciliation when the greatest sacrifice of reconciliation is brought forth. And this picture serves to illustrate the godly wonder of our redemption. We too have a High Priest, who reconciles us with God. This High Priest, this mediator between God and men, is Jesus Christ. But the sacrifice he brings is his own body and blood: "Behold, the Lamb of God who takes away the sins of the world!" [John 1:29]. He brought this sacrifice to Golgotha and has gone to the heavenly sanctuary. With that he paved the way for us, and opened the door to God. "Therefore, brothers, since we have confidence to enter the holy places by the blood of Jesus, by the new and living way that he opened for us through the curtain, that is, through his flesh, and since we have a great priest over the house of God, let us draw near with a true heart in full assurance of faith, with our hearts sprinkled clean from an evil conscience and our bodies washed with pure water. Let us hold fast the confession of our hope without wavering, for he who promised is faithful" (Heb. 10:19–23).

Yet, while we hear this word, the hard and serious question looms large over our souls. Will this proclamation be understood at all in our time? To what extent should this that was first written to "the Hebrews" be applied to the Germans of the twentieth century? How long will it be until a generation has grown up that is not able to sing "Daughter of Zion, Rejoice"[75] and "Jerusalem, O City Fair and High?"[76] How soon will the knowledge of the Bible, the knowledge of the Old Testament, become so small that there won't be one out of two experts who will know any longer how it looked in the temple and what happened there? Does the Church then have any other option other than to teach our young people? Here we stand before the great question that is quickly becoming Germany's fateful question, a question concerning the Christian Church in Germany and also the German culture. It is the question of Scripture. It is good that we clear this up on the threshold of the new Church Year. Behind the political problem of the Jewish people, over which we have not spoken about here, appears the question of the Bible that we have in common with the people of Israel. I say the question of the

---

[75] 1. "Zion's daughter, O rejoice! Shout aloud, Jerusalem! Lo, thy King doth come to thee, Yea, He comes, the Prince of Peace! Zion's daughter, O rejoice! Shout aloud, Jerusalem!" The Wartburg Hymnal, hymn 85 (Chicago: Wartburg Publishing House, 1918). MH

[76] *Jerusalem, Du Hochgebaute Stadt*, Johann Matthäus Meyfart 1590–1642, *LSB* 674. MH

Bible, and not only the question of the Old Testament, because even though the difference between the Old and New Testament is certainly great—as great as the difference between the word of the prophets and the proclamation the apostles, between the promise of the Messiah and the incarnation of the eternal Son of God—yet no one is able to tear apart the two components of Scripture without completely destroying it. He who rejects the Old Testament, he must, as is the point of our Epistle, also destroy the New Testament.[77] He must also reject the Epistle to the Hebrews, the letters of Paul, yes all the letters of the New Testament, also the Book of Revelation and the Book of Acts, and in the end, even the Gospels. Yes, he must also reject Jesus Christ, the real Jesus Christ, who was a son of David according to the flesh. At best, he holds the lingering crazy thought of an ideal Christ, who has never lived, one that men made up in the Gospel. So it is that the German people today wrestle with the question of the Bible as never before, not since the days of the Reformation. It is certainly not an accident that all the German people ask this question, everyone will discuss it, all Christians in Germany, the Catholics as well as us Evangelicals. It is certainly not an accident that the Catholic Church in Germany experiences a powerful biblical movement today. The question of Holy Scripture is the most controversial, the most burning question regarding our worldview in Germany today. It is, at the same time, a real question of

---

[77] A pointed rejection of the "German Christians" or "Christian" Nazis. MH

life, a question that actually deals with life and death. Because if the assumption that the Bible is God's Word is false, then that means that the destruction of its authority was a great loss, because now the wrong path followed for a millennium and a half since the Gothic Bible was published is coming to an end. Or the Bible is God's Word. That means that its destruction and rejection is the rejection of God. Then what is proclaimed in the streets and markets concerning the Old Testament and the God of the Old Testament today is blasphemy and must pay the consequences that all blasphemy has. When the Word of God, as it says in Hebrews (4:12) "is living and active, sharper than any two-edged sword," when it, as the whole Bible testifies and as Christian Germany has believed through so many centuries, is really the great power of all the world's history, then we must all perish on the power of this Word when we despise it. That is the fateful seriousness of the biblical question put before our people. It is good, in fact it is dire, that we remind ourselves of it at the beginning of the new Church Year. The fight over the Bible will give this Church Year its rich Church historical context because of this question. It is because it so stands that we are called from our text to a joyfulness of holy, faithful certainty that bears confession. That is what is demanded today from our Church, what is demanded from us as a Christian congregation, and from every one of us individually because we can't prove to anyone that Holy Scripture is the Almighty God's almighty Word. However, we can and should testify to it. Our church testifies to it by

God's Word

53

selecting such texts for its pastors to preach. And we as a Christian congregation testify to it when we gather around this preaching. And so we hear it then as an exhortation that we send out on the threshold of the new Church Year in a time of refusal and denial, this exhortation to the joyful confession: "Since we have a great priest over the house of God, . . . let us hold fast the confession of our hope" [Heb. 10:21, 23].

Yes, we confess ourselves to his, the true High Priest's, the only mediator between God and man about whom this tenth chapter of Hebrews in another verse says, "By a single offering he has perfected for all time those who are being sanctified" (v. 14). We confess that "Jesus Christ, true God, begotten of the Father in eternity and also true man, born of the Virgin Mary, is my Lord, who has redeemed me a lost and condemned man."[78] "With true hearts let us hold fast to the confession of our hope." But can we go into the new Church Year with such joyfulness? We would like it so much. We have such a lively feeling for that which our church must be today. Oh, that we would be a church that could confess with such a power, with such a joyfulness and joyful certainty. But how we feel our helplessness. Our German Church is like a great field of ruins. The refuse of faith. The refuse of enthusiasm! How can such a church exist?

However, we must also confess joyfully in view of these facts. And that is just what our Epistle will say to us. He is judge of the Church, who knows the refuse.

---

[78] SC, Creed II.

"Therefore lift your drooping hands and strengthen your weak knees" (12:12). Here the Church, wherever she lives, learns about who her Lord is, about whom she waits for despite all disappointment. And she can wait for him because he is with her. That is the mystery of the expectation of the Early Church. She could wait, because she was with him, hidden under the means of grace, in the Lord's Supper. That is the mystery of the coming of Christ.

Come, Lord Jesus!

"Surely I am coming soon!"

Advent's Ageless Question
3rd Sunday in Advent
December 17, 1933[79]
Matthew 11:2–11[80]

Now when John heard in prison about the deeds of the
Christ, he sent word by his disciples and said to him, "Are
you the one who is to come, or shall we look for another?"
And Jesus answered them, "Go and tell John what you hear
and see: the blind receive their sight and the lame walk,
lepers are cleansed and the deaf hear, and the dead are
raised up, and the poor have good news preached to them.
And blessed is the one who is not offended by me."

As they went away, Jesus began to speak to the crowds
concerning John: "What did you go out into the wilderness
to see? A reed shaken by the wind? What then did you go
out to see? A man dressed in soft clothing? Behold, those
who wear soft clothing are in kings' houses. What then did
you go out to see? A prophet? Yes, I tell you, and more
than a prophet. This is he of whom it is written,

"Behold, I send my messenger before your face,

---

[79] In August of 1933 Sasse and Bonhoeffer had composed the "Bethel
Confession," the most significant of the documents of the Church
protesting Nazism prior to Barmen. Sasse's *Kirchlisches Jahrbuch* (the
annual then went to every clergyman in Germany) was censored
because of his outspoken rejection of Nazism in the '31 and '32
volumes. His appointment to the Erlangen theological faculty was
nearly aborted when the Nazis intervened and withheld approval over
Sasse's rejection of the constitution of the DEK (German Ev. Church),
a forced union constitution adopted by the increasingly Nazified church
in September 1933 in Wittenberg. Sasse appeared before Bavarian
Minister of Culture Hans Schemm. The approval came on April 25.
Loewenich described it as a "miracle." Feuerhahn, *Sasse as an
Ecumenical Churchman*, op. cit., p. 47.
[80] *Predigt: 3. Sonntag im Advent (17 Dez 1933). "Eine Adventsfrage
Aller Zeiten."* Feuerhahn 117a. MH

who will prepare your way before you."
Truly, I say to you, among those born of women there has arisen no one greater than John the Baptist. Yet the one who is least in the kingdom of heaven is greater than he." (Matthew 11:2–11)

For a thousand years, this Gospel has been read from the altars in the chancels of Western Christendom, and the Church's Advent message of the coming Christ has been brought to heart. And the message of Advent is none other than this: that the historical man, Jesus of Nazareth, who was executed before the gates of Jerusalem during the reign of the great Tiberius [Caesar, ruled AD 14–37] and under the government of Pontius Pilate, is the Christ, the true Redeemer of the world, who will come again in glory to judge the living and the dead, whose kingdom will have no end. Everything we associate with the message of Advent, all the pretty poetical Advent customs to which our souls have clung since childhood, all the symbols of this charming season in the Church Year, the evergreen of the Advent wreaths with their burning candles, our children's first Christmas carols and their blessed joy for the Christ Child, all get their meaning from the message of Advent. Yet all this should be done away with and completely forgotten if it becomes a substitute for the true celebration of Advent. Just as the Church of Jesus Christ has the duty to extinguish all the candles on the Christmas tree forever if they become a substitute for the true light, the illumination for every man, which came into the world and will be the light of the entire world on the greatest day of Jesus Christ

57

for which we wait. The Church lives on this message alone. She does not know of any German Advent or of an American Advent or Chinese Advent. She only knows the Advent of Jesus Christ. She has waited for him since the days of the apostles. Already, nineteen centuries have passed and yet she still waits for the end of the world. She will not grow tired of praying the last words of the Bible, "Amen. Come, Lord Jesus," and believing in His promise, "Surely I am coming soon" [Rev, 22:20]. This Advent the Church proclaims the day of Jesus Christ to the world. It was with this message that she once stepped into the world and went to the Jew, the Greek, and the Roman. She also came to the people of the North. With this message, she went to the great cultures of the East and the people of Africa. She has only one message, and it is for all people and for every age. The world changes, races come and go, people come to life, and people die. The spiritual lives of men experience the deepest changes. The systems of philosophy, the worldviews, the religions, the knowledge of science, all is in flux. They all change, but the message of the Church is always the same. Therefore she works the same way in every culture, the ancient and the modern, the European like the Asian, monotone and backwards, uninteresting and improbable. And men shake their heads at the Church, because she remains undismayed, never doubting year after year, century after century, always the same confession and proclamation: "And he will come again in glory to judge the living and the dead, whose kingdom will have no end."

But it is interesting. So often men have said, "This proclamation is no longer relevant; no one can understand it. Man is definitely done with it: the humanity of today is finished with it." But you cannot lay this message aside like a philosophical system. It forces you to take a position. Wherever this message is proclaimed it creates unrest, violence, and fights. When Paul proclaimed it to the educated Athenians, they told him with polite understanding that they would have nothing to do with it [Acts 17]. But then everything, even the great philosophies of the Greeks became affected by this message. Is Jesus really the Redeemer, "Light of Light, God of God, very God of very God"? Ever since that time this has become the great theme of philosophy. When the message became known to the authorities of the Roman Empire, they dismissed it with a formal gesture. But then the question "Is Jesus Christ Lord?" became the great question of the Roman world. And everything that this world power still experienced in history became bound to this question. And so it was, wherever this message went. This question echoes among humankind everywhere throughout history and until the end of the world: "Are you the one who is to come, or shall we look for another?" [Luke 7:20]. That has been the profound question of humanity since the first time the message of Advent rang throughout the world. It is a question of life, a true question of life for every man and for all peoples, a question that is really about life and death. It is a question of life for you and me, beloved Christians; it is the question of life for our German people even in the

59

age of the Third Reich.

This question was asked by one man in our Gospel. He asked it not only in his name, but also in the name of his disciples, in the name of his people, and in the name of humanity. Who is this man? Who was this John? The person asking the question is obviously not inconsequential. Jesus himself, so reports the evangelist, began to speak to the people about this noteworthy questioner [Luke 7:24–35]. "What did you go out into the wilderness to see? A reed shaken by the wind?" [v. 24]. Why did you journey out to the desolate wilderness on the banks of the Jordan River where the wind shakes the reeds? "What then did you go out to see, a man dressed in soft clothing?" [v. 25]. A distinguished man, a modest man who enjoys the popularity of the church? Behold, those who wear soft clothing are in the houses of kings. No, for that you must go elsewhere. Famous men are not found in the wasteland of the deserted wilderness. Did you want to see a prophet? Yes, that he was.

Do we still know what that means: a prophet? We men of the twentieth century, we members of the Church, in which the gifts of the prophets are nearly extinguished? Certainly, there are no longer any prophets in the old sense of the word, not since the eternal Word of God became man in Jesus Christ or the witness of the apostles have pointed us to him. However, there is a prophecy that is promised to the Church of Christ and by which it is served. Were it living among us our church would not be so devastated by false and fanatical prophets as she is today. We would understand what the nature of God's greatest prophets was: Why then did men come from every region and go out to John in the wasteland? To hear an enthusiastic speaker, a religious guru, a popular evangelist? No my friends no one goes to the desert for that. Pretty religious speeches are heard in warm auditoriums. An evangelist is expected to go to the masses, and therefore do not wait for the masses to come to them. That is why he searches for the right meeting place for his hearers to come: "You brood of vipers" [Luke 3:7]. That is why he takes into consideration their feelings, wishes, and values and does not proclaim the wrath of God, the end of the nation, and the end of the world. That is why he does not preach so one-sidedly the Second Article, but expounds upon the first beginning and the order of creation. No, an evangelist John was not. The people did not go to him for this reason. What drove them to him? It was their hunger and thirst for that which the prophet Amos had once spoken, a hunger and thirst that is not natural to man but sent by God himself: "Not a famine of bread, nor a thirst for water, but of hearing the words of the LORD" (Amos 8:11).

Do we Germans of the twentieth century still know this hunger and thirst as our people once knew it during the Reformation? Do we still know something of the languishing for the Bread of Life, for the Spring of Life, when men literally lived on the Word of God? This hunger and this thirst made the people journey to the Jordan, because this bread was there. Here the Word of God happened. Here occurred the Word of God. Here was a man who served God with his Word. He didn't discuss his wisdom, his thoughts, his feelings and experience. He was one who was solely a vessel of the living God. He only proclaimed the eternal will and counsel of God. He proclaimed God's justice and God's mercy. He did not elevate his own will, did not lust after wealth. He didn't elevate his claim on life. He was only a voice—a powerful impression went out from him, and a great congregation gathered around him. He had a circle of disciples, and had given his disciples a prayer, just as Jesus gave us the "Our Father." He had given them the Sacrament of Baptism for the forgiveness of sins, which Jesus took over from him and gave again to his Church. And yet an echo of the question is still ringing in this Gospel: is it possible that he was the Redeemer of the world? Centuries later an Eastern religious community of the last century had seen in him the greatest prophet of God.[81] But he only desired to be a path-maker for the Coming One. "He must increase, but I must decrease" [John 3:30] remained written over the life of the great and humble man, the greatest of all prophets. "Yes, I tell you, and more than a prophet" [Matt. 11:9]. Jesus said this of him, a great compliment, the greatest that he said of any man! "Truly, I say to you, among those born of women there has risen no one greater than John the Baptist" [Matt. 11:11]. The greatest of all men before the beginning of the kingdom of God! How this judgment violates our idea of what it means to be a great man.

This judgment shows the great difference between the

---

[81] Mandaeanism. MH

judgment of God and man in regards to great men. In this spirit let's place the great men of world history, the great creative geniuses, next to John the Baptist. Place Plato [ca 428–348 BC], Buddha [ca. 563–483 BC], or Goethe [1749–1832] next to him. Compare John the Baptist to the great leaders of the world, whose names have been recorded in the history of man. Then hear this judgment, which will be revealed to all men before the judgment seat: "Truly, I say to you, among those born of women there has arisen no one greater than John the Baptist."

And now we find this great man in the deepest misery of captivity. Now he has been locked behind the dungeon doors forever. Now his voice has been silenced. He would have stopped being God's prophet if he had not also proclaimed God's will and God's justice to the powers of the world, even as the Church stops being Christ's Church when she no longer dares to speak God's eternal Word to the powers of the world. He dared to do this. He told one of the powers of the earth that the Sixth Commandment was meant for him also [Matt. 14] and that the wrath of God would strike him for disregarding it with the so-called gentleman's standard. Now he would be a casualty of the gentleman's standard. Now "night is coming, when no one can work" [John 9:4], but this was not the deepest misery. but the other, that God would not spare him the deep anxiousness through which he has led all his saints. We can't comprehend what went through this man's soul at that time. We now have a premonition of just how very hard the fight must have been. Now we hear the question, which he sent his disciples to ask Jesus after hearing of Christ's work: "Are you the one who is to come, or shall we look for another?" [Matt. 11:3; Luke 7:19]. Is that which happened in Galilee the dawn of the new kingdom? Is this Jesus, the Christ, the Coming One, the Redeemer of the world? During this period of deep angst in his life, he asked the fearful question. It was a question of life for him, literally a question of life, because if Jesus is the Christ, then he is also his Christ, his Lord, and his Redeemer. Then the promise must be fulfilled in him. "The Spirit of the Lord is upon me, because he has anointed me to proclaim good news to the poor; he has sent me to bind up the brokenhearted, to proclaim liberty to the captives and recovering of sight to the blind, to set at liberty those who are oppressed" (Luke 4:18; Isa. 61:1 [author's translation]). To bind up the brokenhearted, to proclaim liberty to the captives! Yes, if he is my Redeemer then he must open the doors of my dungeon. "Are you the one who is to come, or shall we look for another?" Truly this is not a theoretical question. The question of who Jesus is is never a theoretical question. It is a question of life. Has he ever heard a drowning person cry for help? With a voice that is no more than a man's voice? Has he heard a seriously wounded soldier cry for a paramedic on the battlefield?[82] Does he

---

[82] Sasse served as a chaplain in WWI in the horrid battle of Passchendaele. See *Letters to Lutheran Pastors I*, liv–lv. "I shall never forget that wet autumn day in Belgium, when we were assembled before we went into the great battle of Passchendaele. . . . After the service, the Lord's Supper was celebrated; some people went to receive Holy Communion, and then we went up to Passchendaele. We were

know this voice? That is John's question. And the greatest of all men asked it, but not just in his name. He binds together all the miserable, the crushed, the imprisoned, the blind, and the poor of this world with the "we" of this question. He not only asked this question for himself, but for everyone. This is everyone's question: "Are you the one who is to come, or shall we look for another?"

With what frightened expectation he must have waited for the answer. What disappointment he must have felt when the time came and he heard the answer: "Go and tell John what you have seen and heard: the blind receive their sight, the lame walk, lepers are cleansed, and the deaf hear, the dead are raised up, and the poor have good news preached to them. And blessed is the one who is not offended by me" [Luke 7:22–23]. What does this answer mean? Is it a "yes"? John had known all this before. Even with all these things happening he asked. Why didn't Jesus give a clear answer? There was only one time when Jesus answered this question frankly: as he stood before the judge's bench. "I am, and you will see the Son of Man seated at the right hand of Power, and coming with the clouds of heaven" (Mark 14:62; [see also] Matt. 26:64). Why doesn't he answer the question so frankly now? Perhaps because he is a different kind of redeemer than the world thought: A different kind of redeemer than John

---

one hundred and fifty men, fully equipped and a full company. On the sixth we came back and six men reported. The others were killed or had disappeared in the fire, the water and the gas of one of the worst battles of the First World War. When we came back, we heard of the Russian Revolution." "The Impact of Bultmannism . . ." p. 4. MH

thought of him. In his words, as in the entire story and the Gospel, is the deep riddle of hidden glory. "The blind receive their sight, the lame walk, lepers are cleansed, and the deaf hear, the dead are raised up, the poor have good news preached to them" [Luke. 7:22]. His disciples, who lived through this, could not have helped but to see the beginning of the new world, of which is promised: "And death shall be no more, neither shall there be mourning, nor crying, nor pain anymore" (Rev. 21:4). They could do nothing but confess, "We have believed, and have come to know, that" "you are the Christ, the Son of the living God" (John 6:69; Matt. 16:16), and attest to the word, "We have seen his glory, glory as of the only Son from the Father" (John 1:14). But hundreds of thousands of others have also seen him and have not seen the glory. How many lame, blind, and deaf? And all of the sick people who died! What kind of Redeemer is he? How does it help me, John would have thought, that in Galilee the dead are resurrected? Between him and Jesus was a three-day walk. Between Jesus and us there are nineteen centuries of world history! How does it help us that at one time such things happened on earth? What then has become of others through the appearance of Jesus Christ? Does the world look like the Redeemer's feet have walked on it? And if the great days of Jesus Christ were the morning light, why doesn't the sun rise up? "Watchman, what time of the night?" (Isa. 21:11). That is the greatest disappointment Christ has given us. Certainly, this disappointment has been felt throughout time by John the Baptist, by Christ's disciples, his people,

66

and his Church. "Where is the promise of his coming? For ever since the fathers fell asleep, all things are continuing as they were from the beginning of creation" (2 Peter 3:4). Why is it that men again and again become confused about him? Why are they confused about him today? The whole modern world of the last two centuries deduced: he must have been a great teacher, but even so, he was not what the New Testament says he was. Millions of men in every land have lost their faith since the world war. And all that our people have lived through since the spring of 1933[83] has influenced the people very deeply, the view our people have of Christ will be nothing else. The doubt about him clothes itself in a new form. Still, nothing has changed. Men turn from atheism to some other worldview. Is not the departure to pre-Christian religions in our time a meaningful sign that the doubt about Jesus remains? There will be more Christmas trees burning in Germany this year than the Christmas before. In many houses there will be more Christmas carols sung, houses in which they haven't been heard for a long time. There will be many who become homesick for the long forgotten Christmas. Perhaps it will bring more people to church, but will it also cause more to join in the Church's confession of Jesus Christ, in the incarnation of the eternal Son, "begotten of his Father before all worlds, God of God, Light of Light, very God of very God"? Or will they also raise humanity's old question to heaven on this Christmas? "Are you the one who is to come, or shall we look for another?" [Luke 7:20].

---

[83] When Hitler took over dictatorial power. MH

But today, as before, it will be up to men to discern a "yes" from his Gospel. Men who understand "the poor have good news preached to them. And blessed is the one who is not offended by me" [Luke 7:23–24]. Foolish perhaps in the eyes of the world, but foolishness in Christ (1 Cor. 4:10). Men who hear his Word throughout all the past centuries that separate us from him. Men who are called by his name, to whom he said, "Your sins are forgiven" [Matt. 9:2]. Men who ask him, "Are you the one who is to come, or shall we look for another?" And while they are speaking to him, he begins to speak. And they understand the mystery of faith in him: "I believe that I cannot by my own reason or strength believe in Jesus Christ, my Lord, or come to him, but the Holy Spirit has called me by the Gospel, enlightened me with his gifts, sanctified and kept me in the true faith."[84] Men who have heard the words of Jesus, "You did not chose me, but I chose you" [John 15:16]. They understand his silence, because we have not asked him, but he has asked us. He does not need to be justified by us, but we need to be justified by him. We are not his judge. He is our judge. We have not forgiven him. He has forgiven us. We do not decide to make him our *Führer.*[85] No, he chooses to be our Lord.

---

[84] SC, Creed III.

[85] *Führer* is German for leader and probably should be translated as such, except that in translating it you would lose the obvious dig at Hitler who demanded to be called *Führer*.

The Mysteries of God
Third Sunday in Advent
December 15, 1940
1 Corinthians 4:1–5[86]

This is how one should regard us, as servants of Christ and stewards of the mysteries of God. Moreover, it is required of stewards that they be found faithful. But with me it is a very small thing that I should be judged by you or by any human court. In fact, I do not even judge myself. I am not aware of anything against myself, but I am not thereby acquitted. It is the Lord who judges me. Therefore do not pronounce judgment before the time, before the Lord comes, who will bring to light the things now hidden in darkness and will disclose the purposes of the heart. Then each one will receive his commendation from God. (1 Cor. 4:1–5)

In Advent of 1930, a professor in a northern German university was lying on his deathbed. He was one of the foremost experts and keenest observers of the modern world's spiritual life. Growing up in a Catholic home, he had been alienated from his church as a young man, only to return to the faith of his childhood later in life. But now he was lying at last in a sickbed at the height of his life, stricken by an incurable disease and in full view of his impending death. There he wrote with the last of his strength a short farewell to his school on the day before Christmas. The letter he wrote belongs to the most humanly

---

[86] *Predigt: 3. Sonntag im Advent (15 Dez 1940). "Gottes Geheimnisse."* Feuerhahn no. 224a. MH

moving documents in the history of philosophy. Therein he searched to point to the deepest meaning of our age when he said, "That as we experience the most intense stage of the Western Advent, this great and deep affliction of a Europe in the wake of the failed Enlightenment, we should once more return to and ponder our simple inheritance from Bethlehem . . ." "Metanoeite, Repent!" The letter continues, "This call has been heard since the days of Napoleon. It calls even louder to the European intelligencia. *Metanoeite*, repent—this call has rung throughout the entire nineteenth century. It has become even more intensive in the twentieth century, screaming over the thundering cannons of two world wars. It will be with great astonishment that some will look back on the last 150 years, and see how at first it was but a small spiritual movement, but then larger sections of the western intellegencia began to see at last that the age without Christ has not brought the freedom so many others had promised." It should be pointed out that many very unlucky men have had their lives destroyed by the question of God, because of men like [Heinrich von] Kleist [1777–1811], [Johann Christian Friedrich] Hölderlin [1770–1843] and Friedrich Nietzsche [1844–1900] who were leaders in the spiritual life of Germany. Their lives were destroyed by the question of Christ. This should call to mind for us the deepest words of Augustine [354–430]: "You had it so organized, O God, that you yourself will punish an unorganized spirit."

Whatever one might say about these points, he is right about one. If there was ever a time in which the question of

Christ has moved the spirit and separated the spirit, it is our age. This is evident by the fact that many men can simply no longer bear the fact that we use a Christian calendar that counts the years beginning with the year Christ was born or that secular newspapers mention the Christian Christmas, that Christian books also appear in bookstores and Christmas catalogues, that German children sing Christmas carols and bow their knees towards the Christ Child's crib in Bethlehem—I say that many people can no longer bear this. Here, we simply acknowledge this fact without any bitterness or accusation—this is evidence that we are already in the middle of an age in which the spirit is divided over Christ. In the midst of the noise accompanying this great war is the great spiritual battle that follows every great war of the West. The fight is really about whether there will be any room in Germany after this war for this child in the crib. It is about whether or not there will be any room for the inheritance of the Christian West in the new Europe when it steps out of this sea of blood and tears. This fight is more than a wrestling of human spirits.

This is why the Church celebrates Advent in a different manner today than it did a generation ago. At that time Advent was a time to quietly prepare for the most beautiful feast of the year. Who at that time understood the meaning of the Advent message? Who still understands that the Advent of Jesus Christ has two sides? That we celebrate both his arrival in humility and his return in glory during Advent? Who understands that the Gospel and the Epistle for Advent call the Church and world to repentance because Advent is actually a time of great repentance in the Church?

The ancient Epistle for the Third Sunday in Advent also calls the Church to repentance before God, to the deep reflection on her own nature and commission. She does this because the Church lives in between the First and Second Advent, in between the arrival of Christ in humility and his return in glory because the time of the Church is this time between the incarnation of God's Son and his return on the Day of Judgment. This Church is a congregation of poor sinners wandering through the centuries of history, despised and abused by the world. No one but God sees any glory in it, because the world does not understand what she keeps in her hands. The world does not understand this truth they retain from century to century and millennium to millennium because it is the mystery of God.

Yes, a congregation of poor sinners! That is the Church our Epistle places before our eyes now. Many churches, like the Church of Corinth did not look like the Church of God to the world, but they were saints in Christ Jesus. The apostle Paul even addressed the Church of Corinth as holy in his letter. "For consider your calling, brothers: not many of you were wise according to worldly standards, not many were powerful, not many were of noble birth. But God chose what is foolish in the world . . . ; God chose what is low and despised in the world, even things that are not . . ." (1 Cor. 1:26–30). But it isn't only on the scale of the Gentile world that the Church fails to make a good impression. We Christians like to idealize the Church and then search for this Church in the pages of the New Testament. But the Church wasn't even perfect in the beginning. That is pointed out to us by the example of the Church of Corinth and the few churches near Jerusalem of which we have real pictures. There the Christians brought each other to trial in the Gentile courts [1 Cor. 6:1–8]—like we do. They would relapse, falling prey to the awful vices of the Gentile cities—like we do [1 Cor. 5; 6:12–20.]. There were denials of the resurrection—as we have today [1 Cor. 15:20ff.]. There were also excommunications [1 Cor. 5]. We, in fact, owe the first account of Holy Communion, the first teaching about the Sacrament [1 Cor. 11:17–34.], to the fact that at that time, some twenty years after the institution of the Lord's Supper, this Sacrament was already decaying to such a point that Paul had to write the Church in Corinth: "When you come together, it is not the Lord's supper that you eat" [1 Cor. 11:20]. There were splinters, movements and parties—as with us. "I follow Paul," said one. "I follow Apollos," said the other. "I follow Peter," said the third. And the apostle had to intervene: "Is Christ divided? Was Paul crucified for you? Or were you baptized in the name of Paul?" (1 Cor. 1:12–13). "What then is Apollos? What is Paul? Servants through whom you believed as the Lord assigned to each? I planted, Apollos watered, but God gave the growth" (1 Cor. 3:5–6). "So let no one boast in men. For all things are yours, whether Paul or Apollos or Cephas or the world or life or death of the present or the future—all are yours, and you are Christ's and Christ is God's" (1 Cor. 3:21–23). And then he goes on to join himself with the other apostles: "This is how one should regard us, as servants of Christ and stewards of the mysteries of God" (1 Cor. 4:1). The Church does not belong to men, but to God alone. Men don't have power over you, but only your Lord Jesus Christ. The Corinthians were worshiping men. There is no room for this in Christ's Church. The world likes to admire heroes, and lives on hero worship. In the Church there is no hero worship. Paul, who was a genuine genius, a brilliant man, a product of the classical era's spiritual life, put himself on the same level as Apollos and the other apostles even though these men were not geniuses. In the Church the heroes of the faith are no higher than the desperate man who prays with folded hands, "I believe; help my unbelief!" [Mark 9:24]. In the Church, St. Francis of Assisi [1182–1226] and Saint Elizabeth are no higher than the simplest deaconess consumed by the service of the poor and distressed. The intellectual giants of Christendom, like Augustine and Thomas Aquinas [1225–1274], are no higher than the poorest of the intellectually weak children in the bottom wing of an institution who can't learn anything more than to sing a Christmas carol to their Savior. There is no hierarchy in the Church, no chain of command, no nobility of blood or spirit. There is only the poverty of nothing that Augustine expressed with his favorite verse of the New Testament. He writes about this chapter: "What do you have that you did not receive" [1 Cor. 4:7]. And Luther, in the last words that he ever wrote: "We are all beggars. This is true."[87] There is only the wealth that God has given us: "without Him all that pleases is valueless on earth; the gifts I have from Jesus Alone have priceless worth."[88] In the Church, men count for nothing, and God for everything. And all the natural gifts the Creator has given us men—without any merit or worthiness—find their greatest worth in the service of God.

"This is how one should regard us, as servants of Christ and stewards of the mysteries of God." That was the task of the apostles and the task of those who are ordained to this service of Word and Sacrament: to be servants of Christ and stewards of the mysteries of God. The churches' chancels are not there for us to bring our own wisdom and small thoughts to the people, but it is there for us to proclaim the message entrusted to us. The Sacraments of Baptism and the Lord's Supper, which we perform, are not cultic actions that men thought up. Rather, we celebrate Baptism and the Lord's Supper as Christ commanded us.

---

[87] See Sasse's "Luther's Legacy to Christianity," Feuerhahn no. 252 (1946) in *The Lonely Way II*, pp. 171ff. "Nobody can understand Virgil in his *Bucolics* and *Georgics* unless he has first been a shepherd or a farmer for five years. Nobody understands Cicero in his letters unless he has been engaged in public affairs of some consequence for twenty years. Let nobody suppose that he has tasted the Holy Scriptures sufficiently unless he has ruled over the churches with the prophets for a hundred years. Therefore there is something wonderful, first, about John the Baptist; second, about Christ; third about the apostles. 'Lay not your hand on the divine Aenied, but bow before it, adore its every trace.' We are beggars. That is true.' " These were the last thoughts of Dr. Luther on the day before he died." WA TR 5.317. No. 5677; AE 54.476. This "divine Aenied" is the Holy Scriptures. MH

[88] "*An mir und meinem Leben ist nichts auf dieser Erd; was Christus mir gegeben, das is der Liebe wert.*" "If God Himself Be for Me." Paul Gerhardt 1607–1676. *LSB* 724. MH

The world does not understand this message nor does it understand these actions. She started to mock them already in the days of the New Testament, and she will mock them until Judgment Day. It is impossible for her to do anything else as long as she doesn't understand the mystery of God. What is this mystery? It is for example, what the triune God, the Father, the Son, and the Holy Ghost, has done and will do as the Creator, Reconciler, and Sanctifier of the world. First Timothy contains a perfect expression of this mystery as the focal point in one of the oldest hymns of the Church, where it is written, "Great indeed, we confess, is the mystery of godliness:

> He was manifested in the flesh
> vindicated by the Spirit,
> seen by angels,
> preached among the nations,
> believed on in the world,
> taken up in glory." (3:16)

Yes, that is the mystery of all mysteries, the mystery of world history: God became flesh. That the eternal Word, the eternal Father's eternal Son became flesh is truly a mystery, a mystery in the strict sense incomprehensible to reason.

> Now in the manger we may see,
> God's Son from eternity,
> The gift from God's eternal throne
> Here clothed in our poor flesh and bone.

> The Virgin Mary's Lullaby,
> Calms the infant Lord Most high.
> Upon her lap content is he,

Who keeps the earth and sky and sea .[89]

Human reason finds this to be a complete contradiction. It is only grasped in faith, the faith which the Holy Spirit works in us, causing our hearts to confess in humility and simplicity: "I believe that Jesus Christ, true God, begotten of the Father from eternity, and also true man, born of the Virgin Mary, is my Lord."[90] It was at this point during the mass that the ancient choirs singing the Nicene Creed would fall silent before the words "et incarnatus est."[91] Because mere human voices are silent before the ineffable mystery. "And was conceived by the Holy Spirit, born of the Virgin Mary and became man." Out of this one mystery, the incarnation of God, every mystery flows: all the miracles of the Christian faith, the mystery of Good Friday, Easter, Pentecost, the miracle that occurs today in the working of God's Word, the miracle of the forgiveness of sins, and the miracles which Christ still does today in the Sacraments of Baptism and the Lord's Supper.

This miracle is to be proclaimed by the steward of the mysteries of God. That is the task of Christ's servants, the

---

[89] *Gelobet seist du Jesus Christ.* "We Praise You, Jesus, at Your Birth." Martin Luther. WA 35.147; *LSB* 382. "The eternal Father's only Son, In a crib is found smiling on, Lord almighty, the eternal Good, Clothed in human flesh and blood, All the worlds could never contain He, who in Mary's lap is lain, Who now an infant child small Is yet *the* Creator and Lord of all. (The translator's more literal translation.)
[90] SC, Creed III. MH
[91] "And was incarnate . . . ." Translated "conceived" in the English. The Latin is a more accurate rendering of the original Greek: καὶ σαρκωθέντα ἐκ Πνεύματος Ἁγίου καὶ Μαρίας τῆς παρθένου. MH

77

task of the entire Church: "This is how one should regard us, as servants of Christ and stewards of the mysteries of God. Moreover, it is required of stewards that they be found faithful" (1 Cor. 4:1–2). And now the apostle dares to oppose his critics, the critics of his apostolic proclamation, not on the basis of human wisdom, the wealth of thought, the sweetness of speech, or as some would comment, on the organization of this message, but on truth alone. "But with me it is a very small thing that I should be judged by you or by any human court. In fact, I do not even judge myself" (1 Cor. 4:3). No one can stand before this faithful judgment. There can, at last, be no one to judge except he who is the message, the Lord, Christ himself.

"I am not aware of anything against myself" [1 Cor. 4:4], Paul says. What does he mean by these very controversial words? Does he mean to say with some: "I have a perfect and clean slate on which to be judged?" Does he no longer know that he is a poor sinner who lives by the daily forgiveness of sins? Has he forgotten what he taught Christendom, that we are sinners and remain so until death? Has he forgotten the deeply painful experience he spoke about so tremendously in the seventh chapter of Romans: "I have the desire to do what is right, but not the ability to carry it out. . . . Wretched man that I am! Who will deliver me from this body of death?" [v. 18, 24; see vv.15–25]. No, he hasn't forgotten that. Rather, he knows that we men belong to two aeons, two worlds, the old world of death, which we still live in, and the new world to which we have been rescued, but in which we do not yet live.[92] He knows that through Baptism we are born again into a new life, but also that the old man is still living inside of us. So the apostle also knows that we are justified children of God by faith in Christ, and yet we are still sinners so long as we bear this dead body. He knows that we will all step before the judgment seat with empty hands, and then this truth will apply:

> Jesus your blood and righteousness
> My beauty are, my glorious dress
> Mid flaming worlds in these arrayed
> With joy shall I lift up my head.[93]

Yes, he said it here himself, that though he is not aware of anything against himself, he is not thereby acquitted: "but I am not thereby acquitted. It is the Lord who judges me" [1 Cor. 4:4b]. But then, what does he mean by these proud-sounding words: "I am not aware of anything against myself" [1 Cor. 4:4a]? Only that he also knows what this means: "Who can discern his errors? Declare me innocent from hidden faults" (Psalm 19:12).

Just what he means Luther is able to make clear to us. He also knew what it means to a sinner unto death. The same Luther, who knew that we come before the judgment seat of God with empty hands, once said in his *Great*

---

[92] Sasse wrote the entry for "aeon" in *Kittel's Theological Wordbook of the New Testament*. Αἰών, αἰώνιος. Th.WbNT 1 (1933) 167–68; English: TDNT 1 (1964) 168. Feuerhahn no. 108. He had also written an S.T.M. thesis at Hartford Seminary 1925/26, titled "*Der Begriff des Aion in der Bibel*," which has never been found. MH

[93] Zinzendorf, "Jesus' Blood and Righteousness," *Lutheran Worship* 362 (St. Louis: CPH, 1982); *LSB* 563.

Confession on the Lord's Supper to men who held the words of institution literally and didn't change anything: "Consequently, you can boldly address Christ both in the hour of death and at the last judgment 'My dear Lord Jesus Christ,' a controversy has arisen over thy words in the Supper. Some want them to be understood differently from their natural sense. But since they teach me nothing certain, but only lead me into confusion and uncertainty, and since they are not willing or able to prove their text in any way, I have remained with thy text as the words read. If there is anything obscure in them, it is because thou didst wish to leave it obscure, for thou hast given no other explanation of them, nor hast thou commanded any to be given. No one finds anywhere in Scripture or in any language that 'is' should mean 'signifies,' or that 'my body' should mean 'sign of my body.' Now if there should be anything obscure about these words, thou wilt bear with me if I do not completely understand them, just as thou didst forbear with thine apostles when they did not understand thee in many things—for instance, when thou didst announce thy passion and resurrection. And yet they kept thy words just as they were spoken and did not alter them. Thy beloved mother also did not understand when thou said to her, Luke 2[:49], 'I must be about my Father's business,' yet with simplicity she kept these words in her heart and did not alter them. So have I also kept to these thy words.' "[94] So a poor sinner can also speak to Christ as Luther did in his hour of death and Day of Judgment. It was in this sense Luther spoke of

---

[94] AE 37.305–6; WA 26.447.

right preaching, saying that when he was finished preaching he would not pray for forgiveness, "but would say and boast with Jeremiah, 'Lord thou knowest that which came out of my lips is true and pleasing to thee' [Jer. 17:16]; indeed, with St. Paul and all the apostles and prophets, he should say firmly, *Haec dixit dominus*, 'God himself has said this' " [1 Cor. 1:10].[95] And here is the basis of his reasoning: "It is, of course, quite true that if judged by its way of life, the holy church is not without sin, as it confesses in the Lord's Prayer, 'Forgive us our trespasses'; and John writes [1 John 1:8, 10], 'If we say we have no sin, we lie and make God a liar [1 John 1:10], who calls us all sinners'—also Romans 3 [:23], Psalm 14 [:3] and 51 [:7]. But doctrine should not be sinful or reproachable. It does not belong to the Lord's Prayer and its petition, 'Forgive us our trespasses' [Matt 6:12], because it is not something we do, but is God's own Word which cannot sin or do wrong."[96] I leave the question open whether we pastors today should be "correct preachers" in the manner of Luther's thought. But there was, in any case, a time in our church when our pastors were confessing in this sense, as Luther and every man did. "Therefore, in the presence of God and of all Christendom among both our contemporaries and our posterity, we wish to have testified that the present explanation of all the foregoing controverted articles here explained, and none other, is our teaching, belief, and confession in which by God's grace

---

[95] AE 41.216; WA 51.517.
[96] AE 41.216; WA 51.516.

we shall appear with intrepid hearts before the judgment seat of Jesus Christ and for which we shall give an account."[97]

Cheerfully, "with intrepid hearts," we step before the judgment seat of God—so speaks the confession of the old Evangelical Church, because they knew that they stood on the Word of God. This sheds some illuminating light on these words of Paul: "I am not aware of anything against myself." He knew that he was a poor sinner, but he also knew that he had preached the Word of God. He could also say, "I stood on your Word." That is the sense of that verse. He will not praise his faithfulness. He will only praise God's faithfulness. Because it is God who entrusted this Holy Word to him and who keeps him in this Word. It is because we cannot remain in God's Word by our own strength that the Church prays, "Lord, Keep Us Steadfast in Your Word."[98]

"This is how one should consider us, as servants of Christ and stewards of the mysteries of God. Moreover it is required of stewards that they be found trustworthy, but with me it is a very small thing that I should be judged by you or any human court." How serious an exhortation to the servants of the Church, no, to the whole Church, is contained in these words! Think of what we theologians have done to the mysteries of God, the mystery of the incarnation in the last century! Certainly, no one wanted to

---

[97] F.C. S.D. XII, 40; BKS 1099–1100.

[98] Martin Luther, *Lord, Keep Us Steadfast in Your Word (1541/42)*; *Erhalt uns Herr bey deinem Wort*, AE 53.304f.; WA 35.467–468. *LSB* 655. MH

destroy this mystery, they only wanted to understand it a little better, to make it in some way plausible. But then it stopped being a mystery. It was, therefore, no longer a mystery of God. How is it that in the nineteenth century the strong faith of the Reformation and the old Evangelical Church became an inoffensive religion of the bourgeoisie? During that time, the confession of the Church was stripped like a Christmas tree, of which there is hardly anything that remains but a little old wood. "Conceived by the Holy Spirit, born of the Virgin Mary." This was no longer understood by the enlightened citizen of the nineteenth century. So then the path was set, and all the articles of faith fell one after another! That Christ's death is atonement for our sins; that Jesus is risen from the dead, "that He sits at the right hand of God, from whence He shall come to judge the living and the dead." Every one of these fell down the slope. That the Holy Ghost is true God—when that article fell, the Holy Trinity and everything associated with it was abandoned. This is the real reason the Evangelical Church in Germany fell. Do we wonder how these men hollowed this out and threw the contents away like an old garment? That which today is called the myth of the twentieth century is the fruit of destruction of the Church's dogma.[99] Do we think

---

[99] See Sasse's "The Impact of Bultmannism on American Lutheranism, with Special Reference to His Demythologization of the New Testament" (lecture to a free conference, Bethany Lutheran Seminary, Mankato, Minnesota, March 8, 1965). Feuerhahn no. 418. "The intellectual disposition of the modern world has developed through a long, difficult struggle against ecclesiastical dogma—be it that of

somehow, that it was only the theologians who no longer kept true to the Christian faith? What are we pastors, what are we teachers of theology without the Christian Church? And where was the Church? Where is she today? When the shattering report of the Evangelical Church is heard in this Sunday's Divine Service, that the Lord's Supper, Holy Baptism, the children's Divine Service, the catechesis of the confirmands slowly dies, then the heart is crushed. How will it look in this house of God thirty years from now? Yes, God can and will keep his Church before all who would like to destroy her. Christ can and will protect his Church, even today. But it is his order by which he keeps his faithful, who believe in him. You mothers who in these days prepare your children for Christmas; you fathers whose children perhaps no longer study the Bible in school, do we know what God expects of his faithful? The nineteenth century coined the phrase: "Religion is a private matter."[100] But the Christian's religion is never a private matter. This phrase carries less weight today than it did before, because today it is well known that there are no private matters: Christ is not a personal Savior, but the Savior of the world. He will return, revealed in glory, to judge the living and the dead, the members of his Church as

---

Roman Catholicism or that of old Protestant Orthodoxy. This explains the deep aversion of modern man toward dogmatic Christianity, indeed toward everything which confession, doctrine and dogma mean." "The Confession of the Church" (1930) in *The Lonely Way I*, p. 101. Feuerhahn no. 56. MH

[100] A watchword advocated variously by Marx, Engels, and other socialists/communists and used by the Social Democratic Party in Germany (SPD) in the nineteenth century. MH

well as other people, the German people as everyone else. You young men, looking into the future, thirsty for action—do you really think the Church is a thing of the past? That to believe in Jesus means to believe in a man or a message of the past? No, if anything has a future in the world, it is the Church.[101] Perhaps, it is a future that no one can foresee, a future with a completely different outlook than we have now. But a future, which only when it is past, when all is said and done, will we men in the future be able to look back and describe, because the future of the Church is the future of Christ. She travels through the angst and distress of this world, from his incarnation to his return. Yes, the future of our Lord Jesus Christ is the blessed future of the Church. Amen.

---

[101] Hermann Sasse, "The Presence of Christ and the Future of the Church," (1938) in *The Lonely Way I*, pp. 461–70. Feuerhahan no. 205. MH

The Congregation of the Redeemed
Oculi
February 28, 1937[102]
1 Peter 1:13–21[103]

Therefore, preparing your minds for action, and being sober-minded, set your hope fully on the grace that will be brought to you at the revelation of Jesus Christ. As obedient children, do not be conformed to the passions of your former ignorance, but as he who called you is holy, you also be holy in all your conduct, since it is written, "You shall be holy, for I am holy." And if you call on him as Father who judges impartially according to each one's deeds, conduct yourselves with fear throughout the time of your exile, knowing that you were ransomed from the futile ways inherited from your forefathers, not with perishable things such as silver or gold, but with the precious blood of Christ, like that of a lamb without blemish or spot. He was foreknown before the foundation of the world but was made manifest in the last times for the sake of you who through him are believers in God, who raised him from the dead and gave him glory, so that your faith and hope are in God. (1 Pet. 1:13–21)

The First Epistle of Peter, from which our Epistle

---

[102] By this time Sasse was banned by the Nazi government from attending conferences outside of Germany or even traveling outside of Germany. He wrote to a fellow member of the Faith and Order Executive Committee on January 25, 1937, "I have been informed by some authority that it would be better for me not to apply for the permission just now." He was writing to inform Hodgson that he would not make the meeting in Paris scheduled for February. The Nazis wanted one view of German affairs promoted abroad, and Sasse's was not it. Feuerhahn, *Sasse as an Ecumenical Churchman*, p. 38. MH

[103] *Predigt: Sonntag Okuli (28 Feb 1937) "Die Gemeinde der Erlösten."* Feuerhahn no. 188a. MH

reading for today was taken, is one of the oldest documents from the history of the Church of Rome. At that time Rome, the cosmopolitan city in which all languages and dialects of the Mediterranean world were spoken, the Babel of its time, the center of all anti-Christendom, hid itself behind the mysterious Babylon at the end of this letter: "She who is at Babylon, who is likewise chosen, sends you greetings" (1 Pet. 5:13). Peter, as it is reported to us through Silvanus, the Silas of Acts, wrote this epistle to the Christians of Asia Minor to encourage those true to the faith, those who suffered as they waited for the fullness of time. As soon as this letter arrived in one of the sea ports of the eastern Mediterranean, copies of it would be sent to the congregations of Asia Minor, from the crowded old cities of culture on the Mediterranean coast to the small towns and villages of the Anatolian plateau and the harbors and trade cities of the Black Sea. So this epistle is a monument to that which Peter himself once called the "brotherhood throughout the world,"[104] the worldwide brotherhood, and what we in our confession of faith confess as the communion of the saints. "Knowing that the same kinds of suffering are being experienced by your brotherhood throughout the world" (1 Pet. 5:9). The men who read this letter during the period of persecution knew that when they were so unified: it was a communion of saints. In the Church of God, we are all bound together with those who

---

[104] "Resist him [Satan], firm in your faith, knowing that the same kinds of suffering are being experienced by your brotherhood throughout the world" (1 Pet. 5:9). MH

confess the same true faith as us. We are bound with them even if we do not know their faces, people we have never seen and will never see while on this earth. We are bound in a communion that is something completely different than anything else we might know of human communions.

What kind of communion was it that knew to whom this letter applied? It was of course, not merely intended for quiet private lectures, but as with all the congregational letters of the New Testament, yes as with all the letters of the entire Holy Scriptures, it was meant for oral reading in the congregation, and that means during the Divine Service. Therefore we have to be clear about this, beloved congregation, if we want to understand why this letter of the Holy Scriptures was written, and what it means for us. The most ancient of churches did not yet have any written New Testament. Therefore the Old Testament alone was the Holy Scriptures of the Church. The New Testament was still a completely oral message: "A good news and cry that rang out into the world through the apostles." As Luther said, "For before they wrote, they first of all preached to the people by word of mouth and converted them, and this was their real apostolic and New Testament work."[105] But now the Church, called through the spoken word, faces a different problem—it is scattered amongst the millions in the kingdom, amidst constant temptation; many are falling away from the Christian faith; and it is perpetually threatened by false teachers misrepresenting the faith. Now it was rare that an apostle could be with them, not to

---

[105] AE 52.206; WA 10/1/1.626.

mention the fact that the generation of the apostles was dying. The prophets and teachers that served the Word with them were no longer there either. In such a case an apostolic letter or a prophetic book like the Revelation of St. John or the writing of a teacher such as Hebrews would become a substitute for the living voice of the first proclaimers. So the New Testament began with the letters of the apostles. The letters of Paul were read during the Divine Service well before the four Gospels were written. And this became the case more and more. They were, of course, meant to be read aloud in the Divine Service in front of the congregation from the very beginning as a substitute for the oral speaking of the apostles. This is also the reason that they conclude with the oldest form of the Christian liturgy. So at the close of First Corinthians is found the oldest piece of the Christian liturgy for the Lord's Supper. And this is why the end of our letter reads, in the same style as First Corinthians [16:20; Rom. 16:16]: "Greet one another with the kiss of love" (1 Peter 5:14). This is a reference to the celebration of the Lord's Supper with which they would end the reading. The Lord's Supper began with the kiss of peace, which the bishops and the deacons gave one another, the men to one another and the women to one another. The writer of such a letter and the congregation that conveyed the greeting were then present together in the Spirit. They included themselves in the communion of saints, who were gathered around the Lord's Table as one despite great distances between them. So we, too, though we are living centuries later, are included in this communion when we read or hear the old Epistle in worship. This is the great communion of the saints in which the whole Church of God through all times and in all places is one. A communion that is completely different from all such human communities, because it is the communion of the Body of Christ.

This communion of the saints envelops us when we hear the warning of our Epistle: "Therefore, preparing your minds" [1 Pet. 1:13a; German and Greek, girding up the loins of your mind]. That is the same exhortation Jesus gave his disciples: "Stay dressed for action [German and Greek, let your loins be girded] and keep your lamps burning, and be like men who are waiting for their master" [Luke 12:35]. The exhortation is to be ready for the arrival of the Lord. "Being sober-minded, set your hope fully on the grace that will be brought to you at the revelation of Jesus Christ" [1 Pet. 1:13b], particularly the revelation of his glory on the day of his return. "As obedient children, do not be conformed to the passions of your former ignorance" [1 Pet. 1:14]. These people once lived as Gentiles according to the wisdom of the Gentile world. "The desires of the flesh and the desires of the eyes and pride," as 1 John [2:16] once in the deepest knowledge of man described the desire of natural man, were the motivations of their lives. But now they are children of God, and that applies the great "but" to them that they should be separate from the world: "But as he who called you is holy, you also be holy in all your conduct" [1 Pet. 1:15]. Therefore the apostle spoke to the congregation what God had once given to Moses,

"Speak to all the congregation of the people of Israel and say to them, You shall be holy, for I the LORD your God am holy" [Lev. 19:2]. In the place of Israel, who had rejected the Messiah and therewith God's righteousness was undone, the Church marches as the true Israel as it says in the second chapter: "But you are a chosen race, a royal priesthood, a holy nation, a people for his own possession . . . . Once you were not a people, but now you are God's people; once you had not received mercy, but now you have received mercy" (1 Pet. 2:9–10). The people of God are called out of the people of the world, the Church, a true chosen race, a people for his own possession, and therefore they are holy. But only in fear and trembling can the Christian carry this dignity: "If you call on him as Father who judges impartially according to each one's deeds" (1 Peter 1:17a). Yes, before his judgment seat all people will finally stand, also the Christian, and the first righteous. Because all judgment begins in the house of God [1 Pet. 4:17], and the terrible judgment in the court of disciples will pass over the sins that happened within the Church of Christ. Because it is so, because the Christian is also on the way to judgment, therefore, "Conduct yourselves with fear throughout the time of your exile" (1 Peter 1:17b). Or when one may translate it word for word: "in fear, conduct the time of your exile!" And then follows the great exhortation, you must be aware of, where salvation calls: "Knowing that you were ransomed from the futile ways inherited from your forefathers, not with perishable things such as silver or gold, but with the precious blood of Christ, like that of a lamb without blemish or spot" (1 Peter 1:18–19).

Let us pick out three exhortations from this for further and more detailed consideration. There is *the exhortation to sober-mindedness,* on which our apostle gave particular stress. It is found often in this letter. Apparently, he himself had obeyed this, "being sober-minded" [1 Pet. 1:13]. Sober-mindedness belongs so firmly to a New Testament epistle that it displeases many souls longing for the poetic and the aesthetic. But the New Testament is not a book of religious poetry for the nightstand. Rather it is very sober, very real. It is a catalogue of virtue and vice, a table of duties for men and women, for elders and children, for lords and slaves. It speaks of the real lives of people, not only of those whose souls are moved on Sunday, but of those whose gray days of the week bring them sin and worry. It speaks to those whose souls are distressed with pangs of conscience, duties and struggles, temptation and transgression. And so it is good. Otherwise the Gospel could not help in the real distress of life. We all come to church on Sunday after a hard week of work. We come laden with the heavy inner and outer distress of these times. How many tears have been cried in the past week in our congregation? How many worries have depressed our hearts? With all these burdens we come to church. And you may, you should come too, beloved Christians. It is for this reason we have houses of God and the Divine Service. The house of God is the place where you can shed your worries. But even with that we can and should hear this exhortation to be sober-minded!

The opposite of soberness is intoxication. And according to the opinion of men, their worries are best lost with intoxication. Today, humanity has tried this on a large scale. They have intoxicated themselves with the radio and movie theater. They have consumed the greatest music from the generations that created greater masters in a few years as intoxicants and anesthetics. They intoxicate themselves on great words and ever increasing superlatives, on conversation and worldviews. But this did not happen first in our days. How many religions of the world are nothing but an intoxication in which the people forget the realities of their lives? The first readers of our Epistle had certainly known to a great extent the intoxicating mystery religions the old Gentile world learned to know.[106] But one doesn't need to think only of these. To a great extent, that which is called the Christian religion is nothing more than one such intoxication. This is why the apostles fought with such determination against the *Schwärmerei*,[107] against Enthusiasm as Paul did in Corinth, because in intoxication, even in the holy drunkenness of the *Schwärmerei* of Christendom, one forgets reality. He forgets the load of his life, but he doesn't lose it. He lives in a dream world. He no longer stands before the real God, but before a dreamt-up god. He no longer sees the real, but a dreamt humanity. But

---

[106] E.g. the Cult of Mythra. MH

[107] A technical term literally meaning "swarming" like bees, used by Luther particularly for those who seek evidence of God's will where he has not promised to give it (his Word) and reject the clear teaching of Scripture on the Sacrament, for instance. See SA III, VIII.3f. and BKS p. 454, note 1. MH

the New Testament will have nothing to do with such dreams. It points us to the real humanity and places us before the real God. Only the real God can take up the burden of your life, never an imaginary god. And you must come to him with the real burdens of your life, with all your burdens. You cannot say to him: "Look Lord, here is the burden that life has imposed on me. Here is the distress, which other men have caused for me." But you must know that the hardest burden and the deepest distress of your life is something completely different. It is the burden that you have imposed upon yourself, and which you daily impose upon yourself anew. It is the distress that you cause yourself. It is that which your eyes will not see. It is your guilt. It is the sin slumbering in the depth of your soul in opposition to God.

"Be sober!" What then led the men in the days of the apostles to the Church of Jesus Christ? What leads them today in India, where every week a thousand men join Christian congregations? Religion that men raise above the weekday they also have. They have moving worship with which to help men awaken the divine within themselves that promise them immortality and holiness and give meaning to their poor lives. Only one thing it does not give. It does not give the forgiveness of sins. And therefore it doesn't give freedom from the burden of life. Forgiveness of sins is only given by Jesus Christ. This is why the first readers of our Epistle came to the Church of Christ. And this is why there is no other way for you to shed the heavy burden of life, but that you come to him, your Savior, he who with all your worries, all your suffering, all the hurt of your soul, the mourning of your life, the complete distress of your life, which by his cross he took upon himself as he went to Golgotha and died for you there.

"Being sober-minded" [1 Pet. 1:13]—only when we understand this exhortation and all that it encompasses, then and only then will we also understand the other enormous and great exhortation in our Epistle that holds everything together. The exhortation they gave the congregation: "Be holy" [v. 15]. "But as he who called you is holy, you also be holy in all your conduct, since it is written, 'You shall be holy, for I am holy' " [vv. 15–16]. Truly, this requires a sober mind; it requires the complete, clear, and illusion-less biblical assessment of man to not have a false understanding of this. There had once been a people in this world to which God had promised, "You shall therefore be holy, for I am holy" [Lev. 11:45]. This people ended up nailing the Holy God to the cross when He came and thought that this proved their holiness. Then it became a pharisaical people. If one wants to know how the oldest Church understood "you shall therefore be holy, for I am holy," then one has to think about the highpoint of the Divine Service. Already in the first century, the Church sang the *Sanctus* during the Divine Service. This is the song that the seraphim sing in the presence of God, as Isaiah heard in his call: "Holy, holy, holy is the LORD of hosts; the whole earth is full of his glory!" [Isa. 6:3]. Where that rings, there the space in the earthly house of God widens, and the Church on earth becomes one with the crowds of heavenly hosts and with the Church Triumphant in heaven. So it is also articulated in our liturgy, when the *Sanctus* is introduced with the words "It is truly good right and salutary that we should at all times and in all places give thanks to you, holy Lord, almighty Father, everlasting God, through Jesus Christ our Lord, who ascended into heaven and sitting at your right hand, poured out on this day as he had promised the Holy Spirit on the chosen disciples. At this the whole earth rejoices with exceeding joy. Therefore with angels and archangels and with all the company of heaven we laud and magnify your glorious name ever more praising you and saying." Of course, these words, like the preceding exchange, "The Lord be with you. Let us thank the Lord, our God. That is meet and right," belong to the oldest parts of the Christian liturgy. For eighteen centuries they have been spoken Sunday after Sunday in many languages throughout the world, and right at the most celebrated moment of the Christian Divine Service, just before the words of institution for the Lord's Supper are heard, and Jesus Christ, the Lord, truly present, gives his body and his blood under the forms of bread and wine to his Church to eat and drink. There heaven and earth become one. There he, the Holy One, in the power of his forgiveness is among his own, and they are his holy people. They are this only on account of him. Were he not there, then they would be nothing but a small gathering of poor unholy people. This came to be expressed in the words of the liturgist during the old Communion liturgy, when he introduced the reception of the body and blood of Christ, saying, "The Holy for the holy." And the congregation would answer "One is Holy, one is the Lord, Jesus Christ to the glory of the Father." And then the congregation stepped before the Altar and received what the old Roman Church order around the year 200 called, "the cure for your soul, whereby sins are forgiven."[108] No, there is no other holiness of the Church but the holiness of Jesus Christ who with the power of his forgiveness is in our midst. This is how the oldest Church understood it, and this was also true when she closed the Communion table to the hardened sinner. Because then she, the Holy Church, never ceased to plead, "For our brothers, who are in the presence of evil, and that you forgive their sins and ours." So the oldest Church remained sober in her self-judgment, even when she knew by faith she was the people of God to whom the words applied, "you shall be holy, for I am holy" [1 Pet. 1:16; see also Lev. 11:44].

God's holy people: that is the Church of Christ in the world. That was the Church in the days of the apostles. That was every chosen stranger of Asia Minor, the small congregations who lived amongst the distractions of the

---

[108] Ignatius of Antioch (d. ca. 112) says of the Lord's Supper, "Breaking one bread, which is the medicine of immortality, the antidote that we should not die [$\phi \alpha \rho \mu \iota \kappa o \nu \ \alpha \theta \alpha \nu \alpha \sigma \iota \alpha \varsigma$], but live forever in Jesus Christ." Letter to the Ephesians 20. Lake, *The Apostolic Fathers I* (London: Harvard University Press, 1912), p. 195. See the *Apostolic Constitutions* VIII (ANF VII.488) and related contemporary liturgies, particularly the Ancient Egyptian liturgy (Ludolf), which contains these precise words. Rietschel, *Lehrbuch Der Liturgik,I. Die Lehre vom Gemeindegottesdients* (Berlin, 1900), p. 287. M H

great Roman Empire. God's holy people, that is the Church of Christ today. And we belong to this Church. Therefore we will remember the last exhortation of our Epistle: *Forget not, that you have been redeemed!* "Knowing that you were ransomed from the futile ways inherited from your forefathers, not with perishable things such as silver or gold, but with the precious blood of Christ, like that of a lamb without blemish or spot. He was foreknown before the foundation of the world but was made manifest in the last times for the sake of you who through him are believers in God, who raised him from the dead and gave him glory, so that your faith and hope are in God" [1 Pet. 1:18–21]. You are redeemed. Soul, forget that not! Before the world's foundations were laid [Rev. 13:8], God had foreknown that he, as the lamb without blemish or spot, would bear all the sin of the world. God had chosen you, faithful soul. As his beloved Son wandered about the earth, there he enveloped you in his merciful salvation, as he carried the arduous burdens of calling everyone to him. And then he also thought of you when he cried, "It is finished" [John 19:30]. And when you were baptized, the heavenly Father called you by your name and had given all of you everything that Jesus Christ had acquired for you, and these commitments remain to stay. And when you leave him, the door to the Father's house is still open to you. Heaven and earth shall pass away, but the Word of his mercy never fades, and trusting in this Word you may rejoice:

O wonder love, who chose me

Before the world began
And me to your children counted
For whom you the kingdom ordered
O father's hand, o mercy's desire
Who in the book of life did me write![109]

"Forget it not." One should think this exhortation is superfluous. How can one forget that, when one has once known it! And yet, the apostle is right when he calls his congregation to remember it evermore. At the end of the century, it was reported to Rome by the Roman governor of one of the provinces in Northern Asia Minor that is mentioned in our letter that in his province so many took to Christianity that the heathen temples had been deserted. In the same report, however, it is also read that there are former Christians who have not gone to church in twenty years. Yes, men can even forget this. As children, we all learned Luther's explanation to the Second Article, that glorious part of the catechism that has been called the most beautiful sentence of the German language, a sentence based on our Epistle. "I believe that Jesus Christ . . . is my Lord, who has redeemed me a lost and condemned person, purchased and one me from all sin, death, and the power of the devil, not with gold or silver but with his holy precious blood and his innocent suffering and death, so that I may be his own and live under him in his kingdom and serve him in everlasting righteousness, innocence, and blessedness, just as he is risen from the dead, lives and reigns to all

---

[109] *O Wunderliebe, die mich wählte vor allem Anbeginn der Welt.* Johann Gottfried Herman. MH

eternity. This is most certainly true."[110] Four hundred years later, millions of German people are brought up in this faith. Even before ten years of age, every evangelical child has learned this sentence in school. And today? And tomorrow and the day after tomorrow?

When our people forget their Christian faith, then it happens because they are no longer living in the Christian congregation. Then our church has sunk to the level of uniting religious interests with those of church taxpayers, and is no longer the Church of the Lord Christ. It is attested before the world that you are redeemed from sin, death, and the devil, not with gold or silver, but with the precious blood of Christ as a lamb without blemish or spot. And when our congregations no longer know that, then it must fall fully on the shoulders of us pastors. It is heard more and more: "Christian? Yes, I would like to remain one. But that we are reconciled to God through the sacrifice of Christ at Golgotha is something that I cannot understand. That must be some relic of Judaism." Just as if the Judaism of all times went mad for the last nineteen hundred years. Or one says, "That would be the imagination of the master theologians." Oh, just the opposite! The theologians have all they can do to put this incomprehensible matter in the fore and point to it! It has always brought their imagination to nothing. Yes, it is contrary to all reason.

If there was ever one in whom this teaching was grounded, then it was him who said, "The Son of Man came not to be served but to serve, and to give his life as a

---

[110] SC, Creed III. MH

100

ransom for many" [Matt 20:28]. He went to his death with the intention to at last fulfill what had been spoken through the prophet: "Surely he has borne our griefs, and carried our sorrows; yet we esteemed him stricken, smitten by God, and afflicted. But he was pierced for our transgressions; he was crushed for our iniquities; upon him was the chastisement that brought us peace, and with his wounds we are healed" (Isa. 53:4–5).

To stand still before this last deep miracle of the Christian faith, that is what our Epistle exhorts us to do. And if you have had nothing to do with it for a long time— do it this year, beloved Christians. As you go through these hard times, straight through, through the week of the Passion this year, stand still before the deep miracle of godly love. Here and here alone will the heavy burden be left, and you can thankfully say,

> Within my heart's foundation
> Thy name and cross alone
> Shine forth each day and hour
> For which I can rejoice.[111]

Amen.

---

[111] Bach, Johann Sebastian, "In Meines Herzens Grunde"; BVW 245, St. John's Passion. MH

The Incomprehensible Easter News
Easter Sunday
April 17, 1938[112]
Mark 16:1–8[113]

When the Sabbath was past, Mary Magdalene, Mary the mother of James, and Salome bought spices, so that they might go and anoint him. And very early on the first day of the week, when the sun had risen, they went to the tomb. And they were saying to one another, "Who will roll away the stone for us from the entrance of the tomb?" And looking up, they saw that the stone had been rolled back— it was very large. And entering the tomb, they saw a young man sitting on the right side, dressed in a white robe, and they were alarmed. And he said to them, "Do not be alarmed. You seek Jesus of Nazareth, who was crucified. He has risen; he is not here. See the place where they laid him. But go, tell his disciples and Peter that he is going before you to Galilee. There you will see him, just as he told you." And they went out and fled from the tomb, for trembling and astonishment had seized them, and they said nothing to anyone, for they were afraid. (Mark 16:1–8)

I saw a sight once while visiting New York during Easter that has been forever burned into my memory. In

---

[112] Sasse was editor of a theological journal titled *"Lutherische Kirche."* Early in 1938 an issue was published with only the cover, containing this announcement: "By order of the Secret State's Police, State's Police Office, Berlin, the bi-monthly journal *'Lutherische Kirche'* in Erlangen was forbidden for three months" (i.e., Feb 15 to May 15, 1938). Feuerhahn, *Sasse as an Ecumenical Churchman*, p. 73, note 393. MH

[113] *Predigt: Ostersonntag (17 Apr 1938) "Die Unbegreifliche Osterbotschaft."* Feuerhahn no. 214a. MH

one of the busiest areas of the city, a center of traffic, where a countless number of people pass by night and day, someone had hoisted an inscription between two high-rises. "Christ is risen." So read the gigantic letters over the sea of buildings day and night in this cosmopolitan city for the entire season of Easter. Not a single person out of the hundreds of thousands of those passing by daily could avoid this message. "Christ is risen! – He is risen indeed!" That has been the Easter greeting of the Church since the days of the apostles. "Christ is risen! – He is risen indeed!" This greeting and response is still used today by the Eastern Church during the season of Easter, not only in the church (we also began our Divine Service singing this greeting), but also in their houses and on the street. You might wonder whether the means of modern propaganda should be used to literally write this greeting over our city, but this picture has been permanently engraved into the memory of every person that saw these words displayed above the city lights.[114] They will never again be able to rid themselves of the question that nags our souls today, on this Easter Sunday: What does the message of the resurrection of Christ have to say to the world? Is there any room for it in a world where the thinking of the modern natural sciences is

---

[114] For similar thoughts by Sasse about such means, see "*American Christianity and The Church*" in *The Lonely Way I*, pp. 29ff. Sasse wrote this essay after visiting America in 1925/26. The German Evangelical Church Committee (*Deutscher Evangelischer Kirchenausschuss*) under an initiative by Julius Richter arranged the exchange of six theologians. Sasse, Peter Brunner, and Wilhelm Pauck were among the Germans. Sasse did an S.T.M. at Hartford Theological Seminary. MH

definite and where life and the contemplations of man's reason are shaped by the inventions of our technical understanding? Does this message still have meaning for a world of radical political and social change in which the new worldview has gained authority over the spirit? Or does this message merely live today as a venerable monument to the religious life of the past? Can it be anything other than the object of the modern Enlightenment's mockery and Faust's[115] doubt in the twentieth century?

With these questions, we approach the ancient Gospel for the holy feast of Easter, and stop before the message of the risen Christ to say that it is the most incomprehensible and disconcerting message ever proclaimed to the world. At the same time, it is the most important and the most noteworthy message that can be proclaimed. It is also a message that the world fights against with hand and foot, a message she does not believe, and yet from which she unknowingly receives life.

It is a very disconcerting and incomprehensible message. Yes, there is something about the ancient Easter story that is deeply disconcerting and not only to a few people in our era. "And they were alarmed." "And they went out and fled from the tomb, for trembling and astonishment had seized them, and they said nothing to anyone, for they were afraid." These women were scared because they experienced something they never expected. It

---

[115] Faust is a character of German legend who makes a pact to trade his soul for hedonistic indulgence. MH

shocks us too when their story is told, because there is something about it we do not expect. Here people experience Easter, the first Easter of Christendom, something that is not experienced in nature.

Is it possible to think of Easter as one of God's great miracles of nature, a poetic reminder of nature's newly awakened life? What would you think of an Easter sermon today in which there was no mention of spring, nature's new life, the first flowers in all their glory, or of the birds singing the songs of spring? Would you think that it was an awful sermon, a sermon lacking the Easter spirit? Now that is what you would have to say of the Easter sermons of the apostles, those that are found in the New Testament. They do not speak of nature or of spring. The same goes for Luther's Easter sermons. I cannot find any indication in them that Easter and spring belong together. This is also true for the songs of the Church. The Easter hymns found in our hymnals do not mention spring. Ditties such as "Easter Easter, Winds of Spring"[116] were not found in our hymnals before the nineteenth century. That was when the Enlightenment had first destroyed faith in the resurrection. Easter then became a celebration of spring.

Perhaps you still don't think that can be right. Maybe you think that Easter and spring have to belong together; that it is no accident that the Church celebrates the resurrection of our Lord in spring at a time in which ancient cultures already celebrated the awakening of life in nature.

---

[116] *Ostern, Ostern, Frühlingswehen*; Gottlob Ferdinand Maximilian Gottfried von Schenkendorf, 1783–1817.

To that the answer is that the Church celebrates Easter in spring because Jesus died as the Paschal Lamb during Passover according to his will. As Paul says, "For Christ, our Passover lamb, has been sacrificed" (1 Corinthians 5:7). If Jesus were crucified on the Day of Atonement [Yom Kippur], we would celebrate Easter in the fall. This is when the entire Church of the Southern hemisphere celebrates Easter because Easter comes in the fall there. For example, our Lutheran sister church in Australia, which is celebrating its hundredth anniversary,[117] is also celebrating Easter in the fall for a hundredth year. There it is celebrated along the lines of a harvest festival, and it works. It works just as well as when we celebrate Sunday the whole year through because every Sunday is, of course, a small Easter, a celebration of the resurrection.

But doesn't that ruin the beautiful symbol of the resurrection in nature? Yes, it does, but there is no damage when the resurrection of nature is not written about so much in the papers. No one should ever talk about that. The resurrection of nature is a sentimental fabrication, by which the faithless bourgeoisie of the nineteenth century tried to hide the fact that they no longer believed in the resurrection, whether it be the resurrection of Christ or their own resurrection. Dead things do not rise again in nature.

---

[117] An Australian/German student of Sasse, Siegfried Hebart, was promoted to Doctor on January 27, 1939, at Erlangen University. *Siegried HEBART, Wilhelm Löhes Lehre von der Kirche, ihrem Amt und Regiment. Ein Beitrag zur Geschichte der Theologie im 19. Jahrhundert. Neuendettelsau 1939.* Unfortunately, the dissertation remains untranslated. MH

Our Germanic forefathers knew that much better than today's thoughtless newspaper readers. They knew of death with deep horror. They knew that we live in a world in which there is no resurrection. No, the resurrection does not belong to nature; it is above nature. The resurrection is supernatural. It is against nature. It is, according to all the laws of nature, impossible. That is why naturalists are shocked and oppose the message of Easter, this shocking incomprehensible message, which we worldly people say we don't know. "For they were afraid" [Mark 16:8].

Yes, the message is a bit frightening and mysterious, because it is beyond our understanding and thoughts. We are incapable of incorporating it into our picture of the world. If it is a truth of this world, then it should conform to the formerly held general truths of human wisdom by which we are consoled from the frightening mystery, distress, and agony of this world. We have all been taught the proverbs of this wisdom in our grandmother's parlor. With these, we seek the most of life in this world. "Every cloud has a silver lining." "Do right and fear no one!" "Live as you will wish that you had lived after you die." These you can write in a scrapbook, hang on a wall, or sew into a sofa cushion. People even write books about them and call it philosophy. They seek out such proverbs, such cheerful and joyous truths, and examine every message they hear for such truth. Would not the Church's Easter message contain such truth? Does not every religion of the world contain such truth? Death and resurrection are not only spoken of in Christendom! The myths of the ancient world also spoke of these things. Celebrations of resurrection are also found in other religions. Marvelous liturgies, radiant ceremonies, deeply meaningful myths describe death and resurrection in the myths of Osiris[118] and Attis.[119] Yes, there is something really moving about the longing for life and resurrection that lived in these myths. It is an indication that the soul of men yearned for that which the message of Easter spoke.

But there is something different about this message. This is made clear in one of the great scenes of the New Testament, the hour Paul stood on Mars Hill and preached the tremendous sermon about the unknown God to the Greeks of Athens (Acts 17:23–32). They listened attentively to him as long as he spoke of God, who "is actually not far from each one of us for 'in him we live and move and have our being' " (vv. 27–28). But then he started to speak of Christ, the "man whom he has appointed; and of this he has given assurance to all by raising him from the dead. Now when they heard of the resurrection of the dead, some mocked. But others said, 'we will hear you again about this' " (vv. 31–32). When he came to the message of Easter their patience ended. These were the same men who, in order to be certain of the resurrection, ran to other mystery religions over and over

---

[118] The earliest record of this Egyptian myth is found on the walls of Egyptian pyramid burial chambers from the twenty-fifth century BC. MH

[119] Phrygian god of vegetation, first referenced ca. 1250 BC. "In his self-mutilation, death, and resurrection he represents the fruits of the earth, which die in winter only to rise again in spring." "Attis," Wikipedia. MH

again to hear beautiful myths about gods who die and rise again. But in the blink of an eye, there was opposition when he said the resurrection is not a myth, but fact, and said that there is one who was raised from the dead during the reign of Pontius Pilate and before the gates of Jerusalem. So it has been since the days of the New Testament and the controversy between Origen [AD 184–253] and the assertion of Celsus,[120] who thought it must have been the mistake of excited women. The world has nothing against Good Friday and Easter as long as they are presented as myth and clothed in poetic expressions of death and life, defeat and victory, night and day. The world has nothing against Good Friday and Easter presented in that way. However, when the cross and resurrection, Golgotha and the empty grave, are not poetic illustrations but hard facts, then you hear the relentless, "no." It is heard today, just as it was in the days of the apostles, by contemporary Germans who are the same as the Jews and Greeks of the classical era. The Easter message appeared just as strange and incomprehensible to the world of that era as it does today. This message was not a poetical expression of common wisdom, but the unheard-of assertion that the grave was empty and Christ is risen.

The world is not alone when it finds this message to be incomprehensible and fearful. The Church knows it also and warns us when we no longer hear and pass on the

---

[120] We know of the Platonist Celsus' work "The True Word" solely from its quotation in Origen's "Contra Celsum." It is the earliest known extensive attack on the Christian faith. *The Ante-Nicene Fathers*, Roberts and Donaldson, eds., vol. IV.395ff. MH

Easter message, the most awesome act of God, with fear, trembling, and deep anxiety. The three women heard the first Easter message with deep anxiety: " 'Do not be alarmed. You seek Jesus of Nazareth, who was crucified. He has risen; he is not here. See the place where they laid him. But go, tell his disciples and Peter that he is going before you to Galilee. There you will see him, just as he told you.' And they went out and fled from the tomb, for trembling and astonishment had seized them, and they said nothing to anyone, for they were afraid" [Mark 16:6–8]. It is amazing that throughout the Easter Gospel there is no ringing sound of joy, but only this deep fear. If there is proof for the authenticity of this Easter story, then it is in part the fact that nowhere was an attempt made to separate this fear from any description of the resurrection. It is amazing that the [oldest] manuscripts prove the "Gospel of Mark" once ended with these verses. How can it possibly end here?

The oldest written Gospel is silent about many things the evangelist knew well. He was silent about the birth of our Lord, about most of his conversations and parables. He hints at quite a bit in a single sentence. For example, the story of the temptation of Christ is told in only a few words. "And he was in the wilderness for forty days, being tempted by Satan. And he was with the wild animals, and the angels were ministering to him" (Mark 1:13). So his Gospel is also silent about the appearance of the resurrected Christ, and only hints at it. "But go, tell his disciples and Peter that he is going before you to Galilee. There you will see him, just as he told you" [Mark 16:7]. He doesn't record any of the great experiences the disciples had, in which the risen Christ was revealed to them in Jerusalem [John 20:19–31] and Galilee on the lakeshore [John 21] and on the Mount of Ascension [Luke 24:50–53.], individually to Peter and the circle of apostles, in the locked room [Luke 24:33–49], or on the country road to the disciples from Emmaus whom he broke bread with [Luke 24:13–32.], or to the five hundred brothers [1 Cor. 15:6]. None of these were entrusted to paper in the earliest of times. They were told face-to-face during the Lord's Supper. But when that generation of blessed eyes began to dim they were written down out of necessity. So we received these short and curt statements in the New Testament.

It is not sufficient, and will not be sufficient enough to give a full historical picture of the event. It is and will be nothing other than a witness to the tremendous experience these men were allowed to have. "But blessed are your eyes, for they see, and your ears, for they hear. For truly, I say to you, many prophets and righteous people longed to see what you see, and did not see it, and to hear what you hear, and did not hear it" (Matt. 13:16–17). This word of the Master to the disciples becomes clear when you take into account the joy of the Early Church's Easter liturgy. This will help you picture what the eyes of these men saw and the ears of these men heard. The deep wonder that occurred was too inconceivable, and so also the New Testament, to be written down. God the Father had awakened his Son, who suffered as the Lamb of God

111

bearing the sins of the world from the dead. Through the blood of the eternal testament, he took the great Shepherd of the sheep from out of the grips of death. He rose as the firstborn of many brothers. He is the head of the Church, and his Church knows that, "For where the Head is, there as well I know his members are to dwell, when Christ will come and call them."[121] With that, the end of the world began. The firstborn is risen from the dead, and all will follow him. However long it takes is of no consequence. The new era began with Christ's resurrection. The old world perished. The Church lives between these two worlds, between these two eras. It is still night, but the first rays of light are dawning. Now the sun will rise. It is no accident that the only relationship between the resurrection and nature in the Church's ancient liturgy is the mention of light. "Very early on the first day of the week, when the sun had risen, [the women] went to the tomb" [Mark 16:2]. That was the first Sunday of this world. Just as God created light on the first day of the week [Gen. 1:3–5], so the new creation began on the great Sunday of the holy Easter festival. For this reason, the first candle on the Eve of Easter was lit in the dark of the church during the Early Church's Easter Vigil, (a custom which the Church would do well to keep even today) with the liturgical announcement: "The light of Christ. – Thanks be to God."

That is the message that is proclaimed throughout the world today in the tolling of the Easter bells, in the prayers

---

[121] Latin hymn tr. John Chandler, "On Christ's Ascension I Now Build," *Lutheran Worship* 150 (St. Louis: CPH, 1982).

and songs of the Church, and in the preaching of the Easter Gospel. It rings throughout the lands of the extreme North and the extreme South of our planet in the lands of early Christendom and on the mission fields of Asia and Africa where the light of Christ is dawning for the first time. It rings throughout the wide-open lands of the Russian Empire, where men still greet each other, but in secret, with the ancient greeting, "The Lord is risen! – He is risen indeed!" It rings through the cosmopolitan cities of modern civilization, and at the same time through tiny country villages. It is for the rich and powerful people as well as the poor and oppressed. It is for the learned and the unlearned, the men of every race, all peoples, and all languages without any exception, because we are all on the way to the grave our earth places before us. We are all on the way to the grave in which all human differences end. That means the end, the end of all history, the end of the eternal Germany,[122] and the end of the eternal Rome. To the grave that no human wisdom, no human power opens. To the grave that devours all of us, and from which only one has risen on this Easter Vigil, as over a dark world where [the sun comes up, when the joyful message of this day is proclaimed: "The Lord is risen! – He is risen indeed!" Amen.][123]

---

[122] Sasse is referencing *"Es lebe das Ewige Deutschland."* "Long live Eternal Germany!" A popular Nazi slogan and the last words of Hitler's cabinet member Wilhelm Frick before his execution after the Nurenberg Trials. MH

[123] Because the last page is missing, the bracketed sentence has been added to finish the sermon. FWH

On Hearing the Word of God
Rogate
May 18, 1941
James 1:22–27[124]

But be doers of the word, and not hearers only, deceiving yourselves. For if anyone is a hearer of the word and not a doer, he is like a man who looks intently at his natural face in a mirror. For he looks at himself and goes away and at once forgets what he was like. But the one who looks into the perfect law, the law of liberty, and perseveres, being no hearer who forgets but a doer who acts, he will be blessed in his doing.

If anyone thinks he is religious and does not bridle his tongue but deceives his heart, this person's religion is worthless. Religion that is pure and undefiled before God, the Father, is this: to visit orphans and widows in their affliction, and to keep oneself unstained from the world. (James 1:22–27)

It is well known that Luther called the Epistle of James, from which the Epistle lessons for the Sundays of Jubilate, Cantate, Rogate, and Exaudi come, "an epistle of straw"[125] because he found nothing of the nature of the Gospel in it. Even if this Epistle were a good letter, teaching no mere doctrine of men and driving home the Law of God, he still could not regard it as an apostolic letter, as this was also disputed in the Early Church, because it only preached the Law and not the Gospel. For: "Whatever does not teach

---

[124] *Predigt: Sonntag Rogate (18 Mai 1941) "Vom Hören des Gotteswortes."* Feuerhahn no. 235a. MH

[125] AE 35.362; WA DB 6.10.33. Luther's reference of "straw" is to 1 Cor. 3:12. MH

Christ is not yet apostolic, even though St. Peter or St. Paul does the teaching. Again, whatever preaches Christ would be apostolic, even if Judas, Annas, Pilate, and Herod were doing it."[126] How important Luther's judgment is that we all feel a little of it during these Sundays, the great time of joy for the Church between Easter and Pentecost. During this time, when the Church focuses on the great unspeakable miracles of Easter, Ascension, and Pentecost, when the Jubilate and Cantate, the Rogate and Exaudi of these Sundays like the chimes of a heavenly world rings throughout the earthly spring, at this time the simple exhortation of this pericope from the Epistle of James, this somewhat straw and wooden preaching of the Law, acts as a foreign body in the Divine Service.

In this simple yet somewhat awkward and occasionally thought-provoking speech, we miss the prophetic momentum of the Pauline Epistles, such as in the fifteenth chapter of First Corinthians, the great resurrection chapter Luther so happily preached on during the season of Easter. But there is a deeper reason for why, on these Sundays during her season of great joy, the Church places the Epistle of James next to the Gospel lesson concerning our Lord's farewell speech, next to the unspeakable beauty of this profound section of the Gospel of John transcribed with profound inspiration. Alongside this super-earthly glance into the eternal Father's house, there is placed this wholly simple text of James with its firm earthly instruction by which the very simple people that came to Jesus Christ

---

[126] AE 35.396; WA DB 6.10. MH.

from the Gentile world once learned the ABCs of Christian life as children learn letters from a primer.

And just as in the days of the Early Church when the newly baptized were reminded that they still lived on earth and not in heaven as they celebrated the Easter Vigil for the first time, and for the first time partook of the Holy Communion singing "Holy, Holy, Holy," with all the angels and archangels and all the company of heaven while receiving the body and blood of the Lord, so also our Epistle reminds us that we celebrate this joyous season of the Church here on earth in a world of sin and death, in a strange land that is not home. "Till our road in Canaan ends, through this wilderness of dangers."[127] And so we also hear our old text warning and exhorting us in worship, as it speaks to the whole Church on earth, of the futile hearing of the divine Word and on the sanctified hearing of the divine Word.

"But be doers of the word, and not hearers only . . . , being no hearer who forgets but a doer" [James 1:22, 25]. One may not understand this word as if it would put hearing and doing in opposition to one another: here the hearing and there the doing, here the Christendom of hearing and there a Christendom of doing, here a theoretical and there a practical Christendom. This would make the Epistle of James to be an epistle of straw. The writer was not as foolish as the wise people of our day, who are famous for wanting to ransom "practical Christianity" from the seriousness of the Christian belief, from the very

---

[127] Benjamin Schmolck (1672–1737), *Himmelan!*

seriousness of repentance. He knew that there is no life without teaching, no Christian life without the divine Word, no doing the divine will without hearing the Word of God. No, the Early Church knew that, also there, where she had not looked as deeply into the unfathomable depths of the Christian faith as Paul and John: only from hearing, from deep, devotional immersion in God's command can the action of obedience come. The self-deception, of which James warns, is a hearing that remains only a hearing, a hearing that is not really a hearing. He warns against those superficial hearings that are also found in the church, hearings that don't bring fruit and remain empty. "But be doers of the word, and not hearers only, deceiving yourselves."

Yes, there is a great self-deception, even in the church. There is a dreadfully empty hearing of God's Word. Jesus Christ himself has said this, as he spoke of the deep, unfathomable mystery of unrepentance: "They may indeed see but not perceive, and may indeed hear but not understand, lest they should turn and be forgiven" (Mark 4:12). He spoke of it again in the parable of the sower in the same chapter [Mark 4:3–20], of fields where no fruit remained. This happens not only in the world outside the church. No, it especially happens inside the church, and here it is a self-deception, as our Epistle says.

We all know this. We know the hearer of whom our text speaks, the hearer, who one likens to a man "who looks intently at his natural face in a mirror. For he looks at himself and goes away and at once forgets what he was

117

like" [James 1:23–24]. And this man is not some neighbor of yours in the church or your opponent. No, "you are the man" [2 Sam. 12:7]! When you leave your house you steal a quick look in the mirror, a fleeting glance, to see if your hat and tie are in the right place. And then you sit in the church and hear the Word of God, hear the Scripture readings, hear the sermon—and the impression remains as superficial, as transitory as the impression of the quick look in the mirror before. It is hardly remembered. It doesn't bring any deep experience, at least not a serious, deep experience that shakes one's being. It brings no joy for the Gospel, which is really the source and zenith of all true joy in the world. At best it brings a feeling of uneasiness, perhaps of boredom. Perhaps it leads to an analysis of the sermon and the pastor on the way home. But it has nothing to do with any real spiritual judgment, which according to Paul is the right and duty of the congregation, a judgment determining if what the pastor has said is really true.

Not true, we all—I willingly unite myself—have often been annoyed by the sermon without asking if the real reason for our discontentment is to actually be found in ourselves. When a hearer cannot agree with a sermon, it is not always the sermon and the preacher that are to blame. Listening to a sermon is an activity, an art that needs to be learned. To listen to and receive a sermon properly requires a measure of Christian formation and spiritual open-mindedness that few of us posses in this day. What this formation and open-mindedness means, that I, if I may say so, have experienced most strongly among very simple people, farmers and workers and their wives in Franconian and Prussian village churches. The lack of this spiritual formation, however, leaves nothing to replace it, at the very least the thundering rhetoric and the arousal of feelings with all the means of eloquence many people expect of the preacher so that they don't fall asleep. That we ourselves are really the deepest reason for our not hearing or our empty hearing, is no less the reason that this same incompetence of hearing also stands in opposition to the Holy Scripture. Hand on heart, beloved friends, who of us today can listen to a chapter of Romans the same as our grandparents. I fear many simple farmers in Altmühltal or in Schwabia, in Siegerland or Minden-Ravensburg would put many learned theologians to shame on that. But how long will these people be there with us? Here, beloved congregation is the deepest distress of our church. The deepest distress is not that we can no longer have a church newsletter, but that we can no longer read our Bibles. A distress that becomes more perceptible as we see in our Catholic Christians a hunger and thirst awakened in them by the long missing biblical Word, as we perhaps have not experienced for generations! I think we all know what empty hearing is.

Empty hearing of the Word of God is worse than not hearing. Better never hear the Word of God than listen to it in vain! It would be better for the men and peoples who once heard the Gospel and then fell from Christ to have never heard it. No Gentile is able to blaspheme like the one who has fallen from the faith, a former Christian. No mission field is as hard, as unfruitful, and as hopeless as the region of the old Christian lands where the inhabitants have fallen to Islam. The Word of God can be heard in vain, but it will never be heard without effect. It is either heard as a blessing or a condemnation, for deliverance or judgment. It either brings fruit, or it leads to obstinacy.

If we therefore still need proof, then may it be supplied in our time in unparalleled abundance because our time and our people face the question of whether we can still hear the Word of God or if it is perhaps too late. There is for us no more serious prayer than that God protect us from futile hearing.

We take the warning of our text regarding hearing in vain very seriously, but we note even more profoundly what he has said about blessed hearing, about the hearing of the Word that bears rich fruit. The vain hearer is here contrasted with the right hearer, who does not hear the Word of God in vain. The one of whom it is said, he is "like a man who looks intently at his natural face in a mirror. For he looks at himself and goes away and at once forgets what he was like" [James 1:23–24]. But of the other hearer it is said, "But the one who looks into the perfect law, the law of liberty, and perseveres, being no hearer who forgets but a doer who acts, he will be blessed in his doing" [v. 25]. There is a movement with the Word that is more than a fleeting urgency, more than a superficial look back. There one stands still before the Word of God. He looks into this mirror and it is he, then he peers into a mysterious, unfathomable depth. He recognizes himself in this mirror, he sees himself, but completely different than he sees himself otherwise. He experiences the truth, which Hebrews clothes in the words, "For the word of God is living and active, sharper than any two-edged sword, piercing to the division of soul and of spirit, of joints and of marrow, and discerning the thoughts and intentions of the heart. And no creature is hidden from his sight, but all are naked and exposed to the eyes of him to whom we must give account" (4:12–13).

Where we stand still before the Word, there it seems like standing for hours before the all-knowing God, whose eyes penetrate all, even the hidden depths of our lives, the abyss, which we so happily hide when in front of others because, "no creature is hidden from his sight, but all are naked and exposed to the eyes of him to whom we must give account" [v. 13]. In this the Word says to us that God is our Creator, and we his creature. In this it tells us why he created us and what we ought to be according to his holy will. We see ourselves. Only in the mirror of the Word of God, in the mirror of the divine Law, is there true, deep self-recognition. Where the man seeks to understand himself without this mirror, there he receives a false picture of himself. And whatever has been said by the great philosophers from the day of Socrates [470–399 BC] and his students, what the wholly great poets of Pindar [522–443 BC] and Aeschylus [525-456 BC] are to Shakespeare [ca. 1564–1616] and Goethe about people and the deepest being that contains only as much truth as there is a thought or a knowledge of Law of God that lives in it. In the mirror of the divine Word that corrects us, in which the innermost of our being is laid bare before God, we learn to understand what the people without God's Word never learn to understand: that we are sinners.[128]

How does it actually happen, that a modern man has such deep aversion to the word "sin"? Maybe because he has heard it so often? But how does it happen then that he cannot hear enough of what has been preached day after day now for two centuries, namely that people are good? Since Rousseau [1712–1778], the modern world has tirelessly preached the dogma "that man is good" through its poets and thinkers, through great and small spirits alike. Day after day, this impression, this dogma of the people, is continually hammered into a person by the modern media, the newspaper and the radio: "Man is good. Man is good!"

Why is this not boring? Only because we like to hear it. Because the natural man loves it, to believe this about himself, to speak about himself as being holy, to burn incense to himself. He does not love to descend to the base of the monument upon which he has placed himself. For this reason he needs the living powerful Word of God that is sharper than a two-edged sword [Heb. 4:12]. It shows us the true state of our lives, the sin, of which Luther said, it is "so deep a corruption of nature that reason cannot understand it. It must be believed because of the revelation

---

[128] "Pindar and Sophocles had vanished from our lives, but one book had remained, our Greek New Testament." Sasse thus spoke about the effect of seeing battle in WWI on a generation of theological students. *Reminiscences of an Elderly Student,* quoted in *Letters to Lutheran Pastors I,* p. lv. MH

in the Scriptures."[129] That is the recognition, to which a real, genuine encounter with the Word of God leads us, an encounter that is not merely a quick glance in the mirror, but is a long deep introspection, a peering into the "perfect law of liberty," as James said.

Where man stands still before the Word, and reads his judgment from it, there his eyes will be opened not only to the will of the Holy God, not only to the sin of one's life, to the deep disobedience of will, but there we learn the disobedience of understanding to which our will became obedient. Our Epistle does not expressly speak [of the Gospel]— that is its limitation that Luther had so clearly pointed out—but there is no page of the New Testament in which it is not written, at least between the lines: "Behold, the Lamb of God, who takes away the sin of the world!" [John 1:29]. Even the simple Christians for whom James was written, those who still lived deep in the Greek Old Testament have known and believed in their hearts, "Surely he has borne our griefs and carried our sorrows; yet we esteemed him stricken, smitten by God, and afflicted. But he was pierced for our transgressions; he was crushed for our iniquities; upon him was the chastisement that brought us peace, and with his wounds we are healed" (Isa. 53:4–5). That he became a man is about our will, that he died for us and is risen from the dead, that was also the prerequisite for their new obedience to which they called one another: "We love because he first loved us" (1 John 4:19).

How can one who has been touched by the breath of

---

129 SA III, I, 3; BKS 434. MH

this love remain cold and dead? "O it is a living, busy, active, and mighty thing this faith. It is impossible for it not to be doing good works incessantly. It does not ask whether good works are to be done, but before the question is asked, it has already done them, and is constantly doing them."[130] So said Luther in his preface to Romans. In this sense, we as evangelical Christians understand all the great exhortations of the New Testament to a living, active brotherly love. We know that we never even cooperate in our redemption. We know that we remain poor sinners, who live on the active forgiveness of sins. We know that it literally remains true: "The best and holiest deeds must fail."[131] We know that even the great saints of Christendom, Francis of Assisi, Loehe [1808–1872], and [Friedrich von] Bodelschwing [1831–1910] went to heaven only because of greater grace and mercy, apart from all their service and worthiness. All the works of life that you have done were, yes, only an inconspicuous song of your thankfulness, only a further reflection of the unending love by which you have been saved. "We love because he first loved us."

Only in this sense are all the exhortations of the New Testament to active brotherly love to be understood, even this exhortation of James: "But the one who looks into the perfect law, the law of liberty, and perseveres, being no hearer who forgets but a doer who acts, he will be blessed

---

[130] AE 35.370; WA DB 7.11. MH
[131] Martin Luther, "From Depths of Woe I Cry to Thee," *LSB* 607:2; WA 35.492, AE 53.221. MH

in his doing" [1:25].

And then a very simple and comprehensible example would show wherein the fruit of a blessed hearing exists. "If anyone thinks he is religious and does not bridle his tongue but deceives his heart, this person's religion is worthless" (James 1:26). He who has heard God's Word and then sung "Amen" and "Alleluia" with the congregation, he who has been united in the confession of faith, the confession that all tongues in heaven and on earth and under the earth will one day make, he who has sung the *Sanctus* during communion with all the angels and archangels and the whole company of the heavenly host— how can he still use his tongue to lie, and slander, and speak furious words of abuse?! "With it we bless our Lord and Father, and with it we curse people who are made in the likeness of God. From the same mouth come blessing and cursing. My brothers, these things ought not to be so" (James 3:9–10), it says in the next chapter. Where that happens, there the Divine Service was worthless; there the Word of God has been heard in vain. But where the tongue is tamed and the language sanctified, the conversation is placed in the service of love, there it is a fruit of blessed hearing.

And yet our Epistle adds another example by which to recognize a blessed hearing. "Religion that is pure and undefiled before God and the Father is this: to visit orphans and widows in their affliction" (James 1:27). For the Christians of the Early Church the Divine Service was not yet finished when the Word of God was heard and the

125

Lord's Supper celebrated and the confession, prayer, songs of praise, and blessing were done. The deacon and deaconesses went from the altar into the houses of those who could not partake of the communion of the congregation. They went to the sick and to the dying and brought them the blessed bread of the greeting of peace of the congregation. As in all times, also in the past century, when the deaconess and deacon offices were newly instituted in our church—*diakonia* grows from the liturgy. Sacrificial service of the poor, sick, and forsaken arises from the living Divine Service. That is already shown in the fact that our deaconess houses were the actual places of the liturgical renewal and the new understanding of the Lord's Supper. In the great cities of the ancient world, in which the Church was great, there were as many individual, destitute people as at any other time of history. But those who belonged to the Church were not deserted. They were not alone. How can a member of the Body of Christ be destitute? And when it happens with us, when it would be different for us, when we no longer visit the widows and orphans, the poor and the sick, the despairing and the worrying, when we will not at least visit the members of Christ's Body who live alone somewhere in the world with our thoughts and gifts and include them in our prayers, then our hearing of the Word of God has gone bad. Then our Divine Service will not be a pure and undefiled Divine Service, but, as the patient words of James say, a self-deception.

And our text adds yet another example to tell us what

the blessed hearing of God is. To pure and undefiled Divine Service belongs this, "to keep oneself unstained from the world" (James 1:27). Naturally, this does not mean leaving the world as it has so often been understood in the history of the Church. Yet experience has always shown that this is not possible. One can leave the cities of men and go out into the deserts, but the world goes with him. One can leave the hustle and bustle of men and withdraw into a cloister. But the world goes with him. No, to keep oneself unstained from the world never means to leave the world. Neither does it mean to live without sin. So often, in the history of the Church, Christians have sought to do this also, and have learned through painful experience that this too is impossible. "To keep oneself unstained from the world" means to be a citizen of heaven in this world. It means to live on the daily forgiveness of sins and faith within the world where sin and death live. So we are told, "In the world you will have tribulation. But take heart; I have overcome the world" (John 16:33).

That is the pure Divine Service, the fruit of the blessed hearing of the divine Word. How does it happen? Our Epistle doesn't tell us how it happens. It doesn't tell us how an empty hearing becomes a blessed hearing. But the answer that is missing in our Epistle is given to us in the Gospel for the Sunday of Rogate: "Truly, truly, I say to you, whatever you ask of the Father in my name, he will give it to you" (John 16:23). There is a prayer in which the hearing is promised, and this Sunday calls us to it. It is a gift for which we will never pray in vain. "If you then, who are evil, know how to give good gifts to your children, how much more will your Father who is in heaven give good things to those who ask him!" (Matthew 7:11). O let us pray for this gift in Jesus' name! Let us pray for our congregation, for our church, for the whole Church of God in the world, that God would bless the course of his Word in the middle of the distress and war in this world. That he himself would open ears and hearts and blessedly exchange empty hearing for true hearing. Let us pray for our people, that God would not take his Word from them. O let us pray that we ourselves would be spared an empty hearing and become doers of the Word. Let us then pray the prayer to which this hearing is promised with certainty, the Pentecost prayer of the Church of Christ: come, Holy Spirit, fill the hearts of your faithful and light in them the fire of your heartfelt love. Amen.

The Comforter
Exaudi Sunday
May 29, 1938
John 15:26–16:4[132]

But when [the Comforter] comes, whom I will send to you from the Father, the Spirit of truth, who proceeds from the Father, he will bear witness about me. And you also will bear witness, because you have been with me from the beginning. I have said all these things to you to keep you from falling away. They will put you out of the synagogues. Indeed, the hour is coming when whoever kills you will think he is offering service to God. And they will do these things because they have not known the Father, nor me. But I have said these things to you, that when their hour comes you may remember that I told them to you. I did not say these things to you from the beginning, because I was with you. (John 15:26–16:4)

"The Comforter," that is how Luther, with great care, translated *paraklete*, or "advocate," the strange name for the Holy Ghost that our Gospels use: "But when the Comforter has come, whom I will send you from the Father, the Spirit of truth" [John 15:26, author's translation]. Luther once explained this name in a Pentecost Sunday sermon this way: "The word 'comforter,' in the Greek *paraklete* (which is almost as one in Latin says 'advocate,' or 'patron') is what one such man is called, who is the legal advisor of the accused or defendant, who takes him on, to defend him, to get his things in order, to serve

---

[132] *Predigt: Sonntag Exaudi (29 Mai 1938) "Der Tröster."* Feuerhahn no. 215a. MH

and help him, to admonish and strengthen him where it is necessary. That, Christ said, should be the office of the Holy Spirit. After I leave you, you will not have comfort or assistance in the world. But the whole world will be against you. The devil will harass you, and speak to you with his poisonous, blasphemous, and annoying tongue. He will accuse you and cry out before the whole world as a tempter and an insurrectionist. Yes, the Holy Ghost will also be a Comforter."[133] Luther continues, "When your own consciences and hearts are tormented and frightened inside you with the horror of God's wrath, with sadness, with hard thoughts about your own weakness that would like to and must drive you to despair."[134]

In doing this, the Reformer speaks about the deep comfort the Holy Ghost gives a despairing heart in an hour of deep disheartenment and bereavement; with him he will escort the Church through the hardest days of the fight. He will reveal to us a part of his heart, a deep experience in his life. Where the word "comforter" stands in our Bible, there it stands as a powerful, living witness of him, who as the Reformer of the Church, and the Church with him, had once experienced in the days of the Reformation, because the Reformation was not well-known as a shining triumph, but as a chain of very strenuous fights inside the Church. For many at that time, it looked like the breakdown of the Church. At that time the Church hardly saw anything else.

---

[133] WA 21.445.32f. *Evangelium am Pfingstag 1536, Johan. XIIII.* Aland no. Po 244. MH
[134] WA 21.446.4ff. MH

In such times, Luther learned to confess: "I believe in the Holy Ghost"—and he experienced what kind of a comfort this faith could be.

Luther was not always known as the hero of the German nation, not always known as the one who stands on the Luther Monument, but for many years he was known as "the most hated man in Germany." He must have experienced for himself what it meant that, "the devil will harass you and speak to you with his poisonous, blasphemous, and annoying tongue and accuse you. He will cry out before the entire world as a tempter and an insurrectionist."[135] His whole life long, he had experienced how weak and powerless a human heart is, when God's strength and power does not maintain it. The question put to him is always repeated, whether or not he could answer for his teaching. "How often has my heart frightened, punished and reproached me with its strongest and only question: are you alone wise? Should all the others have been wrong and wrong for so long a time? If you are wrong, and tempt so many people into error, who will all become eternally damned."[136] During such hours he experienced that it is literally true that Christ did not leave him alone in the world. "But when the Comforter has come, whom I will send you from the Father, the Spirit of truth, who proceeds from the Father" [John 15:26, author's translation].

Our understanding of the Gospel must come from such

---

[135] WA 21.446.2–4. MH
[136] *Misuse of the Mass (1521)*; AE 36:134. WA 8.482–83. Aland 503.

experiences, which the Church has had throughout all the centuries. And when we think about these experiences, then we can do nothing but what God asks, because he gives us these experiences so that he may also let us live in this rich comfort that comes from faith in the Holy Ghost, the great comfort of the Church, about whom this Gospel for the Sunday of Exaudi speaks.

Where is this comfort? What is this comforting message of the Gospel? It is the comforting promise that the witness of Christ will not be silent in the world. It will be repeated again and again, generation to generation, despite all the weakness of man, despite all the opposition of the world. And is it not true? We need this comfort today amidst all the anxiousness over the future of our church that so often lies heavy on our souls. All these worries of men trespass against the godly promise: that the witness of Christ will not be silent! "But when the Comforter has come, whom I will send you from the Father, the Spirit of truth, who proceeds from the Father, he will bear witness of me. And you will also bear witness, because you have been with me from the beginning" [John 15:26, author's translation].

The witness of Christ—that is the message of the Church. The task of the apostles was to give this witness again. They, who were with Jesus from the beginning, they who ate and drank with him, who witnessed his changes, whose ears and eyes witnessed his words and actions, the holy witness of his resurrection, they would carry his message on. And when they are no longer there, then those who have received the Word of truth from their hands

132

become witnesses. So the proclamation of Christ would go throughout history, from generation to generation. Next to the oral sermon stands the written Word. The witness of the apostles was written down, and the apostolic and prophetic Word of the Old and New Testaments were put next to the oral sermon. It remains the source and norm, the witness of Christ to be carried to all people and races, and to be preserved through all the centuries. So the Church of Christ would be the Church of the apostolic message, the apostolic Church erected upon "the foundation of the apostles and prophets" [Eph. 2:20], a witness for all times, a witness for all people. With sublime monotony the Church would speak this to all alike, the same message to all, to all the testimony of what once happened at the time of Pontius Pilate.

We pause now—and place a question before us. Is that really the message? Is this message not enormously weak? Is it not something wholly monotonous, and should it not become obsolete? Modern man raises this protest against this message: "Man cannot always say the same thing. Men cannot all say the same thing. One cannot be witness Sunday after Sunday, year after year, century after century, to something that happened once in the gray past. What use is a revelation to us that happened once in the past? Must we go back?" It is quite noticeable that this objection is already very old. In the second century in Asia Minor, a powerful movement brought it out. A prophet stood up. A prophet began to speak. The end is coming. God's Spirit speaks now. The Comforter, the Paraklete is appearing. The classic era brought forward two world religions. Mani [ca. 216–276]: "I am the Paraklete."[137] Mohammed [570–632]: "I am the Paraklete." In the Middle Ages, the prophets suddenly sounded, "The time of the spirit comes." In the time of the Reformation: "New truths! Do not stand by the apostles like Luther!" [Gotthold Ephraim]. Lessing [1729–1781] proclaimed the season of Johanine brotherly love, "Wait for the new revelation." Who has then closed the canon (the collection of holy writings) "every holy writing is only a mausoleum of religion," the young [Friedrich] Schleiermacher [1768–1634] said.[138] Where is the Holy Ghost, the real Spirit of God? There, where one only repeats the old story again, or there, where there is new proclamation? That was Luther's fight. The fight that started already in the Early Church: "He will bear witness about me" [John 15:26]. That is the Spirit of truth, who proceeds from the Father. "Every spirit who confesses that Jesus Christ has come in the flesh is from God" (1 John 4:2).

Therefore he explains that the Church's witness to Christ is not merely the witness of men. It is the witness of the Holy Ghost. The Word of the Church is not only man's

---

[137] Mani was Iranian, Gnostic founder of Manichaeism. MH
[138] Quoted from *Reden über die Religion* Göttingen 1799. *On Religion: Speeches to Its Cultured Despisers*, (Harper, 1958), p. 91. "Every sacred writing is in itself a glorious production, a speaking monument from the heroic time of religion, but, through servile reverence, it would become merely a mausoleum, a monument that a great spirit once was there, but is now no more. . . . Not every person has religion who believes in a sacred writing, but only the man who has a lively and immediate understanding of it, and who, therefore, so far as he himself is concerned, could most easily do without it." MH

word. Therefore, it is not subject to the laws governing the words of man. Therefore, it does great wonders. Therefore, it is not obsolete. Therefore, it is not boring. Therefore, it is for all of mankind. Therefore, it is not subject to the past. This Word does not die, because it is God's Word. Therefore, the Holy Ghost calls men with it, over all pleading and understanding. It is always the same Word, the same witness.

English Christianity celebrated a glorious commemoration this past Thursday. That hour on the evening of May 24, 1738, when John Wesley suddenly understood, because of Luther's foreword to Romans, what forgiveness of sins is: "I became certain that He had taken my sins away, and reconciled me from the law of sin and of death."[139] "The Spirit himself bears witness with our spirit that we are children of God" [Rom. 8:16].

Because it is God's Word, the witness of the Divine Spirit, therefore it breaks the opposition. Never before in the history of men's religion has one religion been so fought against. Never has a message motivated such an enraged opposition in the name of religion as the Christian witness. This is not the worldly opposition to the Church. In the text it is the Jews. Luther experienced it inside the church, and he was kicked out. Today it happens in the name of "belief in God." So it must be. God's Word will be recognized straight through as God's Word.

---

[139] *The Works of John Wesley, 3rd ed., vol. 5, First Series of Sermons (1–39)*, journal entry, May 24, 1738 (Grand Rapids: Baker Books, 2007), p. 103. MH

This witness goes on. It cannot die. And God's Word was already so powerful in the Old Testament that trees and plants were ripped out and destroyed by it (Jer. 18: 9). How much more will it do for the Church? Do you think that it doesn't matter, when one builds a modern megalopolis and there is no church in it? When one builds a settlement with no room for the Divine Service? No, the world lives on, because God gives you his Word. God's Word will not delay. It remains the power. The witness remains—and also through martyrs, and thereby wins over the world anew.

"But when the Comforter comes . . ." He came. A million altars sound the prayer *"Veni Creator Spiritus."* "Come, Creator Spirit!" Jesus Christ promised: This prayer would be heard. *Veni Sancti Spiritus.* Amen.

The conclusion of this sermon manuscript is abbreviated and indicates that it was undoubtedly continued orally from his thoughts. FWH

The Miracle of Pentecost
Pentecost Sunday
Old Town Church, Erlangen[140]
May 12, 1940
Acts 2:1–14

When the day of Pentecost arrived, they were all together in one place. And suddenly there came from heaven a sound like a mighty rushing wind, and it filled the entire house where they were sitting. And divided tongues as of fire appeared to them and rested on each one of them. And they were all filled with the Holy Spirit and began to speak in other tongues as the Spirit gave them utterance.

Now there were dwelling in Jerusalem Jews, devout men from every nation under heaven. And at this sound the multitude came together, and they were bewildered, because each one was hearing them speak in his own language. And they were amazed and astonished, saying, "Are not all these who are speaking Galileans? And how is it that we hear, each of us in his own native language? Parthians and Medes and Elamites and residents of Mesopotamia, Judea and Cappadocia, Pontus and Asia, Phrygia and Pamphylia, Egypt and the parts of Libya belonging to Cyrene, and visitors from Rome, both Jews and proselytes, Cretans and Arabians—we hear them telling in our own tongues the mighty works of God." And all were amazed and perplexed, saying to one another, "What does this mean?" But others mocking said, "They are filled with new wine."

But Peter, standing with the eleven, lifted up his voice and addressed them, "Men of Judea and all who dwell in Jerusalem, let this be known to you, and give ear to my

---

[140] *Predigt: Pfingstsonntag (12 Mai 1940) "Das Pfingstwunder."* Feuerhahn no. 225a. MH

words." (Acts 2:1–14)

Is it possible to celebrate Pentecost this year? If Pentecost were a festival celebrating earthly joy, in which we would walk through spring laughing with joyful songs on our lips enjoying the beauty of the world and life, then, no, we couldn't celebrate Pentecost this year. Why should we even be capable of joy, when the greatest conflict in German history rages on the Western battlefields, and every hour our brothers are confronted with the sight of death before their eyes?[141] Neither can we celebrate Pentecost as a celebration of spirit in the sense of the spirit that is able to overcome obstacles and be in control, the wise imaginative spirit of humanity that created the great achievements of earthly culture. We can't celebrate Pentecost in that sense either. Rather, we, as honest men, must hang our heads in deep shame at the mere thought that we could ever sing a song of praise to such a spirit.

But Pentecost is the celebration of a different Spirit, a Spirit who is something entirely different then the spirit of creatures, the spirit of men and their creation. It is the Spirit that is spoken of on the first page of the Bible: "In the beginning, God created the heavens and the earth. The earth was without form and void, and darkness was over the face of the deep. And the Spirit of God was hovering over the face of the waters" (Gen. 1:1–2). It is the Spirit of God, who hovered over the void, a formless and dark world

---

[141] The Germans commenced the *Blitzkrieg* offensive in mid May 1940. MH

in the beginning. It is the same Spirit, who in the last book of the Bible shows John the seer the end of all history: a world returning to the void from which it emerged, an earth which became a monstrous cemetery, and over which the voice of the Spirit, the voice of the Comforter, is heard: " 'Blessed are the dead who die in the Lord from now on.' 'Blessed indeed,' says the Spirit, 'that they may rest from their labors, for their deeds follow them!' " (Rev. 14:13). And behind this world of the dead, the Spirit causes him to see another world: "Then I saw a new heaven and a new earth, for the first heaven and the first earth had passed away, and the sea was no more" (Rev. 21:1). We celebrate the festival of this Spirit on Pentecost. And so we celebrate Pentecost this year and possibly with a deeper understanding and stronger faith than usual.

"I believe in the Holy Spirit, the Holy Christian Church, the communion of saints," so we all learned as children. So we confess Sunday after Sunday with the rest of the congregation in the Divine Service. How often has this confession been a mere confession of the lips! As if what we speak about in the Third Article of the Creed were obvious. The Holy Spirit, the Holy Church, the communion of saints, are not obvious. They are miraculous facts. Perhaps, these hard times during the war are opening our eyes a bit wider to the wonderful reality we confess in these ancient words of the Creed. Is it not an indication that this reality is occurring already, when this confession is spoken across the entire earth in over a thousand different languages? "I believe in the Holy Spirit!" Today this confession bridges all borders of confession, those chasms by which men separate themselves. Whatever may stand between people: hate, enmity, and misunderstanding, old and new guilt; wherever the name of Christ is called upon across the entire face of the earth, there the ancient Pentecost prayer ascends from the hearts of millions to heaven: "Come, Holy Ghost, God and Lord, With all your graces now outpoured On each believer's mind and heart; Your fervent love to them impart. Lord, by the brightness of your light In holy faith your Church unite; From every land and every tongue . . . ."[142]

Our contemplation of the ancient Pentecost story should be helped by the fact that we pray this prayer with one voice. And in the Creed we confess with renewed strength: "I believe in the Holy Spirit." Whoever wants to understand this correctly must keep guard against a great misunderstanding that makes the correct understanding of Pentecost and its message impossible for many Christians. The confession of our church, the Augsburg Confession, once described this misunderstanding when it warned against the mistake of thinking about the Holy Spirit as "a created movement in things."[143] All that we men normally know about spirit is what we know of the spirit of creatures. The spirit of man is a poor sinful creature, and this is the spirit of the deepest thinkers, the sharpest observers of nature, and the tremendous creation of

---

[142] German hymn, thirteenth century, "Come, Holy Ghost, God and Lord" tr. *The Lutheran Hymnal* 1941, alt., *Lutheran Worship* 154 (St. Louis: CPH, 1982); AE 53.266; WA 35.510.
[143] AC I; BKS p. 51, especially note 7. MH

government. There is something great about the spirit of man. He who has dominion over the earth, and to whom creation has been entrusted, has changed the face of the earth. The earth has become quite different since man has appeared, but she has not become better or more beautiful. It is rather questionable whether or not the spirit of man has built more than it has destroyed. "The earth was without form and void, and darkness was over the face of the deep" [Gen. 1:2]. And so it is written at the beginning of earth's history, so it will be written of her end. When the last man disappears from the earth, and this earth is nothing more than a huge cemetery, then the earth will be without form and void as in the beginning. That is what the spirit of man has brought about. He can do no more, because he himself is nothing but a poor, fallen, and sinful creature.

But there is another Spirit. He is not from below, but from above. He is not a sinful spirit, but a Holy Spirit. He is not a creature. He is God, true God, not a distant work of God in his creatures, but God himself, God of God, very God of very God. That is the key to understanding the story of Pentecost. We call what happened "the outpouring of the Holy Spirit," because of the explanation Peter gave of this event: "but this is what was uttered through the prophet Joel: 'And in the last days it shall be, God declares, that I will pour out my Spirit on all flesh' " (Acts 2:16–17). But this outpouring of the Holy Spirit is not an outpouring of a power. It is something the poor words of human language cannot describe. It is the coming of God, the Holy Spirit. The Holy Spirit is not a thing. He is a person; a person in a much higher sense than the spirit of man is a person. He is a person as the Father is a person, as the eternal Son of God is a person. And yet, along with these two persons, he is *one* God.

He is he who hovered over the formless void and the darkness of the deep at the beginning of the world [Gen. 1:2]. It was through him that the chaos of the cosmos was made into an orderly creation. He is he who still surrounds the earthly creations with beauty and order by his creative power and dominion as a testimony to the deadly destruction of sin. He is he who had spoken through the Prophets [2 Pet. 1:21]. He is he who descended in the Baptism of Christ [Mark 1:10]. He is he, who the Lord promised his disciples as the Helper, when they would stand before judges and have to confess their faith. "For it is not you who speak, but the Spirit of your Father speaking through you" (Matt. 10:20). He is he who helps the abandoned disciples, He who will help the persecuted Church: "And I will ask the Father, and he will give you another Helper, to be with you forever, even the Spirit of truth, whom the world cannot receive, because it neither sees him nor knows him. You know him, for he dwells with you and will be in you" (John 14:16–17).

God the Holy Spirit came to man. That is what the disciples experienced. Notice in their accounts how hard it fell on them. Take note of the unexpected, incomprehensible, and absolute wonder in the description of their experience: "And suddenly there came from heaven a sound like a mighty rushing wind, and it filled the entire

142

house where they were sitting, and divided tongues as of fire appeared to them and rested on each one of them" [Acts 2:2–3]. From these words it is apparent that human language is not sufficient to describe the heavenly tone, which filled the house. Nor is it sufficient to make a picture of the expression on their faces with the gleaming light from the tongues of flame shining on each of their heads. None of us can experience that. These words were written for us: "what no eye has seen, nor ear heard, . . . what God has prepared for those who love him" (1 Cor. 2:9). But we comprehend it. This is not written about the spirit of man, about his glory or his experience, but about the revelation of God. God the Holy Spirit came to men who heard him. He did not come down to a few lonely individuals, here and there, only for a moment. He came to stay, to take up residence, "to be with you forever; . . . for he dwells with you and will be in you" (John 14:16–17).

That is the miracle of Pentecost: "And they were all filled with the Holy Spirit" [Acts 2:4]. Henceforth, God the Holy Spirit will no longer merely hover over the world. He will no longer only appear here and there for short moments in the world, but he will live here on earth. He will have his temple in the midst of men. It will not be a sanctuary of stone, yet it will be a real sanctuary, and it will be said of it: "The LORD is in his holy temple. Let all the earth keep silence before him" [Hab. 2:20]. And already here in earthly history some of the truth of the promised new creation is fulfilled: "Behold, the dwelling place of God is with man. He will dwell with them, and they will be his people" (Rev. 21:3). That is the miracle of Pentecost that we confess as often as we speak with the words of the ancient Creed: "I believe in the Holy Spirit, the Holy Christian Church."

"And they were filled with the Holy Spirit." What sort of men were they that experienced that? Later, the Church came into contact with the great spiritual world of the Greco-Roman culture. There she would constantly have to answer the reproach that the spirit still remains with the Church, but not like it did when the unlearned fishermen and tradesmen from Galilee were its first messengers. As a matter of fact, nothing in the history of human spiritual life has ever come close to being as great as this outpouring of the Holy Spirit. And it happened where one would have never expected it. "For consider your calling, brothers," so wrote Paul to the Church in Corinth, "not many of you were wise according to worldly standards, not many were powerful, not many were of noble birth. But God chose what is foolish in the world to shame the wise" (1 Cor. 1:26–27).

The Holy Spirit only comes to the place where men despair of their own wisdom and strength. And that is what those, who are "wise according to worldly standards," as Paul so nicely put it, lack. Yes there are humble men even among the wise of the world, but they are very scarce. They are as scarce as the great Greek poet who spoke so profoundly about the lives of men in a poem, even before the advent of Christianity: "What is a man? What is a man not? Man is the dream of a shadow. But when the brilliance given by God (Zeus) comes, a shining light is on man, and a gentle lifetime."[144] That is one of the few cases where, in the midst of the Gentile world, a longing homesickness was illuminated by grace, an example of a humble wisdom, the wisdom of how poor in spirit man is: "Man is the dream of a shadow." Men who were filled with the Holy Spirit were by no means particular heroes of faith. It is not written that they were anywhere in the Bible. It was quite to the contrary. We remind ourselves of what was said about this in the sermon for Easter, and the Ascension Epistle. It is not written anywhere in the Bible that Andrew, Thomas, Bartholomew, and Simon the Zealot believed more, hoped more, or had more love than other Christians. And still "they were all filled with the Holy Spirit, and began to speak in other tongues as the Spirit gave them utterance" [Acts 2:4].

Certainly though, there does seem to be a requirement for the reception of the Spirit. "They were all together in one place" [Acts 2:1]. That is what it says at the beginning of this story. They had to be together in order for Pentecost to happen. If each remained in their own house, each in their own rooms, there would not have been a Pentecost. Also on the day of Christ's ascension it was already said: "All these with one accord were devoting themselves to prayer [and supplication]" (Acts 1:14). And what is here a prerequisite for Pentecost is also a consequence of Pentecost, an effect by the Holy Spirit. "And [they were]

---

[144] Pindar [522–443], *Pythian Ode* 8.95ff, Special thanks to Prof. Mark Brighton for finding this reference for me.

day by day attending the temple together and breaking bread in their homes" (Acts 2:46).

God the Holy Spirit always comes to the individual, even in our story it is each individual that is filled with the Spirit. The flame of the Holy Spirit blazed over each head, and each individual spoke by him. But God the Holy Spirit comes to individual men where they are together in a fellowship [Gemeinschaft]. As Luther said so beautifully in his catechism: "I believe that I cannot by my own reason or strength believe in Jesus Christ, my Lord, or come to him; but the Holy Spirit has called me by the Gospel, enlightened me with his gifts, sanctified and kept me in the true faith." Here we have both next to each other: The Holy Spirit has called me to the faith. No one else can believe for me, but my faith is never separated from the faith of the others in the Church. "In the same way He calls, gathers, enlightens, and sanctifies the whole Christian Church on earth, and keeps it with Jesus Christ in the one true faith."[145]

The modern world has forgotten this deep connection between the faith of the individual and the faith of the Church. Incidentally, this is as true for the Roman Catholic Church as it is for the Evangelical Church. We have forgotten that we do not sit in church as individuals, each holding their own private devotion—if necessary, that could be done at home in their own rooms—but that we as members of a congregation are together in one accord, with each other in prayer and supplication, together in the

---

[145] SC Creed III. MH

confession of the one true faith. Then all belongs together, the unity of love and the unity of faith. Where the one is missing the other is also missing. Perhaps, the Eastern Church has kept this thinking of the Early Church about Pentecost in its purest form. It is customary for that Church to speak the confession of faith [i.e., the Nicene Creed] in every Divine Service. The pastor starts by saying from the altar, "Let us have love for one another that we may with one accord confess the faith." The choir continues, "In the name of the Father and of the Son and the Holy Spirit," and then the Nicene Creed is spoken.

So on Pentecost the Holy Spirit works on men, who were gathered together in one accord. That is the Church, which is his temple in the world until the end of days. And this Church immediately makes an appearance before the world. "They were all filled with the Holy Spirit and began to speak in other tongues as the Spirit gave them utterance" [Acts 2:4]. We don't know how this speaking in tongues is actually to be understood such that everyone present understood immediately, and that each heard his language, his mother tongue. But it is completely clear: a message was proclaimed and heard here. But the proclamation was not a normal proclamation, and the hearing was abnormal also. The Holy Spirit performed a miracle in the proclamation as well as in the hearing. God the Holy Spirit spoke the eternal and powerful Word in and through human speech. He also performed a miracle in the hearing. Not everyone there understood what was being said. There were some who did not understand, "Others mocking said, 'they are filled with new wine' " [Acts 2:13].

What kind of a message is that? Our Epistle does not say anything more about that, but it comes out in the great Pentecost sermon, in which Peter explains this miracle. It is the simple message of the crucified Jesus, whom God raised from the dead: "Let all the house of Israel therefore know for certain that God has made him both Lord and Christ, this Jesus whom you crucified" (Acts 2:36).

That is the message of the Church. The Holy Gospel is the message that there is forgiveness of sins in Jesus Christ, and in him alone. It is completely free, wherever this message is heard, that God the Holy Spirit is at work calling men and giving them the faith that goes to the heart. He, God the Holy Spirit himself, is the bearer of this message. That is the mystery. Who can explain the fact that he works faith here and finds unbelief there? Who can explain why the spiritual world of the Greeks was closed to Paul in Athens [Acts 17] and then half a century later it was opened in Alexandria? What induced the cultures of the Germanic world to accept it in the time of the migration of peoples? What compels three thousand men to be baptized every week in India! Every week three thousand! Every Sunday a Pentecost? What compels the Chinese Christians to hold on to this in the midst of all the distress in their church, and at such an extreme sacrifice? What compels the educated Japanese, the students and the professors, the officials and the officers, to study this message and to endure so many sacrifices for it? What is the basis for the fact that in the last year there came into existence simple yet moving folk songs praising Jesus in Papua New Guinea? Yes, what is this power? Why does the Pentecost story keep repeating itself in other names?! And how is it that each of us hears in our own native language?!

Yes, what kind of a mystery is behind this? Oh Holy Spirit, we pray to you! Oh Holy Spirit, we confess you, and we never cease to pray in the Babylonian confusion of tongues throughout the centuries:

> Come, Holy Ghost, God and Lord,
> With all your graces now outpoured
> On each believer's mind and heart;
> Your fervent love to them impart,
> Lord, by the brightness of your light
> In holy faith your Church unite;
> From every land and every tongue . . . .[146]

Oh, Holy Spirit, return to us. Amen.

---

[146] German hymn, thirteenth century, "Come, Holy Ghost, God and Lord" tr. *The Lutheran Hymnal* 1941, alt., *Lutheran Worship* 154 (St. Louis: CPH, 1982); AE 53.266; WA 35.510.

The Question before the Church

First Sunday after Trinity

June 27, 1943[147]

Acts 2:42–47

And they devoted themselves to the apostles' teaching and the fellowship, to the breaking of bread and the prayers. And awe came upon every soul, and many wonders and signs were being done through the apostles. And all who believed were together and had all things in common. And they were selling their possessions and belongings and distributing the proceeds to all, as any had need. And day by day, attending the temple together and breaking bread in their homes, they received their food with glad and generous hearts, praising God and having favor with all the people. And the Lord added to their number day by day those who were being saved. (Acts 2:42–47)

When this war is finally over, then this question before the Church will ring out anew over the wasted land and through the exhausted people of the West. So it has always been when great wars have naturally and historically razed a community to the ground, after the Thirty Years' War [1618–1648], after the Napoleonic wars [1803–1815], after the First World War [1914–1918]. In such times, Christianity has been reminded of what is confessed Sunday after Sunday on all her altars: "I believe in the Holy Christian Church. I believe in the communion of saints." What kind of a reality is meant by this? He who has ears to

---

[147] *Predigt: 1. Sonntag nach Trinitatis (27 Jun 1943) "Die Frage nach der Kirche."* Feuerhahn no. 244a. MH

hear, he hears this question today going out through the world already, even among us German people.

Yes, what kind of a reality stands behind this confession? Perhaps none at all? Perhaps it has become an old and senseless formulation, when in the midst of the most terrifying of all wars, a war which has already long since stopped being a decent chivalrous fight, when in the midst of this war, it is confessed in a thousand languages throughout the whole world, Sunday after Sunday, yes, day after day, "I believe in the Holy Ghost, the Holy Christian Church, the communion of saints." No, that is no cliché. There is a reality that stands behind that, a reality which one overlooks, which one can forget, a reality that can make you avert your gaze like the sun when it sinks behind the evening sky. Yet, a reality that is there just as certain as the sun is still there even when our eyes cannot see it. No, even more certain. Because I do not know with full certainty that the sun will come up once more tomorrow, but that God the Father, the almighty Creator of heaven and earth is there—that I know. That Jesus Christ the Lord, to whom all authority on heaven and earth is given is there, that the Holy Spirit who proceeds from the Father and the Son and hovers over the chaos of these times just as he hovered over the darkness of the deep in the beginning, is there—that I know. And therefore I know that there is the Church of which the Creed speaks: the Church, which is the people of God, the Body of Christ, and the temple of the Holy Spirit. But where could we understand and learn this reality better than where the Church of God entered the

151

history of men and became visible to our eyes, visible in as much as the eyes of men are able to see?

So in our text she steps before our eyes, the Church of God with that which the great Pentecost chapter of Acts ends. It begins with the miracle of Pentecost. It follows Peter's Pentecost sermon and the baptizing of three thousand. And then the life of the first congregation is described with brief words, yet in concise hints, so that in the words describing the whole violent experience of everyday tremble, the unspeakable fear of the newly baptized, the simplicity of faith of those who devoted themselves to the teaching of the apostles, the trembling of their hearts before the miracle of the Spirit, the brotherly love with which they did everything, the prayer, the celebration of the Sacrament, the praising of God, one can understand why this text constantly shakes people and caused the deepest movements in the Church's history. As the history of the rich young man [Matt. 19:16–22] has continually moved men to repentance and to surrender all their earthly possessions; as the discourse in Matthew 10, with which Jesus sent out his disciples, constantly held the Church of the Middle Ages before the mirror because in these they recognized their sins, their failings; so it is that what Luke said in the second and fourth chapters of Acts about the first congregation has continued to be understood as a call to repentance since the days of the Ancient Church. "And they devoted themselves to the apostles' teaching and the fellowship, to the breaking of bread and the prayers" (Acts 2:42). And we? "And all who believed were together and had all things in common" (v. 44). And we? "And day by day, attending the temple together [with one accord]"[148] (v. 46a). And we? "With glad and generous hearts, praising God and having favor with all the people. And the Lord added to their number day by day those who were being saved" (vv. 46b–47). And we? So one continues to question and so one must question. Then this history of the first congregation becomes a mirror held before the Church in all times. It will also be a call to repentance.

But they are a real call to repentance only when one understands them correctly. One can misunderstand them just like the story of the rich young man and the speech with which Jesus sent out his disciples have been misunderstood. One understands them falsely when one only sees Law in them. How often does that happen! So should the Church be, as they were. Then they proceed to re-create such a church. How often in the history of the Church have people tried to copy them. The Anabaptist churches of the time of the Reformation, the Philadelphia Society and the other congregational views of Pietism, the Irvingians in England,[149] the great church of the Disciples of Christ in America and countless other sects and communities existed, when in fact there is no type of noble Christian communism in the New Testament. It is written

---

[148] The German has "in one accord."

[149] Edward Irving is considered the founder of the Catholic Apostolic Church, a nineteenth-century English sect. It was basically a form of Restorationism with all the odd quirks that go along with that. They insisted on the "real spiritual presence of Christ in the Sacrament of the Altar."

expressly in the story of Ananias and Sapphira that everyone who wanted could keep their property. There was no law [Acts 5]. It is written only that no one said of his goods that they were theirs, and that many gave up all they had for others, for the poor [Acts 4:32–37.]. It is written there that they (and it was not all) sold their goods and possessions and put the money in a common purse. This was what all had done who had come from Galilee to Jerusalem, those who waited for the return of Christ. Of the mother of John, we hear from Mark, the writer of the oldest Gospel, expressly in the twelfth chapter [of Acts], that she owned a house in Jerusalem. But of communism, mark you, the communism of love, he doesn't say, "What is yours, that is mine," but "What is mine, that is yours." Now this is a very ideal thing. And this ideal would be read into Acts. And now one organizes cheerfully fresh Christian communities in which private ownership is done away with. And what comes of this points to the most unhappy experiences of Church history: congregations that all begin as congregations of Jesus and end as the synagogues of Satan.

Or one reads, "And they devoted themselves to the apostles' teaching . . . and many wonders and signs were being done through the apostles" [Acts 2:42–43]. How can one copy the early congregations when they don't have their most important office [*Amt*], the office of apostle? So let us appoint new apostles! From this insane thinking over the past century has come the British man [Edward] Irving [1792–1834], and so originated the old and new apostolic fellowship [*Gemeinschaft*]. In the Early Church the Christians were not called Lutheran or Reformed, Presbyterian or Congregationalists, Methodists or Baptists, Catholic or Orthodox, but "disciples." So we also founded a church of "Disciples of Christ." So said a pious American pastor a hundred years ago. Disciples of Christ would all be Christian, so one can remove themselves so easily from the splitting of Christendom. But naturally this movement does not merely result in the renewal of the one Church, but only a new, if also a very great and very respectable church. If I were to try, beloved congregation, even to just broadly describe all the communities that have originated from this attempt to understand and follow this text as a law of renewal for the Church, we would still be sitting here in the church twelve hours from now.

No, one cannot understand our text as a law for the formation of the Church's life. If one does, then it ends where all such men of the Law end, either in deeper despair, because the salvation of one of these congregations has of course not yet been attained. And many, many Christians have ended in this way. (I remember during my time as a pastor in Berlin,[150] there was a missionary of the

---

[150] "After being discharged [from the German military], Sasse returned to the University of Berlin to pursue graduate work in NT under Adolf Deissmann, receiving his doctorate in 1923. During that time he was ordained in the Church of the Old Prussian Union in 1920 and served as assistant pastor to parishes in Berlin. His first full pastorate was at Oranienburg bei Berlin, 1921–1928. There he met his wife, Charlotte; they were married in 1924. From 1928 to 1933 he was the social pastor connected to the noted St. Marienkirche in Berlin." Feuerhahn in *The Lonely Way I*, p. 15. MH

people who had the gift to evangelize for the Lord Jesus Christ in a mass gathering of Berlin workers. He had once as a red sailor enlisted members of the Soldier's Council in the wake of the revolution. Then he returned to the Christian faith, and became a missionary to the people. He would reform the church by simply transplanting the reality of what is said of the first congregation. This man then went to Russia, and became an agitator for the Bolsheviks. He doubted it was possible to renew the Early Church today, and thereby reform the Church.) The other consequence of this legalism is the titanic height of arrogance of those who think it is a small thing to renew the ideal Church of the ancient times. In this arrogance lives a secret and unspoken faith in mankind. It is then a small thing to be and to achieve what the first Christians achieved! These early Christians were, of course, only men, and what noble men! Men of perfect faith, men of perfect brotherly love! What hinders us from being who they were?

What hinders us is the same thing that the first Christians had hindering them. We must then be very clear on this, beloved congregation, because we are honest and will not add to false illusions. As in every age, so it is also today that the Church is to be a small gathering [*Häuflein*] of sinners. He who wants to understand the Early Church and its meaning for the Church of all times, must know this, that the men of the Early Church were not any different than we poor sinners. They had no other power than we have. They were not better than the Christians of all times. If they were holy, then they were holy for the very same reason by which the poor sinners of all times are holy, namely, because Christ died for their sins because he "became to us wisdom from God, righteousness and sanctification and redemption" (1 Cor. 1:30). Our wisdom is Christ. Our righteousness is Christ. Our sanctification is Christ. Our redemption is Christ. So it was in the earliest of congregations. They were a congregation of nothing but poor sinners, as the New Testament depicts it, the congregation in which the evil fall of Ananias and Sapphira was possible [Acts 5]. The congregation in which despite the community of love, despite the shining care for the poor, what is written in the sixth chapter of Acts could still happen: "A complaint by the Hellenists arose against the Hebrews because their widows were being neglected in the daily distribution" (Acts 6:1). The first strife that broke out in the Early Church was strife about the Church of Jerusalem's cashbox. One could say the distribution of the gifts in the congregation was unjust.

Then there follows in the Church the strife between Paul and Barnabas [Acts 15:36–40], then comes the strife between Paul and the early congregation [2 Cor. 7:8], then comes the strife between Paul and Peter [Gal. 2], then comes the strife between Paul and Peter on the one side and James on the other side [Acts 15]. And so it goes down through the Early Church. No, the Early Church is something completely different than the Church of the holy in the sense that they were perfect and exemplary Christians for the Church to follow in the coming centuries. The Church of the first century was a communion of saints

157

in exactly the same manner as the Church of all centuries is a communion of saints. They are a congregation of justified sinners. Because even these Christians lived on nothing but the daily forgiveness of sins as we confess in our catechism: "In which Christendom He daily and richly forgives me and all the faithful all their sins!"[151] The holiness of the Church is the holiness of Christ. And the history of the first Church, of the communion of saints in Jerusalem, is only understood rightly if it is not understood as the glory of men, but as it is sung, "Holy, Holy, Holy is the Lord," the eternal song of the Church: "*Tu solus sanctus, tu solus dominus, Tu solus altimus.*" "You alone are holy, you alone are the Lord, You alone are the most high. Only you are holy!"[152]

So it is that the Church is never an organization of pious people, but it is the Church of the Lord Christ. It is not a human religion. No, the highest and most beautiful blossom of human religions, the faith of a Peter or a Paul bases its glory in something else. Our text says what that is in the verse, "And they devoted themselves to the apostles' teaching and the fellowship, to the breaking of bread and the prayers" [Acts 2:42]. The apostles' teaching, the fellowship, the breaking of bread, and prayer, in these four things is hidden the mystery of the Church.

"And they devoted themselves to the apostles' teaching." They would not tire of listening to the Word that came out of the mouths of the apostles, the witness of Jesus

---

[151] SC Creed III. MH
[152] The end of the Gloria in the Latin liturgy of the Divine Service. MH

Christ, about his becoming man, of his deeds and words, and "that Christ died for our sins in accordance with the Scriptures, that he was buried, that he was raised on the third day in accordance with the Scriptures" (1 Cor. 15:3–4). From these words that Paul handed down to us, the oldest form of the apostolic proclamation, we received the beginnings of the later confession, "died, buried, and on the third day rose again from the dead." That was the teaching of the apostles. That was what they repeated day after day. "And we are witnesses of all that he did both in the country of the Jews and in Jerusalem. They put him to death by hanging him on a tree, but God raised him on the third day and made him to appear, not to all the people but to us who had been chosen by God as witnesses, who ate and drank with him after he rose from the dead. And he commanded us to preach to the people and to testify that he is the one appointed by God to be judge of the living and the dead" (Acts 10:39–42).

It was always the same message, told and retold with elevated monotony from the apostles as eyewitnesses, and then after their death from those to whom the continuation of the apostolic proclamation was entrusted because the Church of all times has lived on the teaching of the apostles. Is it really so? Must not the Church fit her message to be relevant to the present? How often has she heard the hard reproach made by German citizens of eighteenth and nineteenth centuries in the naïve belief in progress, that she does not speak contemporarily, but just keeps repeating the same message as Peter in Acts? How many theologians, yes whole churches, have finally come to an end? They are not devoted to the apostles' teaching. They have preached something else. For forty years they have preached Goethe and Schiller. They have preached the corresponding worldview, a worldview most could stumble upon with luck when they were thirty years old. And the church did not become more full, but ever emptier. And rightfully so. Because what the newest and only right worldview is, the least of the German city dwellers since 1848[153] could read in the newspaper each morning with their coffee. For this I do not need to go to church. But where the Church lives on the apostles' teaching, there also lives the congregation.

It is a riddle to the world that the Church lives, even though she always preaches the same thing. In reality, she lives precisely because she always preaches the same thing, namely the teaching of the apostles. Yes, because this teaching is the eternal Word of God for all men, for all people, for all times. It is the Gospel of Jesus Christ, the eternal Son of God, "who for us men and for our salvation came down from heaven and became man, who died for our sins, who rose from the dead for our justification, who sits at the right hand of the Father, whose kingdom will have no end." It is the witness of the enfleshed Word of God. In this witness, in the simple preaching of the Church, Christ, the eternal Word himself, is present. Therefore, the Church lives because of this.

"They devoted themselves to the apostles' teaching and

---

[153] In 1848 there were numerous political revolutions in Germany. MH

the fellowship" [Acts 2:42]. Even in this word "fellowship" there is hidden something of the deepest mystery of God, of the Church, because this word points to something other than what we men normally mean by fellowship. Of course, we know two kinds of fellowship. The one is the natural fellowship into which we were born that remains before us, independent of our will: the fellowship of our family, the fellowship of our people. The other is the fellowship that originates through the determination of our will, that which we enter into of our own free will. When I, of my own free will, join a gymnastics club, a party, or a society to which my sympathies align, then one such fellowship originates. But the fellowship by which the members of the Church are bound never originates this way. Because one is neither born into the Church, nor can one join her. These are two completely evil misunderstandings. "So those who received his word," who were also given Peter's Pentecost sermon, "were baptized, and there were added that day about three thousand souls" (Acts 2:41). They let themselves be baptized. Literally, they *were* baptized. They were added, added to those who through the Gospel call had the light of faith lit in their hearts.

And in the same way we too have become members of the Church, and in no other way. You too were added by the Holy Ghost in the hour of Baptism because Baptism is not merely a symbolic action, a rite of admission created by the human imagination, but the Sacrament of Jesus Christ. And even now at this time God does something to us in this Sacrament that He will do at the end of all things. This

Sacrament is the present becoming future, time becoming eternity. What we receive in Absolution according to the teaching of the Church is the judgment of the disciples. What we receive in Holy Communion, the fellowship of the body and blood of Jesus Christ, will at the end of all things be made perfect. With your Baptism the resurrection has begun. "We were buried therefore with him by baptism into death, in order that, just as Christ was raised from the dead by the glory of the Father, we too might walk in newness of life" (Rom. 6:4). With Christ, therefore, you are already dead, with him buried, and with him you will be raised, with him because, yes, you are a member of his Body. That is the deep mystery of the fellowship of the holy: so we many are one Body. "For just as the body is one and has many members, and all the members of the body, though many, are one body, so it is with Christ. For in one Spirit we were all baptized into one body—Jews or Greeks, slaves or free—and all were made to drink of one Spirit" (1 Cor. 12:12–13). And so another verse here says the same thing: "Because there is one bread, we who are many are one body, for we all partake of the one bread" (1 Cor. 10:17). This is certainly a fellowship the world does not know and will never comprehend. This is the everlasting fellowship of the holy.

Perhaps many of us think, "That is a theological theory. That is a theology that goes too far." We think that because we are children of the modern world, who no longer know of the great and deep reality of the living Christ. The Church, of which our text speaks, knew that. She lived because of it. And our fathers in the Church of the Reformation also lived on that. And all the genuine and deep brotherly love in the Church of all times has grown out of this love. Let me take just one example of this. It is the *deaconate of the Church.* She was the great glory of the Church even among the Gentiles; "See, how they love one another!"[154] There she gave welfare for the sick and poor, for the lonely and helpless who could not come to the church, with the consecrated bread of the Lord's Supper and the loving gifts of the congregation and therewith the comfort, the help, and the fellowship that Christian brotherhood brings. And in the nineteenth century, when the Christian deaconate awakened anew, there the deacons went out from the altar. The deaconess houses, like Neuendettelsau,[155] were the places of the renewed liturgy, the renewed Communion celebration, and one needs to only have experienced a Divine Service in Bethel once to know why Father [Friedrich von] Bodelschwingh [1877–1946] preserved the old Lutheran liturgy with such great devotion.[156]

---

[154] Tertullian noting how outsiders viewed Christians (Apology 39.7), MH

[155] See Geiger, E. *The life, work, and influence of Wilhelm Loehe: 1808–1872,* trans. W. D. Knappe (St. Louis: CPH, 2010). MH

[156] Sasse was in fact in Bethel (an institution for the disabled like Bethesda Lutheran Communities) in late July and August 1933 at the request of the younger von Bodelschwingh. There with Dietrich Bonhoeffer he composed "The Bethel Confession," a precursor to The Barmen Declaration. *Guy Christopher Carter, Confession at Bethel, August 1933: The formation, revision and significance of the first full theological confession of the Evangelical Church struggle in Nazi Germany,* PhD Dissertation, Marquette University, Milwaukee, April

But the deaconate is only one example of the deep connection that remains between the Sacrament and the practical activity of the fellowship of the holy that defies all human reason, the fellowship by which the members of the Body of Christ are bound. Therefore the fellowship belongs to the celebration of the Sacrament of the Altar, which was called here by the old mysterious name, "the breaking of bread." "And day by day, attending the temple together and breaking bread in their homes, they received their food with glad and generous hearts" (Acts 2:46). At first they had no room. And they devoted themselves to the apostles' teaching and fellowship, to "the breaking of bread." And the Church today, even our Lutheran Church, has nothing more important than that which it first possessed, yes the disintegration of the fellowship in her midst and also the power to build fellowship simply hang together, because she hardly understands Holy Communion, because she has pushed it into the background. Yes, she has broken with this celebration, which was the heart of the Sunday Divine Service in Christendom up to the Reformation and for the first two centuries of the Evangelical Lutheran Church. Certainly, the whole congregation neither can nor should commune every Sunday. But in their midst, the Sacrament should be celebrated.[157]

1987 (Ann Arbor, MI & London: University Microfilms International, 1987). Feuerhahn no. 112. MH

[157] "No Christian of the Reformation, apart from the followers of the Reformation at Zurich and Geneva, could conceive of a Sunday Divine Service without the Lord's Supper, just as already in the Church of the New Testament there was no Lord's Day without the Supper." "The

But then, is this not yet another one of the laws that one has ever and again taken from our text? No, it is no law. It is merely law like the exhortation to remain in the teaching of the apostles and in the fellowship and to keep praying. Then also "the prayer." Technically translated our text speaks of "[the] prayers" in the plural. This prayer deeply connected to the celebration of Communion together and without these prayers and the rejoicing and jubilation of the congregation filled with gratitude, without the powerful praise of the great God who does miracles, without the worship of the present Lord Christ, there is no Church. She praises God with joy and simple hearts. All liturgies of the Church, all prayers of the Church are merely an echo of the praise of God, the heaven storming prayers of the first Pentecost of Christendom, where the Spirit of God moved the hearts so they can pray. Yes, because this word also applies to the Church: "Likewise the Spirit helps us in our weakness. For we do not know what to pray for as we ought, but the Spirit himself intercedes for us with groanings too deep for words" (Rom. 8:26). And so it is not for nothing that we invoke the Holy Ghost:

> Thou, Holy Spirit, teachest
> The soul to pray aright;
> Thy songs have sweetest music,
> Thy prayers have wondrous might.
> Unheard they cannot fall,
> They pierce the highest heaven
> Till He His help hath given

Lord's Supper in the Lutheran Church" (Letter 6, May 1949) in *Letters to Lutheran Pastors I*, p. 88.

Who surely helpeth all.[158]

It is a comprehensible picture, this picture of the first Church. But we ought not for an instant forget that this glimmering little ray of light shining on the first congregation of Jerusalem is not only the dawn of the Church, it is also the evening of an earthly people, of a dying people. A generation later, and the judgment that Christ had promised to go over all people would be executed. And the Jewish Christian congregation fled over the Jordan by foot on the basis of a prophetic saying. With that mission came the end of her being bound with the history of her people. But the Church of Christ did not end there. God's Holy Ghost called the people of the Gentile world. And now they experienced what it means: "And they devoted themselves to the apostles' teaching and the fellowship, to the breaking of bread and the prayers" [Acts 2:42]. Yes, the people passed away, but the Church remained. And even where people have no future, there the Church still has a future because the future of the Church is the future of Jesus Christ.[159] Amen.

---

[158] *Zeuch ein zu meinen Toren*, "Oh, Enter, Lord Thy Temple," Paul Gerhard (1607–1676), *TLH* 228:4. MH

[159] See also Sasse's *The Presence of Christ and the Future of the Church* (*Lutherische Kirche*, 20.10, 1938) in *The Lonely Way I*, pp. 461–69. Feuerhahn no. 205. MH

Equality of All Men?!

Second Sunday after Trinity

June 18, 1939[160]

Romans 10:1–13

Brothers, my heart's desire and prayer to God for them is that they may be saved. For I bear them witness that they have a zeal for God, but not according to knowledge. For, being ignorant of the righteousness of God, and seeking to establish their own, they did not submit to God's righteousness. For Christ is the end of the law for righteousness to everyone who believes.

For Moses writes about the righteousness that is based on the law, that the person who does the commandments shall live by them. But the righteousness based on faith says, "Do not say in your heart, 'Who will ascend into heaven?' " (that is, to bring Christ down) "or 'Who will descend into the abyss?'" (that is, to bring Christ up from the dead). But what does it say? "The word is near you, in your mouth and in your heart" (that is, the word of faith that we proclaim); because, if you confess with your mouth that Jesus is Lord and believe in your heart that God raised him from the dead, you will be saved. For with the heart one believes and is justified, and with the mouth one confesses and is saved. For the Scripture says, "Everyone who believes in him will not be put to shame." For there is no distinction between Jew and Greek; for the same Lord is Lord of all, bestowing his riches on all who call on him. For "everyone who calls on the name of the Lord will be saved." (Rom. 10:1–13)

---

[160] *Predigt 2 Sonntag nach Trinitatis (18 Jun 1939) "Gleichheit Aller Menschen?!"* Feuerhahn no. 222a" MH.

The French people celebrate the 150th anniversary of the Great Revolution of 1789 this month. Perhaps we Lutheran Christians of Germany, in whose lexicon the word "revolution" does not occur, do not fully understand how one can celebrate an event that as a human act was such a terrible outbreak of human sin, and as God's work such a terrible judgment upon humanity. But this revolution was one of the most powerful events in the history of the world. The revolutionaries intervened deep in the fate of all people in western lands, also in the inner and outer fate of Germany. Yes, even today their work continues all over the world. They had hurled a thought at the world as if it were a firebrand, a thought that has inspired the hearts of millions of people for 150 years, and they have thought of it as a gospel for the sake of the meaningless life of men and all the people who have sacrificed their happiness.

That is the thought of the equality of all men. All men are by nature equal. Then all of the unlucky distinctions with which men distinguished between themselves were made up. Let us abolish these distinctions! Everyone should be equal, equal in power, equal in wealth, equal in happiness. And whenever someone towers head and shoulders above his fellow men, then off with his head, because all are equal. This teaching of the French Revolution that comes to us is just as senseless as the teaching of the Bolsheviks. But it seems to teach then that men are not equal. There are strong and weak, wise and foolish, gifted and ungifted, brave and cowardly. There are the differences between peoples and races, their languages, their cultures, their religions, their worldviews. What [René] Descartes [1596–1650], the first philosopher of modernity, said in the introduction to his first epoch-making work is simply not true. He said, "Good sense is the most evenly shared thing in the world . . . common sense, or reason, is naturally equal in all men."[162] How strange to life, how far from reality is the teaching of race from the equality of all that bear the face of man.[163]

But why has this teaching gained so great a power over their spirits? Why do people believe in it as if it were the Gospel? Only because it wants to be a gospel, a message of redemption that blind faith longs for. Faith, no longer in the Redeemer, Jesus Christ, but in him who during the days of the French Revolution the Christians West visibly put in the place of Jesus Christ and has endeavored to play the role of world judge and world redeemer with festering self-satisfaction for no more than a 150 years. He who has been made the measure of all things and the lord over all, he has an insatiable desire for all to fall before him and pray, and will never forgive the Church of Jesus Christ because they refuse him this prayer.

Who is this hidden god to whom the Christian faith in Europe has fallen? He is none other than the men themselves, these prideful bold men who have pillaged the

---

[162] Descartes, Rene, *Discourses on Method*, translated by F. E Sutcliffe (London: Penguin Books, 1968), p. 27.
[163] See Sasse's "*Das Volk nach der Lehre der evangelischen Kirche.*" In *Ernst Schubert, Auslanddeutschtum und evangelische Kirche Jahrbuch 1933, München:Chr. Kaiser, 1933*, pp. 20–39; English translation "The Lutheran Confession and the Volk," in *The Lonely Way I*, pp. 121ff. Feuerhahn no. 106. MH

earth and have subdued nature. In the year the French Revolution broke out, [Friedrich] Schiller [1759–1805] greeted him with the moving words:

> How fair, O Man, do you, your palm branch holding
> Stand at the century's unfolding
> In proud and noble manhood's prime
> With faculties revealed, with spirits fullness
> Full earnest mild, in action-wealthy stillness,
> The ripest son of time . . .[164]

How harmless this verse sounds today about "the ripest son of time," who was about to invent the guillotine and chop off some hundred thousand heads so that they would all be equal. A man of our times needs ever starker expressions and poetic clouds of incense in order to keep faith in himself, and to mislead himself and others concerning what he really is, a poor, wretched sinful man, "grass that is renewed in the morning: in the morning it flourishes and is renewed; in the evening it fades and withers" (Ps. 90:5–6).

This is why this teaching of the equality of all men has been such a great success, because behind this hides faith in man. Yes, this faith can also make a gospel out of other teachings. That happens today for example, so as not to be silent about this, where one makes a doctrine of salvation

---

[164] "The Artists," by Friedrich Schiller, translation by Marianna Wertz, (www.schillerinstitute.org/transl/trans_shil_1poems.html).

out of the fact of the natural inequality of men.[165] We ourselves must be clear about this, that this faith in man is the essential opposition to faith in God since the day in Paradise when the voice of the tempter annunciated, "You will be like God" [Gen. 3:5]. But wherever in Christendom one falls to this faith in man, there one always finds a reversal, a spoiling of the great truth of Christian faith instead. So the teaching of the equality of all men is also a satanic distortion of a Christian truth. Because contrary to all differences between men, despite the unbridgeable cleft and difference, there is a point where it has to be said, "There is no distinction" [Rom. 3:22]. And only he who understands that can oppose the delusion of equality and all this faith in man, which now since the second half of the

---

[165] Reminiscent of Sasse's stunning and early rejection of the Ayrian Paragraph of the Nazi Party Platform in the "Year Book" for all of Protestant Germany, of which he was editor: "One can perhaps forgive National Socialism all its theological sins, but his article 24 excludes any possibility of a dialogue with the church, whether Protestant or Catholic. . . . According to the Protestant doctrine of original sin, 'the new-born infant of the noblest Germanic descent, endowed in body and mind with the optimal racial characteristics,' is as much subject to eternal damnation as the genetically gravely compromised half-caste, from two decadent races. And we must go on to confess that the doctrine of the justification of the sinner *sola gratia, sola fide*, is the end of Germanic morality just as it is the end of all human morality. . . . We are not much interested in whether the Party gives its support to Christianity, but we would like to know whether the church is to be permitted to preach the Gospel in the Third Reich without let or hindrance, whether, that is, we will be able to continue undisturbed in our insults to the Germanic or Germanistic moral sense, as with God's help we intend to do." *Kirchliches Jahrbuch* 1932. English text quoted from *The Third Reich and the Christian Churches*, ed. by Peter Matheson (Grand Rapids: Eerdmans Publishing Company, 1981), p. 2. MH

[nineteenth] century has exhausted the heritage of the Christian faith also in our people, and seeks to destroy the Church of Christ also in Germany.

To oppose this faith in man, that is what the Epistle lesson from Paul's Letter to the Romans will help us do. It allows us to look deep into the essence of man, leading us to the place where it becomes crystal clear: "Here there is no difference between men." Whatever the deep, natural, and historical differences between men and peoples may be, in one thing they are all similar: "There is only one Savior, Jesus Christ!" There is no difference between Jew and Greek. There is only one Lord who rules over all and calls to you. There is only one deliverance, the faith. "Whoever believes in him will not be put to shame" [Rom. 9:33]. There is only one way by which to point all men to deliverance: the preaching of the Gospel.

The deepest thing that the Holy Scriptures have to say concerning men is never said in an abstract explanation of men but in the living conversation between God and men, between men and men. Even here in our Epistle, a living man speaks to living men: "Paul, a servant of Christ Jesus . . . To all those in Rome who are loved by God and called to be saints" [Rom. 1:1, 6]. Nineteen hundred years have passed already since the apostle spoke to the Christians in Rome at the time of Caesar Nero [Emperor AD 54–68] concerning the deepest worries that filled their hearts. But we understand the worry even today. "Brothers, my heart's desire and prayer to God for them [Israel] is that they may be saved" (Rom. 10:1). Here a man, who had love for his

172

people, who prayed for his people, spoke in deep anguish. Each of the three chapters: nine, ten, and eleven of Romans begin with a word full of worry. "I am speaking the truth in Christ—I am not lying" (9:1). "I ask, then, has God rejected his people?" (11:1). It is the deepest of worries that a man can have for his people, not concerning material prosperity or their power, their living space, their inner and outer peace, though we certainly worry about all that also, yes, as we do in the Fourth Petition of the Our Father, when we have not yet forgotten our catechism. Paul knows of the greatest worry there can be for all men. "Brothers, my heart's desire and prayer to God for them [Israel] is that they may be saved."

"May be blessed," Luther translates it. But ever since Frederich the Great [1712–1786; Prussian King] delivered the fatal explanation, in his land everyone could be blessed in their own fashion, the old sense of the word "blessed" and "be blessed," the sense that it had with Luther was lost. Ever since the great king, eternal blessedness is no longer taken seriously. He taught his young acolytes to steal the last remnants of the word's old seriousness, so for an example also the word "eternity" is no longer the word of thunder, as the hymn uses it. What Luther translated here, "that they may be blessed," literally means "to deliver." And that is meant in all seriousness. For the deliverance of the disciples, judgment. The men of the New Testament, the men of the Early Church, the Middle Ages, and the time of the Reformation, the men of the German people through many centuries, and millions of Germans also in our day differentiate themselves namely by the enlightened spirit of the eighteenth, nineteenth, and twentieth centuries through which they know of one judgment that all men and all people oppose, of one judgment in which all will be revealed, even the most hidden guilt, of a judgment in which all that cannot be brought to purity in this world will be resolved, of a judgment that will be a wholly just judgment according to the Law that one cannot quickly abandon, and according to books of history that no man can falsify, of a judgment that no man can ignore. One cannot abolish it in the very least, and so they close their eyes because we all now know something of the reality of the judgment standing over men in history already. But if there is a divine judgment over man, then yes there is no greater worry for us men than the question of how we can stand in this judgment, how we can be saved. Then Luther's frightening question, "How do I obtain a gracious God?" is the last, deepest, and most important question of every man's life. Perhaps the blindness of the greater part of humanity in the Christian lands of the West to the reality of the judgment over them, perhaps the peace of the soul sustained by the belief that the judgment is an invention of the Church that it uses to scare men, is already in itself the beginning of the divine judgment over us.

To the means by which Judgment Day will be gotten rid of and the Lord Christ dismissed as judge of the world belongs the thought that the judgment of the world is an invention of men who are too weak to bear this life and this state of the world. It is a dream of men that yearn for a balance, who perhaps thereby long that others would be punished. But this explanation does not work. Yes, because then only others would be punished. But yes, that is the frightening aspect of the thought of the judgment, that it meets *me*. If it is a judgment of God, yes, then I am the accused. That is what men found so poignant about the Reformation and the great doctrine of justification, the great confessors of the evangelical faith that they themselves expressed over and over again: You yourself will have to repeat the confession before God's judgment. But when the heart of man has finally realized the full weight of this thought, then it knows there is no escape: "If you, O LORD, should mark iniquities, O LORD, who could stand?" [Ps. 130:3]. There the first great, "There is no difference," of Romans is realized, the one we read in the third chapter: "for all have sinned and fall short of the glory of God" (Rom. 3:23). There is no difference. As in death all men are equal, just as all distinctions of their social standing and education, of possessions, of power, of race and language dwindle there, so are all men equal before divine judgment, poor miserable and cursed men that decay in eternal decay. There is no difference here.

There isn't even the distinction that is made in this life between those who are respectable and unrespectable, between those we men call good and evil, virtuous and depraved. That, at least, was the difference Israel wanted to hold fast to, the difference between those who held to God's Law and those who despised it. Yes, said Paul, there is a righteousness that comes from the law. Moses also

175

writes, "If a person does them, he shall live by them" [Lev. 18:5]. But where is this man? There is no one who does good, not one. What was a shining, radiant virtue on earth, what here on earth was a shining life of good morals, that is vain darkness in the light of the Holy God: because there is no difference here, they are all together sinners and lack the glory they should have in the presence of God.

Or is there among us here in this church one single person who would venture to step before the judgment seat of God, like the spiritual fathers of the French Revolution pledged to do, to step before God's judgment with the words, "Jean Jacques Rousseau [1712–1778] was a good man"? Is there any man who knows what he is, and what he is not, and who knows who God is, who can say anything but, "Lord, have mercy on me"? No, it is not possible with our own righteousness, with the righteousness that comes from the Law, but there is a different righteousness. Paul calls the righteousness that is valid before God the righteousness of faith [Rom. 1:17]. And he made it a reproach to his people that they had not understood this righteousness. "For, being ignorant of the righteousness of God, and seeking to establish their own, they did not submit to God's righteousness" [Rom. 10:3]. This righteousness is different. "For Moses writes about the righteousness that is based on the law, that the person who does the commandments shall live by them. But the righteousness based on faith says, 'Do not say in your heart, "Who will ascend into heaven?" ' (that is, to bring Christ down) 'or "Who will descend into the abyss?" ' (that is, to bring Christ up from the dead)" (Rom. 10:6–7).

Do not say: "For me there is no salvation." "I have no Redeemer." Do not say: "I have no Redeemer in heaven. I cannot raise a Redeemer from the dead." Do not say: "I have no Redeemer." You have a Redeemer. He is very near. He is with you. He is coming to you. He has become your brother. He has born your sins. His righteousness is your righteousness. Your sin is his sin. That is all there is. It has all happened, all been fulfilled. You only need yet to say to him: "Yes, Lord, have mercy on me!"

"(That is, the word of faith that we proclaim;) because, if you confess with your mouth that Jesus is Lord and believe in your heart that God raised him from the dead, you will be saved. For with the heart one believes and is justified, and with the mouth one confesses and is saved" [Rom. 10:8–10]. That is the Gospel—a Gospel for all men, without difference.

That is the Word of faith that we preach, the most blessed message of this world. That is the Word of faith that we should confess with the mouth. That is the Word of faith that you should preach, you who prepare for the holy preaching office [*Predigtamt*], this and nothing else. No philosophy. No spiritual thought. No religious chitchat. Tell the poor sinners nothing but this Gospel.

The worry that Paul spoke of permeates our souls, the concern for our people. The Jewish people were once entrusted with the Law. Our people in a very special manner have been entrusted with the Gospel. Should it now come to this, that this Word is no longer tolerated in

177

Germany? Every day it is made clear. It is made brutally clear for our theology students today how superfluous it is. We do not know how the great fight that began in the West with the French Revolution shall continue. We decline to be students of Rousseau [1712–1778], Voltaire [1694–1778], and Denton. We confess the Gospel as students of Luther. We decline to erect an altar to the god of reason. We pray to the triune God. We maintain firm faith in the power of the prayer that surrounds our people like an iron wall[166] and the power of the Word. And we ask the Lord of the harvest that he would send workers into his harvest [Matt. 9:38]. We know that he will hear our prayer:

> The glorious work you complete
> As Judge and Savior of the blind
> Wretched man you seek to find
> Despite dark paths at your feet
> So believers unceasing you entreat
> Their souls to you in love to bind.
> Amen.[167]

---

[166] "The prayers of a few godly men intervened like an iron wall on our side." LC, Lord's Prayer, 31. MH

[167] This is my translation of the eighth verse to Carl Heinrich von Bogatzky's hymn "Wach auf du Geist der ersten Zeugen," commonly known in English as "Awake, Thou Spirit of the Watchmen."

The High Point of the Beatitudes
Fourth Sunday after Trinity
June 28, 1942[168]
Matthew 5:7–12

Blessed are the merciful, for they shall receive mercy.
Blessed are the pure in heart, for they shall see God.
Blessed are the peacemakers, for they shall be called sons of God.
Blessed are those who are persecuted for righteousness' sake, for theirs is the kingdom of heaven.
Blessed are you when others revile you and persecute you and utter all kinds of evil against you falsely on my account. Rejoice and be glad, for your reward is great in heaven, for so they persecuted the prophets who were before you. (Matt. 5:7–12)

The Beatitudes start off the Sermon on the Mount. They are the Gospel readings, according to the new order, for the Third and Fourth Sundays of Trinity in the Bavarian State Church. Originally they were the Gospels for the feast of All Saints on the First of November. The Reformation, which began on the eve of All Saints, the 31st of October 1517, removed this feast along with saint worship, but it did not do away with the Gospel for All Saints' Day. On the contrary, it was first to put this Gospel reading in the right light. In many Evangelical churches, it has become the Gospel for the Reformation Day festival, where it has been called the Magna Carta of the Church, her constitution

---

[168] *Predigt: 4. Sonntag nach Trinitatis (28 Jun. 1942) "Der Höhepunkt der Seligpreisungen."* Feuerhahn no. 241a. MH

that would speak to us who belong to Christ's kingdom, to the entourage of the King that is a King like no other.

To this belongs the Beatitudes. In spirit we see a great pilgrim procession, we see them in succession as Jesus their Savior sees them: the poor in spirit, those who mourn, the meek, those who hunger and thirst for righteousness, the merciful, the pure in heart, the peacemakers, those who will be persecuted on account of Jesus. Here we see them being pulled through the angst and pain of this world, and we see them arrive where the promise of blessedness is completely fulfilled. We see with John the great seer how all the Gentiles and peoples and languages that no one can count stand before the throne of God and join in the praise of the heavenly King and his Christ. We hear how the promise is fulfilled in him: "After this I looked, and behold, a great multitude that no one could number, from every nation, from all tribes and peoples and languages, standing before the throne and before the Lamb, clothed in white robes with palm branches in their hands. . . . 'These are the ones coming out of the great tribulation. They have washed their robes and made them white in the blood of the Lamb. Therefore they are before the throne of God, and serve him day and night in his temple; and he who sits on the throne will shelter them with his presence. They shall hunger no more, neither thirst anymore; the sun shall not strike them, nor any scorching heat. For the Lamb in the midst of the throne will be their shepherd, and he will guide them to springs of living water, and God will wipe away every tear from their eyes'" (Rev. 7:9, 14–17). Yes, the Beatitudes are fulfilled in Him. They are the comforted. They possess the promised land. They will no longer hunger or thirst. They have attained mercy. They stand face-to-face with God. They are wholly God's children. The heavenly kingdom is theirs. The "blessed" that was once a promise, and must have been seen as a deception, is now fulfilled: "Behold, we consider those blessed who remained steadfast" (James 5:11). The wandering people of God are coming to the house, his holiness that was hidden under the dirt and dust of the desert, under the sin of the world, is revealed. The Church of Christ, the communion of the saints is fulfilled.

That is what we see in the Spirit when we hear the words of the Beatitudes. They are now ready to be contemplated individually. Let us single one out today, in order to understand it more deeply, and then let it shine light on the others. It is the last, and apparently also the highpoint of the whole procession: "Blessed are those who are persecuted for righteousness' sake, for theirs is the kingdom of heaven" [Matt. 5:10]. This is the last of the precious pearls that are so artistically lined up here. This is clear because the last follows up on the first ending with the same promise, "for theirs is the kingdom of heaven." But the importance of this beatitude is shown in that which immediately follows, "Blessed are you when others revile you and persecute you and utter all kinds of evil against you falsely on my account. Rejoice and be glad, for your reward is great in heaven, for so they persecuted the prophets who were before you" [vv. 11–12]. The evangelist wants to attribute this beatitude first with his duplication. The others are to be brought into alignment with this form, and then once again he returns to the old form, which we still find in Luke (6:20–22). This emphasis is in line with the sense Jesus wanted to give it. Here he looks all of them in the eye, all those who will truly follow him to the cross, and personally tells them: "Blessed are you!"

But this "they" applies to all his disciples in all times. It also applies to us. We ourselves are addressed by him. This serious word speaks to us. We already have all experienced something of what this means, "when others revile you and persecute you and utter all kinds of evil against you" [v. 11]. It is, of course, not as easy for you to publicly confess Jesus Christ and his church today as it was in the days of our fathers. What does it really mean, when a young man who has decided to study theology hears this from people, and not just from those who have nothing to do with him, but also from well-meaning relatives and even from his parents and in-laws? And many faithful churchgoers have had the sudden experience of realizing that some nameless person in a mysterious place has gone through their church visitation book, and then in another ever so nameless, ever so mysterious manner has found the number of their visits to be too high.

Times in which things like this have happened, the history of the Church has already seen, and often. They are times in which churchgoing is no longer a habit, but a confession, and the Christian faith a faith of manly character. This is why such times do not hurt the Church.

One must find then, that the appearance of the Church in Germany amongst the people, though not in the papers (but, yes, they are not the people) is much greater than twenty-five years before. It is not pretty, however, when the abusive talk against the Church goes on, and when all sorts of evil is spoken against men who can no longer mention their Christian faith. It can be ever so bitter when it hurts men who have proved themselves in the hardest fighting of this war, men who are prepared to sacrifice for their people and fatherland, or when it hits those who can no longer defend themselves because they are dying the death of courageous soldiers.

But when such persecution, such evil news hits us, do we accept what our text says about that? "Blessed are you when others revile you and persecute you, and utter all kinds of evil against you falsely on my account" (Matt. 5:11). He asks us to make every defamation into cause for serious self-examination, to ask ourselves in all seriousness before we make ourselves out to be martyrs, to ask carefully, "What truth is there in this defamation?"

The old Father [Friedrich von] Bodelschwingh [1831–1910] had the experience once that a particularly hateful and slanderous article against his deaconate appeared. He called them together and had the article read to them and admitted that the attacker was right. Then he saw in the process that arose from it his case would be gloriously justified. The Church is made of poor sinners, so it is quite easy to find fault or scandal within it, and then to make facial expressions of moral indignation and slander the

183

appearance of credibility. The Early Church already knew this. "Utter all kinds of evil against you falsely." According to the textual evidence, the Greek word that Luther translated here as "falsely" is probably an ancient addition in the oldest handwritten Gospels, a warning to the Early Church against the misuse of this beatitude.

But what then, when it proves to be that they lie? When it really is abuse, which we suffer for his sake, what does Jesus say to this? "Blessed are you." "Rejoice and be glad, for your reward is great in heaven, for so they persecuted the prophets who were before you" [Matt. 5:12]. Blessed are you, for you have been given a place amongst the great gathering of those allowed to bear the beloved holy cross, from the prophets of the Old Testament to the apostles, of whom the New Testament speaks, saying that after their first criminal trial, "They left the presence of the council, rejoicing that they were counted worthy to suffer dishonor for the name" (Acts 5:41). Given a place amongst the great gathering of those who throughout time have been allowed to confess the name of the Lord Christ before the world. Yes, to confess this name and to suffer disgrace for this name, that is blessedness.

The Early Church was right when it believed that a man could have no greater experience of being blessed than to be included in the words of Jesus: "So everyone who acknowledges me before men, I also will acknowledge before my Father who is in heaven" (Matt. 10:32). "Blessed are you," said Jesus. Yes, it must be so. "It is enough for the disciple to be like his teacher, and the servant like his master. If they have called the master of the house Beelzebul, how much more will they malign those of his household" (Matt. 10:25). It must be so. And why can it not be otherwise? This is natural man's opposition to the Lord Christ, an opposition toward God, in which all of Adam's children live, even us. But the Holy Ghost has won you over. The natural man doesn't want a Savior. He thinks he doesn't need him. He doesn't know that he is a sinner, and refuses to acknowledge it when someone tells him. For this reason we have to be clear. There is no greater expression of courage than to admit, "I need a Savior." It is a bankruptcy. It is the admission: "I cannot bring my own life into order. I am nothing. I can do nothing. I know nothing. If I don't have you, then my life is wasted and lost for all eternity." It is literally true: "Without Him all that pleases Is valueless on earth; the gifts I have from Jesus Alone have priceless worth."[169] I have no wisdom of my own, no righteousness of my own, no holiness of my own, and never will have. I myself will never be anything. But I have a Savior. I have the Lord Jesus Christ, of whom the apostles said, "Because of him you are in Christ Jesus, who became to us wisdom from God, righteousness and sanctification and redemption" [1 Cor. 1:30]. Therefore, as it is written, "Let the one who boasts, boast in the Lord" (1 Cor. 1:31).

There is opposition against Jesus Christ precisely because this is so harsh. In any case, one will have him be a teacher, or a model. One wants to adore him and show him

---

[169] Gerhard, "If God Himself Be for Me." *LSB* 724. MH

honor along with Goethe, and even bow before him as the divine revelation of the highest principle of morality. One wants to admire him like the young Schleiermacher as the great author of what is gloriously new in religion. But the natural man in us will not let him be our Savior. There we children of Adam speak with all men made in his image: "We do not want this man to reign over us" (Luke 19:14). And because we don't want him to reign over us, neither do we want him to reign over others. So opposition to him becomes opposition to the Church. But now this opposition expresses itself only a little in the abuse of evil slander. But there is another word in our text also, a much more serious word: "Blessed are those who are persecuted for righteousness' sake" [Matt. 5:10]. "Blessed are you when others revile you and persecute you" [v. 11]. The opposition to the Lord Christ escalates to the persecution of his Church.

Persecution! A sea of blood and tears, a vast sum of meaningless human suffering spreads itself before our spiritual eyes when we say this word. From the terrible terror scenes in Nero's gardens thought up by the sick mind of an insane Caesar to the indescribable horror of the greatest persecution of Christians in history that began twenty-five years ago in Bolshevik Russia.[170] What human suffering! Never have men so suffered as in the great persecution of the Church. But there, where men were not only persecuted because they were Christians, but where this motive banished others, there also remains one of

---

[170] 1917.

reason's most frightening riddles: where does this cruelty come from?

It was not mere national hatred behind this cruelty when during the World War an estimated six million Christian Armenians were murdered in Turkey alone.[171] This is reminiscent of Diocletian [AD 244–305; Emperor 284–305.] and Galerius [AD 260–311; Emperor 305–311]. This happened before the eyes of Western Christendom, and under the shared responsibility of the Kaiser's Germany. That is but only one example among many that we could also list. That is the frightening riddle of the persecution of the Church among the Bolsheviks, the consequences of which we see today in the East.

Oh, how harmless were the persecutions of Christians in antiquity compared to those that take place in our day. Apart from the great persecutions under Decius [201–251; Emperor 249–251] and Valerian [ca 193–260; Emperor

---

[171] "The Armenian Genocide, also known as the Armenian Holocaust, the Armenian Massacres and, traditionally among Armenians, as the Great Crime was the Ottoman government's systematic extermination of its minority Armenian subjects from their historic homeland in the territory constituting the present-day Republic of Turkey. It took place during and after World War I and was implemented in two phases: the wholesale killing of the able-bodied male population through massacre and forced labor, and the deportation of women, children, the elderly and infirm on death marches to the Syrian Desert. The total number of people killed as a result has been estimated at between 1 and 1.5 million. Other indigenous and Christian ethnic groups such as the Assyrians, the Greeks and other minority groups were similarly targeted for extermination by the Ottoman government. . . . It is acknowledged to have been one of the first modern genocides. . . . The word *genocide* was coined in order to describe these events." "Armenian Genocide," Wikipedia. MH

253–259] in the years 250 and 258, and under Diocletian [244–311; Emperor 284–305] and his co-Caesars in the years from 303 to 313, there had never been a persecution that had simultaneously been carried on throughout the entire Roman Empire. Leaving aside the occasional outbreaks of wild and fanatical hatred, not in all of antiquity was there this systematic destruction, not only of the Church's organization, but also of the souls of men while hiding under the hypocritical mask of religious freedom. Officially there is no persecution of the Church in Russia, and if one speaks of it he is liable to be punished. How amateur were the Roman persecutions in comparison to those of [Vladimir] Lenin [1870–1924] and [Joseph] Stalin [1878–1953].

At that time, the Church was allowed to possess houses and catacombs even though she didn't legally exist. In the twentieth century, she doesn't even have catacombs. At that time there was at least a remnant of personal freedom, there was the possibility of instruction. The Church lived by the catechumenate for three hundred years. The Bolsheviks, however, allow no room for the soul of a man, not a small bit of freedom. What mystery stands behind this? Our soldiers, our military chaplains related with deep horror the shape of the younger generation, which has become great under Bolshevism, men who no longer know their Creator. The disgraced and murdered soul of these people is a powerful accusing witness to the consequences of this terribly frightening power, which is stronger and wiser than the wisest spirit of man, and therefore can never be removed from the spirit of man alone. Oh, how the enlightened men of the modern world have mocked and laughed at that which the Bible tells them about Satan. In the East, this laughter has become costly.

In these days, there has fallen into my hands a German article published in Dorpat in 1939, one of the last to make an appearance. It was dedicated to "The Memory of the Baltic Martyrs."[172] In it, a man who had also seen something of the great tribulation wrote about the essence of the persecution: "It is the deadly hate with which Satan hates Christ. It is the thirst for vengeance for which Satan cannot leave Jesus be. We have dealt with Satan in our distress. It is the angst before the Judge Christ, the rage of the mortally wounded beast who has received the *coup de grace* from Jesus and turned against the Church and Christians. Jesus has bound the boundless power of Satan. The Lord Jesus took the dominion of the world from Satan. This Lord Jesus is our brother. Satan can never change that. Satan cannot harm this Lord Jesus. So he rages against the Church and us." Truly it is so. If you will not believe me, believe this voice from the East. Believe "the ones coming out of the great tribulation" [Rev. 7:14]. They tell us nothing but what the Bible attests to from the first to last page.

Because it is so, beloved congregation, this fight against everything, that is everywhere in the West, threatening the once Christian West, this fight is much, much more serious than most think, even most of those in our congregation.

---

[172] Even Google was unable to turn up this text. MH

Because the power, which is standing there, is no human power, men alone cannot defeat it. Tomorrow she can appear in another place on the globe, somewhere where she will not clash against the iron wall of which Luther speaks in the Large Catechism[173] as being the only weapon to use against the devil. It is the wall that at that time saved Germany from going under, namely the power of prayer. It will have to be believed in Germany's future as never before. Germany will need Christians to pray as they have never prayed, we must learn to, we will learn to, and when we learn once again to pray the Fourth Petition of the Lord's Prayer, then we will really learn to pray.

That is also the mystery that stands behind the inhuman cruelty of the great persecution. But there a question is raised. There whole peoples and churches fall to the ground. There people are disgraced and murdered in body and soul. "And God is silent,"[174] as the title of a famous Russian book said. And God is silent. He does not intervene. He does not rescue the innocent. He hears the death cries of the pained children and does not appear. He still allows his sun to shine over mass murderers. He is silent. Is he really silent? Can it be then that the applicable language is the language of his judgment? Does he not speak loud, loud and clear in that which has happened in the East since June 22, 1941?[175] Yes, he speaks warning, warning in gruesome clarity to the peoples. Do you not

---

[173] "The prayers of a few godly men intervened like an iron wall on our side." LC, Lord's Prayer, 31. BKS 669.33. MH

[174] By Edwin Erich Dwinger (1898–1981). MH

[175] The date Nazi Germany invaded the Soviet Union. MH

hear the early cry of your judgment? Do you doubt that every single one of those who are responsible for this suffering in the East will be judged? "And the smoke of their torment goes up forever and ever" (Rev. 14:11). That which happened there is the prelude to hell.

No, God is not silent. He doesn't just speak to people. He speaks to his Church. There are, buried in the ground in the endless plains of Russia next to the miserable villages, because these treasures may not remain in the houses (they can cost life), the old, well-thumbed tattered church books of the Church of Russia. There, buried in the ground, hidden by the old German settlements, are the last Luther Bibles. And in the night they are secretly held. And the last Christians are gathered together, secured by watch posts. What do they read there? What have they read for all these years? "Blessed are those who hunger and thirst for righteousness, for they shall be satisfied. Blessed are the merciful, for they shall receive mercy. Blessed are the pure in heart, for they shall see God. Blessed are the peacemakers, for they shall be called sons of God. Blessed are those who are persecuted for righteousness' sake, for theirs is the kingdom of heaven. Blessed are you when others revile you and persecute you and utter all kinds of evil against you falsely on my account. Rejoice and be glad, for your reward is great in heaven, for so they persecuted the prophets who were before you" (Matt. 5:6–12).

No God is not silent, he had also spoken to his Church

in Russia in the death cellars of the Tscheka[176] in the GPU,[177] in the prison camps by Murmansk, in the forests of Siberia, in the Kyrgystan steps, "Blessed are you. Rejoice and be glad." God said this to you through his beloved Son. And the Holy Ghost has given witness to their spirit because they are God's children, and they have known: "and if children, then heirs—heirs of God and fellow heirs with Christ, provided we suffer with him in order that we may also be glorified with him. For I consider that the sufferings of this present time are not worth comparing with the glory that is to be revealed to us" (Rom. 8:17–18). And when they are too tired in body and soul to pray, then the Holy Spirit intercedes for them all the more with groanings too deep for words (Rom. 8:26). And when they die, then he has opened the door to the Church Triumphant for them, the heavenly kingdom is theirs. And when your mutilated bodies are buried somewhere, then the seed of the future Church is sown. Because every church is built on the graves of martyrs and "the blood of the martyrs is the seed of the Church,"[178] even in our day.

No, God is not silent. He speaks in Law and Gospel, in judgment and grace even today. And as his judgment will not be delayed by any human power, so also are his promises firm and irrevocable. They are all in Christ, "Yes"

---

[176] First in a series of police organizations of communist Russia, founded in 1917.

[177] The "State Political Directorate" of pre-WWII Soviet Russia. MH

[178] A phrase first found in Tertullian's *Apologeticus*, ch. 50. "The oftener we are mown down by you, the more in number we grow; the blood of the Christians is seed." *Ante-Nicene Fathers* III.55. MH

and "Amen." The world says "no" to this, but God says "Yes!" We still cannot understand that. But in eternity the deep riddle will be untied, why God allowed evil, why he allowed the evil in humanity to run free. There in his light we will also understand the way of the holy cross, by which he allowed his Christendom on earth to follow Christ, its Head. Once this way has reached its goal, the Church of God will be complete, the communion of saints. Amen.

Army of God

21st Sunday after Trinity

[Published in] Sermon Book of the Lutheran Church 1936[179]

Ephesians 6:10–17

Finally, be strong in the Lord and in the strength of his might. Put on the whole armor of God, that you may be able to stand against the schemes of the devil. For we do not wrestle against flesh and blood, but against the rulers, against the authorities, against the cosmic powers over this present darkness, against the spiritual forces of evil in the heavenly places. Therefore take up the whole armor of God, that you may be able to withstand in the evil day, and having done all, to stand firm. Stand therefore, having fastened on the belt of truth, and having put on the breastplate of righteousness, and, as shoes for your feet, having put on the readiness given by the gospel of peace. In all circumstances take up the shield of faith, with which you can extinguish all the flaming darts of the evil one; and take the helmet of salvation, and the sword of the Spirit, which is the word of God. (Eph. 6:10–17)

Luther once called our Epistle "a Christian military sermon."[180] He thereby compared Paul with a "pious righteous field captain, who addresses his people in battle formation with a field sermon admonishing them to stand fast, and telling them to be bold and confident."[181] It is so

[179] *Predigtbuch der Lutherischen Kirche. Ein Jahrgang Predigten über die alten Episteln, Erlangen: Martin Luther-Verlag, 1936*, pp. 415–22. In *Zeugnisse, "Gottes kämpfendes Herr."* Feuerhahn no. 148. MH

[180] WA 34/2.372.16. *"Eine Herr predigt fur die Christen."* MH

[181] WA 34/2.372. *Das Sechste Capitel der Epistel S. Pauli an die*

because the Christian estate is no idle vocation, yet it is an estate of peace and certainty. "We do not sit at peace here like a farmer, the bourgeois, or the artisan in his city where he lives free and has nothing to fear. We are in a dangerous place among enemies and murderers, who have serious intentions for us and want to steal our treasure."[182] If Christianity has ever had to take such a "military sermon" seriously, then it is the case today. We come out of a time in which the Church was understood as a place of rest in a restless world. Just as the huge old houses of God stand in the middle of city traffic, the noise bustling around them, so the Church is thought of as an island of peace in the middle of a war-torn world. Now it is certainly right that the Church ought to be a place of rest and peace in the world. But no one can really understand the Church of Christ as a place of divine peace in the world who doesn't know anything of the violence of war that flares up wherever the Church makes an appearance. "Peace I leave with you; my peace I give to you" (John 14:27). The same Lord who says this also says the opposite: "Do not think that I have come to bring peace to the earth. I have not come to bring peace, but a sword" (Matt. 10:34). No war on earth, be it a bloody world war or a heated war of spirits, is as serious or dangerous as the war that Jesus once sent his apostles into, and to which he calls the Church of all times. The Christianity of the last generation had forgotten that. They

---

Epheser, von der Christen harnisch und waffen, gepredigt durch D. Mart. Luther (Eph. 6:10ff). Oct. 29, 1531. Aland no. Pr. 1288. MH
[182] WA 34/2.372.21–25. MH

wanted to have the peace of Christ without the harsh war he orders us to enter. They wanted a church where they could save their souls and live undisturbed by the noise of the world. But thereby they forgot the deep peace that the Redeemer of the world alone can give us, and they forgot the real Church.

Because the Church of Christ is the fighting army of God in this world, and if the Church is no longer that, then she has become just one of many human religious societies, and has ceased to be the Church of Christ. Therefore, it is by the mercy of God that he has once again taught us to understand the teaching of the Reformer during this time of war, that the state of the Christian is no state of peace and security. We, along with the entire Church on earth have cause to hear this powerful "Military Sermon" again, with which this Sunday's Epistle has called the Church of Christ to war as the army of God. God gives his Holy Spirit to all of us that take up the call. He issues him to each and every one of us, if we now hear what the apostle says to us about the *enemy of God,* about the *force of the Church* and about the *victory of Jesus Christ.*

The world we live in is in a state of war. Everyone knows that. War rages between the living things of our earth. War is the history of peoples and states. But we have to distinguish everything we men call "war" from the war that the Church has to fight: "For we do not wrestle against flesh and blood, but against the rulers, against the authorities, against the cosmic powers over this present darkness, against the spiritual forces of evil in the heavenly places" [Eph. 6:12]. "Flesh and blood"—by this the Holy Scriptures mean natural man. A war against flesh and blood would be a war against men, against myself or others, a war against human powers, human desires, human thoughts. Even a war between the great powers of the human spirit, a war between the highest ideas, a war with high-minded religions and worldviews would be, according to the use of these words in the Bible, a war against flesh and blood. Because the word applies even to the highest height and the most powerful performances of man's natural spirit: "That which is born of the flesh is flesh" [John 3:6]. It would be a war against flesh and blood if the Church of Christ only had to fight against human opponents like in the first centuries with the Roman Caesars, who demanded divine admiration, or as in our days with the atheism of Bolshevik Russia. If the Church only had to fight with other religions, with worldviews that were hostile to Christendom, if they only had to fight with philosophical schools or with false doctrines of human origin in her own midst, then her war would be a war against flesh and blood like all other wars in world history. But that is simply not the case. Behind the earthly enemies of the true Church stands one that is even more enormous, a super earthly and superhuman power: the enemy of God.

In modern society, and even in the Christendom of the last generation, it has become customary to silence or even to mock belief in this enemy of God that the Bible calls Satan or the devil and those who "still believe in a devil." That is similar to saying that we Christians do not believe in the devil, but in God. One can't "believe" in the devil. But he who believes in God, (not in a conception of God thought up by men, but in the living God to which the Bible attests, the Creator and Completer, the Judge and the Redeemer of the world) also knows of the gruesome reality of the evil enemy who as the enemy of God attempts to destroy the work of the Creator and Redeemer. From the first to the last book of the Bible, from the fall into sin to the judgment of the disciples, in the witness of the prophets and the apostles, in the history of the Old Testament people of God and the Church of the New Testament: all attests to this reality. It is not only that there is evil in the world, but there is *the* evil one, which Luther translated as "villain" in our text. How will anyone understand the Gospel, how will anyone understand the redeeming work of Christ, when he no longer takes seriously what Jesus Christ himself says about his fight with Satan and his kingdom?

Certainly, no human can point out the devil and his kingdom. The Bible doesn't even make the attempt to teach us about this. No, it is not the textbook of a [scientific] worldview [*Weltanschauung*], and neither will it mediate any "knowledge of the higher worlds" to us. Therefore, we should not enquire after things that are hidden from our earthly eyes and will remain hidden according to God's will when even now the nature of humanity and the spirit of man remains an unsolvable mystery to our reason; how much less able are we to penetrate the sphere of the superhuman and supernatural spirits and understand the nature of angels, the servant spirits of God, and the demons, the servants of God's adversary? When even now human reason remains an unfathomable mystery in our thought, how much more the superhuman intelligence of other natures! In any case we modern men, who would like to know and explain everything, and only accept what our limited understanding can comprehend and explain, should learn to be a little modest. There are spirits in the world that are wiser than the wisest human spirit. There are powers in the world that are more powerful than the most powerful men in the history of the earth.

"The lords of the world,"[183] Paul calls these spirits. Thereby he used a title that the mightiest lords in the ancient world assumed for themselves. Luther made it clear to his Wittenberg congregation why "Paul called them, 'lords of the world,' from the Greek *cosmokratoras*, not, as our princes are called, princes of the world, or worldly lords, but such lords who have the power of the world, and the whole world under them. And he named not one, but many who are more powerful and stronger than all the Caesars and kings with the power they have under them."[184] Only the history of the world makes it possible to understand the works of this reality, "lords of the world, over this present darkness." And history knows with the New Testament and Luther that "the rulers" and "the authorities," the "lords of the world" [Luther's translation], "the spiritual forces of evil" [Eph. 6:12] are only, as Luther

---

[183] Luther translated the word *Cosmokratoras* as "the lords of the world" (*Herren der Welt*), rather than "cosmic powers" as it is translated in the ESV.

[184] WA 34/2.390.7ff. MH

expressed it, "servants" [*Hofgesinde*] of the devil, who Paul called elsewhere a "god of this world" [2 Cor. 4:4]. "All his servants rule with him and serve him as his electors, councilmen, and statesmen of the kingdom whom he uses as his regiments, each one according to his skill and purpose. Because they are not all equal among themselves, even though they are all powerful and mighty spirits, one is more cunning and mischievous than the other."[185]

No, our Epistle does not speak about these powers to teach us about the supernatural mysteries of the world. It wants to remind us of the blessed Gospel of the God and Father of our Lord Jesus Christ, "He has delivered us from the domain of darkness and transferred us to the kingdom of his beloved Son" (Col. 1:13). It wants to help us put our whole confidence in the Son of God, who came "to destroy the works of the devil" [1 John 3:8]. It wants to call us with the great exhortation that constantly rings throughout the whole New Testament in new and ever changing words, and applies to the Church in every century whatever the worldview of that time: "Finally, be strong in the Lord and in the strength of his might. Put on the whole armor of God, that you may be able to stand against the schemes of the devil. For we do not wrestle against flesh and blood, but against the rulers, against the authorities, against the cosmic powers over this present darkness, against the spiritual forces of evil in the heavenly places" (Eph. 6;10–12).

Do you hear this exhortation, beloved Christians? Do you hear this exhortation, you congregation of the Lord?

---

[185] WA 34/2.390.25–30. MH

Does the Church in Germany, the Church on earth still hear it? It is the masterpiece of the devil that he has made the humanity of our day too wise for his existence. Has he already finished his masterpiece by making Christendom numb to such an exhortation? Because according to the witness of Jesus Christ himself, it belongs to the reality of Satan that he takes the Word of God out of our hearts. No, he will not succeed in that. We want the powerful word of our Epistle to remain in a fine, good heart. As the light of a lighthouse shines over the sea and points the way over the dark abyss for ships, saving them before they sink, so this Epistle shines over the history of the world and helps us find the way over the dark abyss of the world. We see the powerful struggle playing out behind the history of the world, hidden behind all wars and conflicts in the history of people, the history of the spiritual life and the hidden economy also behind the battle for our lives and our hearts. We see how our miserable little lives, how the life of our people is connected to the great fight, which is the essential and last theme of world history, the fight between the living God and his adversary. And we secure the exhortation deep within our hearts: "Finally, be strong in the Lord and in the strength of his might" [v. 10].

"In the strength of his might," because in such fighting this bitter truth is the deepest experience of all serious men: "With might of ours can naught be done, soon were our loss effected."[186] Where should we, were we to rely on

---

[186] Martin Luther, "A Mighty Fortress Is Our God." WA 35.455; *LW* 298.

ourselves alone, take up arms against this opposition? When human eyes and the spirit of humanity cannot recognize him, when human reason is so endlessly foolish and blind that it fails to even notice the existence of its worst enemy, and then even disputes his existence, when he delivers the last deadly blow to man, how can we stand by means of our own fortitude in such a fight? No, all human strength fails here. Here, we need the strength of God. "Put on the whole armor of God, that you may be able to stand against the schemes of the devil" [Eph. 6:11]. "Therefore take up the whole armor of God, that you may be able to withstand in the evil day, and having done all, to stand firm. Stand therefore, having fastened on the belt of truth, and having put on the breastplate of righteousness, and, as shoes for your feet, having put on the readiness given by the gospel of peace. In all circumstances take up the shield of faith, with which you can extinguish all the flaming darts of the evil one; and take the helmet of salvation, and the sword of the Spirit, which is the word of God" (Eph. 6:13–17). How often did the apostles describe the Christian position so vividly to their young Christians? They, who so often had seen a Roman cohort or a legion with all their armor, the sparkling ornamentations of force clanging as they passed by, filled with pride to be part of the greatest and most disciplined army in the world. This army protected the great power of "Eternal Rome," as the capital city was called in the British Isles and in the heat of Africa, on the Rein and on the Persian border. These young Christians knew all the insignias and the different squadrons and legions when they were only children. Take this picture in: The Church fighting as God's army in the world, armed with the invincible military armament God gives his saints, to equip them for the great battle with the adversary and his kingdom of darkness.

Paul gives particular emphasis to two of these weapons, the shield of *faith* and the sword of the Spirit, which is the *Word of God.* He calls faith the great weapon of defense against the fiery darts shot in a cunning ambush. It is the shield "with which you can extinguish all the flaming darts of the evil one" [Eph. 6:16]. Do we know, beloved congregation, about the power of this faith? Or must the world shame us in the strength of faith? When already a worldly faith, an earthly trust does powerful things, apparently making the impossible possible, removing invincible obstacles, and seems to be able to defeat the most powerful adversary, how much more must be possible on account of faith in the one who has been given all power on heaven and earth! Is not the apostasy of so many people from the Christian faith to a great extent a consequence of our altogether weak faith? Where, if at all, have these people seen strong, deep, real, mountain-moving faith in the living God and the one he has sent, Jesus Christ? Faith gives light to faith. For this reason, Christ the Lord did not send books and letters into the world to awaken faith, but believing men. Where does the intense, believing Church of the Lord still remain in Germany? How different would it be for the inner life of our people if those who are still in the churches could see all who put their trust in Jesus and have solid faith in Him for the forgiveness of sins, life and, salvation and live greater and fuller lives for it? If the devil wants to undermine the glory of Christ and erect his kingdom in the midst of a people, he begins by taking the power of faith from the church of that people. And where the shield of faith is no longer serviceable, how will one extinguish the flaming darts of the evil one? Then no one can do anything to hinder his destructive work.

But the other weapon to which Paul gives particular attention is "the sword of the Spirit, which is the word of God" [Eph. 6:17]. It is the weapon of attack with which the Church conquers the world for the kingdom of God. The only weapon! Woe to the church that uses other weapons, and would even borrow them from the world! She is no longer a Church of her Lord. No theological learning, no "Christian culture," no wise church politicking, and no attempt to win "influence" in the world conquers the world for Christ and defeats the kingdom of darkness, but the Word of God alone. *The Word of God is the greatest power in the world.* It is more powerful than the most powerful force of nature. Because, yes, through this Word all things are created, and the Word of God alone preserves the immense universe in which we live. It is more powerful than all world powers that have ever appeared in history. Therefore, God the Lord said to his prophets, who would proclaim his Word, and the same applies to the preaching of the Word through the Church, "See, I have set you this day over nations and over kingdoms, to pluck up and to break down, to destroy and to overthrow, to build and to plant" (Jer. 1:10). So powerful is the justifying and saving Word of God in history, "like fire . . . and like a hammer that breaks the rock in pieces" [Jer. 23:29]. It is more powerful than all the powers that have appeared in the spiritual life of men. It is the sword of the Spirit that is still at work, where all the powers forged by the spirit of man have failed. "For the word of God is living and active, sharper than any two-edged sword, piercing to the division of soul and of spirit, of joints and of marrow, and discerning the thoughts and intentions of the heart. And no creature is hidden from his sight, but all are naked and exposed to the eyes of him to whom we must give account" (Heb. 4:12–13). Because, yes, it is the Word of truth. It is the Word in which he is present, who says about himself: "I am . . . the truth" [John 14:6], and he himself is this Word. Do we understand now why this weapon is invincible, why it is the only weapon to use against the kingdom of darkness? Oh, that we with Luther and the true Church of all times would learn again from the Word of truth that God's Word is the greatest power in the world.

This "military sermon" from Ephesians speaks to us of God's fighting army, not of the individual soldiers, because this fight cannot be fought by the individual Christian; rather, every man has his place. That is what the "you" in this address means [it is a plural you]. We have heard about the fighting army, we have also heard about the enemy of God and about the power of the Church. And now, finally, we hear how from afar the fanfare of victory is heard through the clatter of the fight and the din of battle:

"Therefore take up the whole armor of God, that you may be able to withstand in the evil day, and having done all, to stand firm" (Eph. 6:13). The victory song is only heard from afar. It is still the time of laborious wrestling, where one is happy if one's position is held. Our eyes do not yet see a victory. So the Church of all times must fight. Her human eyes have seen so little of the victory, she is like the Spanish soldiers in Alcazar of Toledo,[187] who could no longer offer a brave defense until they heard the liberating sounds of victory. As they waited for their liberator, so the Church waits for her Lord. And she knows that the victory will belong to him when he comes. That is the faith and the hope of the Church as God's fighting army in the world: Our fight follows his victory. And so we look to the glorious day of victory, "Then comes the end, when he delivers the kingdom to God the Father after destroying every rule and every authority and power. For he must reign until he has put all his enemies under his feet" (1 Cor. 15:24–25). Amen.

---

[187] An imposing fortress on the highest spot in Toledo, Spain, a Roman palace in the third century. Sasse may be referring to events of the Spanish Civil War, 1936–39. MH

The Church of God in Motion
Annual Celebration of the Society of Domestic and
International Mission in the Sense of the Lutheran Church
Gunzenhausen
July 14, 1937[188]
Matthew 24:14

And this gospel of the kingdom will be proclaimed
throughout the whole world as a testimony to all nations,
and then the end will come. (Matt. 24:14)

Beloved Festival Congregation!

It is the glorious prerogative of the children of God that
they can always be thankful for everything. With songs of
thanks and praise on their lips, Jesus Christ enlisted the
apostles in the world. Their prayers of thanks are still heard
today through the letters of the New Testament. "About
midnight Paul and Silas were praying and singing hymns to
God" (Acts 16:25). So it is said of the apostles in prison.
With the *Deo Gratia*, "Thanks be to God," the martyrs also
received their death sentences from the mouths of the
heathen judges. Out of the wreckage of the migration of the
peoples and the sinking of the ancient world,[189] the Church
learned to sing the *Te Deum Laudamus*, just as the great

---

[188] *Predigt, gehalten von Universitäts Professor D. Sasse – Erlangen,*
beim Jahresfest der Gesellschaft für Innere und Aeussere Mission im
Sinne der lutherischen Kirche am 14. Juli 1937 I der Stadtkiirche zu
Gunzenhausen (Matt. 24,14). In Freimund 83.28 (15 Jul 1937) 219–22.
Also in *Zeugnisse.* Feuerhahn no. 175. MH
[189] See *Letters to Lutheran Pastors I,* pp. 200ff; no. 12, *Ecclesia*
Migrans, 1950. Feuerhahn no. 277. MH

songs of thanks and praise of the Evangelical Lutheran Church rang out during the days of the Thirty Years' War [1618–1648]. There is no Christian faith without the daily praise of God. It wasn't for nothing that the Early Church called the Communion celebration that formed in the middle point of the Divine Service the "Eucharist," "a prayer of thanks."[190] Wherever the Gospel comes to a people, lips open to the great praise of the divine mercy. And where the Gospel goes silent and the church dies, there also die the songs of thanks and praise. Should ever (as the Lord in his grace has thus far prevented) God want to repudiate the German people, there would never again in the German language chime forth a song of thanks or praise of the Church of Christ because great songs of thanks and praise only ring in the Church.

Because it is so in this hour, beloved festival congregation, we can do nothing but offer that one voice in great praise that the Church always brings before God and the Father of our Lord Jesus Christ. Over the past year we began the fifty-year celebration of our Neuendettelsau Mission with the praise of divine mercy. It was no easy year for German missions in general, neither for our "Society for Inner [domestic] and Outer [foreign] Mission in the Spirit of the Lutheran Church."[191] The deep distress of the Church that every branch of church work has born together weighs on this mission in a very particular way.

---

[190] The word "eucharist" is first used of the Sacrament by the *Didache* (ch. 9). MH
[191] Löhe founded the society in 1849. MH

For this reason we have also experienced in a particular way the sympathy that God has given his Church at this time: "*In all ways you have a way, you never lack the means; your action is pure blessing, your way is pure light, no one can hinder what you do, your activity never has to rest, when you want to do what is beneficial for your children.*"[192] Truly, all of us, our brothers and sisters on the mission field and the mission workers at home, the congregation and individual friends must continue the praying and helping that stands behind our work. We all must thankfully confess, "Where our sorrows are great, there your blessings are still greater. Where our strength wanes, there your help begins. Where we walk through the darkness deep, there your light guides us."[193] "Lord we are not worthy of all the mercifulness and loyalty you have shown for your servants."[194] This is because in this hour we can and must confess that we are happy about the future despite all the worries. Today we lay all these worries in God's hands, all worries great and small without exception. All the questions that confront us concerning the work of the mission we tell to him. Thankful and happy, we come to him as sinners, who can only pray, "Kyrie Eleison!" With disheartened and feeble faith, we, like the apostles, ask, "Increase our faith!" [Luke 17:5]. And God took what

---

[192] Gerhard, Paul *Befiehl du deine Wege*, translation by Francis Brown 2006
(http://www.bach-cantatas.com/Texts/Chorale066-Eng3.htm); for six verses in English see *LSB* 754.
[193] Another stanza of Gerhardt's *Befiehl du deine Wege*. MH
[194] Allusion to Genesis 32:10.

is ours upon himself: he, who will forgive our sins according to his living Son's will; he, who will help us in all our weakness with the power of his Holy Spirit; he, who on this day of celebration leads us by the great word of our text out of the everyday hardships to a height from which we have a view to the end of the earth and to the end of the world. He shows what the mission of his Church is. He shows us his wonderful way and your glorious goal: "And this gospel of the kingdom will be proclaimed throughout the whole world as a testimony to all nations, and then the end will come" (Matt. 24:14).

In this prophetic word, Jesus describes what the mission of his Church is. Thus the mission appears when one looks to God. The eyes of the world see something else: "And this gospel of the kingdom will be proclaimed throughout the whole world as a testimony to all nations." That is something that is not understood outside the Church. We must therefore be clear on this, beloved mission congregation, what a hopeless undertaking it is to make clear to a person who does not believe in Christ what the essence, right, and duty of the mission is. Yes, because he can only understand the Christian faith as one religion among many others, and he would never see why all people should have one religion. People have so many different languages, different forms of government, and different cultures. Why shouldn't they have different religions? Is there not for every people according to their kind, one religion, one faith, one Divine Service that is appropriate for their souls? Is it not a barbarism when one takes a faith from a people and gives them another one that is completely foreign to them? So our contemporaries ask us, and we all know that thereby it is the Christian mission that is placed in question.

What do we reply to this? First, we have only to simply stress that this is a theory of bookish men. The real life of people in the world tells of something else entirely. Certainly, the religious lives of people hang together with the mooring of their souls. But it is not as if the importance of their particular religion grew out of this mooring. History knows of a death of religion. When the ancient Greeks stood at the high point of their culture, the religion of their fathers died. Today when airplanes thunder over the primitive worlds of Africa and New Guinea, it means not only a change in their worldviews, but also a deep tremor in the religion of their fathers. And something else hangs together with this: "the migration of religion." The great religions cross over the borders of peoples and races. Buddhism was born in India, but had hardly any devotees in its homeland. But it has wandered deep into inner-Asia and the Far East. Islam stretched out of the Semitic world to India, and today wins devotees among the black Africans. When the native religion of the Greeks and Romans went extinct, they accepted the religions of Egypt, Syria, Asia Minor, and Persia. Yes, the great history of human religions is based on this migration of religions, and on their struggle for the souls of the peoples. Already this simple fact of history should warn us concerning the superficial idea that every people should have a religion in accordance with their location and that it is a tactless interference in the souls of foreign people when we bring them the Gospel. If the peoples of Africa were not Christian, then in all probability they would be Mohammedans or Bolsheviks, but they would not remain what they were.

But of course, the right of the Christian mission is still not proven by this. Should not, we are told, Christianity only be one of these proselytizing world religions too? Perhaps the most successful among them, but in any case only one of them? Is not the Church again extinct in the wide regions of the earth that were once Christian? This is what happened in the land of North Africa and the Near East, which was the showplace of the great Church history of the ancient world. As in the Roman cities of Germany one can find the ruins of temples of the Persian god Mithras here and there, which the Roman soldiers once worshiped, so lay the rubble of old Christian churches in the desert sands of Africa. One can pursue the tracks of old Christian mission churches deep into Central Asia, to India, Ceylon [since 1948, Sri Lanka], and East Asia. During the Thirty Years' War, the Jesuits found an inscription in Singanfu, China, written in Chinese and Syrian from the time of Charlemagne [742–814; first Holy Roman Emperor] that identified a great number of Christian clergy.[195] The name of the Syrian Patriarch in the Persian Empire is known to us, the first to ordain an archbishop in China. His name

---

[195] A Nestorian-Syrian inscription in China, dated AD 781. MH

means "The crucified has victory!"[196] The Christians in Asia bore such a name. The Crucified has victory! But the great church in Asia sunk half a millennium later. They had experienced the fate of the church that would be destroyed by Islam, the fate that so many other religious communities have had. Is the Christian faith then something really all that different from the other religions of humanity?

So the world asks us, beloved friends. They can only see in the best intentions of Christian mission nothing other than the propaganda that one of humanity's religions uses to propel itself, and its natural limits are reached when it runs up against the propaganda of another faith to which it is opposed. We have no human means to teach the world better. No evidence of the side effects of mission, or on the cultural meaning of the mission work, or the indisputable blessing that the medical mission brings will make friends of mission out of enemies of mission. This is the particular meaning of the present hour for mission that is so important for Christianity that one must concentrate only on that which propels the Church's mission. Mission is not about any cultural values. We are not driven to mission out of a desire to force our worldview on others. Rather, the Church of Christ is driven to mission only because Jesus Christ is Lord [Phil. 2:11], to whom all authority on heaven and earth has been given. And he has given his Church the command to preach his Gospel to all peoples to the ends of the world. The Church is driven to mission because she

---

[196] Sliba-zkha was patriarch of the Church of the East 714–28, "the Nestorian Church." MH

believes in "one Lord Jesus Christ, the only-begotten Son of God, begotten of his Father before all worlds, God of God, Light of Light, very God of very God, begotten not made, being of one substance with the Father, by whom all things were made; who for us men and for our salvation came down from heaven and was incarnate by the Holy Spirit of the Virgin Mary and was made man; and was crucified also for us under Pontius Pilate.[197] He suffered and was buried, and the third day he rose again according to the Scriptures and ascended into heaven and sits at the right hand of the Father. And he will come again with glory to judge the living and the dead, whose kingdom will have no end." If we did not believe Jesus is "God of God, Light of Light, very God of very God," were he only a great teacher, the greatest prophet that ever was upon the earth, then there would be no mission, because then there would be no Gospel. The Gospel is not just a religious message like so many others. It is not a teaching that says there is a God who forgives sins and someday will erect his kingdom. The Gospel is much more the message that God has come to man. It is the message that there is Savior of sinners, who calls men from all races and peoples to himself, and that "whoever believes in him should not perish but have eternal life" [John 3:16]. The Gospel is the message of Christ himself. Just as he called "all who labor and are heavy laden" [Matt. 11:28] to himself in his earthly days, so he calls them today in the proclamation of his Church. So it is that the Church is not free to choose her message.

---

[197] Fifth Prefect of the Roman Province of Judaea AD 26–36. MH

She cannot make it like the other religions of the world, who in their glory stir up fantasies, who get at the heart with compelling myths, today with this message, tomorrow with another message, once with the myth of Edda[198] and today with the myths of the twentieth century and later with the myths of the twenty-first century. The Church always has the same message, for all times, for all peoples, for all races, for the healthy and the sick, for the happy and the sad, for the strong and the weak, the learned and the unlearned. She has nothing more to say to a [Otto von] Bismarck [1815–1898; first chancellor of the German Empire] than she has to say to the poorest, sickest child. The world is outraged by this "boring" message that never changes. But the Church cannot change it. Yes, because it is not her message, but Christ's message. The Christian missionary is like an envoy who travels to the prisoners of Siberia—those who are languishing in the prison, who no longer remember or know anything of freedom, and no longer hope for freedom—with orders to proclaim, "You are free. The war is over. Come home with us!" That is the Gospel, the joyous message. It is everywhere the same, but where one comprehends it there it is the greatest thing that men can hear. So the Christian mission proclaims the wonder of redemption, the miracle of all miracles, the God who becomes man. "That is, in Christ God was reconciling the world to himself, not counting their trespasses against them, and entrusting to us the message of reconciliation.

---

[198] Mythology written in Iceland in the thirteenth century, though from the earlier Viking period. MH

Therefore, we are ambassadors for Christ, God making his appeal through us. We implore you on behalf of Christ, be reconciled to God. For our sake he made him to be sin who knew no sin, so that in him we might become the righteousness of God" (2 Cor. 5:19–21).

That is also the Gospel that would be preached in the whole world. Our text calls it the Gospel of the Kingdom. In the early Roman imperial age, during the earthly life of Jesus, "gospel" was used for the news of Caesar Augustus [Roman Emperor 27 BC–AD 14] and his empire, encompassing the *"oikumene,"* the entire world, guaranteeing peace for humanity. Here another kingdom is meant, that is to be established in the entire *oikumene*, the entire world and wherever there is already the reality that Jesus Christ rules over the hearts of men through his Gospel and Sacraments. It is a kingdom that, as the confession of our Church says, is now hidden under the cross ["*cruce tectum*" Ap. VII.18], but will be revealed when throughout the universe it rings: "The kingdom of the world has become the kingdom of our Lord and of his Christ, and he shall reign forever and ever" (Rev. 11:15). That is the Gospel of the kingdom that that will be preached in the whole world. "And this gospel of the kingdom will be proclaimed throughout the whole world as a testimony to all nations" [Matt. 24:14]. It will be preached whether or not it is legal, whether or not the powers of this world will suffer it. It will be preached in the ancient world even though the Roman Caesar did not allow it. It will be preached today here and there in the houses of

Moscow and in the prison cells of Siberia, despite all the opposition of the godless. One can throw his messengers in prison and kill them, as it was done in the days of the apostles. But then the word of the apostles proved true: "But the word of God is not bound!" (2 Tim. 2:9). One can outlaw and punish the preaching of the Gospel, as they did during the Reformation. There is a deeper sense to this because a death sentence hung over the German Reformer his whole life; because the imperial law of Worms that singled him out of the ranks of the German citizens, yes, out of the ranks of the living, was never rescinded.[199] But one thing could not be accomplished: one could not fetter the Gospel. That belongs to the incomprehensibleness of the divine Word. It has a life of its own so to say. It remained a power even when the ability of its messengers to speak was taken away. The history of missions is full of examples of this. God's Word can exist without the helpful means that every other word demands, without the means of writing, of book publishers, or whatever else they might be, because it is not the word of men, but the Word of the Almighty God, and therefore, "Living and active, sharper than any two-edged sword, piercing to the division of soul and of spirit, of joints and of marrow, and discerning the thoughts and intentions of the heart" (Heb. 4:12). It is the Word that can build and plant, destroy and uproot (Jer. 18:9). It is the Word that created the world; how can the world oppose it or stray from its course?

---

[199] The Edict of Worms, March 25, 1521, declared Luther's writings banned and him a heretic. MH

Now we understand what the essence of the Church is. The mission is, as Wilhelm Loehe [1808–1872] said, "The church of God in motion."[200] In the preaching of the Church, the Word of God wanders over the earth and comes to the peoples. It "will be proclaimed throughout the whole world as a testimony to all nations, and then the end will come" [Matt. 24:14]. Then the day will come in which all men, all people, will be questioned as to what they have done with the Gospel. If they have believed the voice that called them out of the darkness to light, out of the darkness of sin to the light of grace, out of prison to freedom, out of death to life. Or if they have ridiculed the true Word of the Gospel, and if then the word of salvation must become a word of judgment.

"And then the end will come," with intense seriousness, this Word of the Lord brings awareness of the responsibility that is laid upon all of us. There is an end to all history. There is a judgment we are all heading towards, the individual and the peoples, the church fellowships [*Kirchengemeinschaften*] of Christendom and their mission work. In this judgment everyone will be asked, "What have you done to preserve the Gospel among your people?" Should our beloved German people belong to those peoples that are only remembered because of the ruins, that the

---

[200] "For mission is nothing but the one church of God in its movement, the actualization of the one universal, catholic church. . . . Mission is the life of the catholic church. Where it stops, blood and breath stop; where it dies, the love which unites heaven and earth also dies. The catholic church and mission— these two no one can separate without killing both, and that is impossible. Wilhelm Loehe, *Three Books About the Church* (Philadelphia: Fortress Press, 1969), p. 59. MH

Church of God once experienced a great history there? Should the word that the German Reformer once had spoken about the un-thankfulness of Germany to God who had given them his Gospel come to fulfillment? "And where we have no better honor, but to continue to despise and be unthankful, then it would mean: You have not recognized the time of your visitation. Then it is over and the devil has already won. Because if we so despise the Word, so it will despise us in return, and separate itself from us, as we separate ourselves from it. From this, God graciously forbids us."[201]

So today Germany stands before the great decision that God has placed before her in history. Yes, seriously, the hour of decision has come upon us, and so the task of missions will be greater. Today, home mission and international mission, inner and outer mission move together. Never before has the task of missions been greater. If we despair, it is because we do not know that the work is not ours, but his alone. The prophecy of the Lord still rings over our people and our church: "And this gospel of the kingdom will be proclaimed throughout the whole world as a testimony to all nations, and then the end will come" (Matt. 24:14). In this we hear this [fateful Word]. Together we hear the Word. By this Word he calls us anew to his service, us sinners, us weaklings, us of little faith: "Peace be with you. As the Father has sent me, even so I am sending you" (John 20:21). Amen.

---

[201] *Vorrede auf Joh. Sutels Auslegung des Evangelii von der Zerstörung Jerusalems, 1539*; Walch II, 14.389; WA 50.666; Aland no. 707. MH

Jesus Intercedes for His Church
Church Consecration During the War,
Together with a Convocation of the Martin Luther Bund.
John 17:6–23[202]

I have manifested your name to the people whom you gave me out of the world. Yours they were, and you gave them to me, and they have kept your word. Now they know that everything that you have given me is from you. For I have given them the words that you gave me, and they have received them and have come to know in truth that I came from you; and they have believed that you sent me. I am praying for them. I am not praying for the world but for those whom you have given me, for they are yours. All mine are yours, and yours are mine, and I am glorified in them. And I am no longer in the world, but they are in the world, and I am coming to you. Holy Father, keep them in your name, which you have given me, that they may be one, even as we are one. While I was with them, I kept them in your name, which you have given me. I have guarded them, and not one of them has been lost except the son of destruction, that the Scripture might be fulfilled. But now I am coming to you, and these things I speak in the world, that they may have my joy fulfilled in themselves. I have given them your word, and the world has hated them because they are not of the world, just as I am not of the world. I do not ask that you take them out of the world, but that you keep them from the evil one. They are not of the world, just as I am not of the world. Sanctify them in the truth; your word is truth. As you sent me into the world, so I have sent them into the world. And for their sake I

---

[202] *Predigt: [1941/42] "Jesus Fürbitte für seine Kirche. Kirchweihfest in einem der Kriegsjahre, verbunden mit einem Diasporatag des Martin Luther-Bundes."* Feuerhahn 243a. MH

consecrate myself, that they also may be sanctified in truth.

I do not ask for these only, but also for those who will believe in me through their word, that they may all be one, just as you, Father, are in me, and I in you, that they also may be in us, so that the world may believe that you have sent me. The glory that you have given me I have given to them, that they may be one even as we are one, I in them and you in me, that they may become perfectly one, so that the world may know that you sent me and loved them even as you loved me. (John 17:6–23)

How inexhaustibly rich are the Holy Scriptures! There are texts of Scripture that one can not only spend his whole life studying without completely exhausting their depths, but whose full understanding requires the work of many centuries of Christianity. For a millennium and a half the Church read the apostle Paul's letters to the Romans and Galatians. Pious Christians were edified by them in the Divine Service. Profoundly learned Church Fathers of antiquity and the great theological masters of the Middle Ages explored them. Then after fifteen hundred years, the hour struck in which the complete depths of the doctrine of justification as these letters taught it was understood during the Reformation. Perhaps something similar happens with the other great texts of the Bible, like the divine mystery of the Church as it is spoken of in Paul's Letter to the Ephesians or with the extraordinary seventeenth chapter of the Gospel of John. August Vilmar [1800–1868], the great nineteenth-century Lutheran theologian, repeatedly stressed that only from the current, enormous struggles concerning the Church, only from the living experience of

Christendom, would the full understanding of the New Testament statement concerning the Church blossom, and that this new knowledge, this new understanding of the Third Article of the Creed, would be ever so great a turning point in the history of the Church as the new understanding of the Second Article of the Creed was in the Reformation.

So today, as we celebrate the consecration of this church, let us ponder what our text says to us concerning the mystery of the Church—us, we who stand in the midst of a fierce struggle concerning the Church. For thirty years now, this house of God has stood. That is a short time compared to the age of other churches.

Our text speaks of the preservation of the Church as a miracle. The preservation of the Church is no less a miracle than the foundation of the Church, as the preservation of the world is no smaller miracle than its creation. It is not self-evident that the Church should remain. In many parts of the world it is nearly or completely sunk, and many people who once had a flowering church in their midst have pushed this Church away from themselves. There are no harsher scenes than the ruins of old churches found in Asia in the lands that have fallen back into paganism. And no less a significant figure than Martin Luther himself had reckoned with the possibility that the Church might one day be taken even from our people. "God's word and grace," so he had once said," is like a passing rain shower that does not return where it has once been.[203]" He knew then of the

---

[203] AE 45.352; WA 15.31–32. The "passing rainshower" remark occurs at AE 45.352; WA 15.32.7. See *At Home in the House of My Fathers*

lands of ancient Christendom that had sunk back into paganism, and spoke these words of caution: "And you Germans need not think that you will have it forever, for ingratitude and contempt will not make it stay."[204] No, it is not self-evident that the Church should remain where she once has been. It is true that the Church of Christ is given the promise that the gates of hell shall not prevail against it [Matt. 16:18], but no congregation, no individual church can say that of itself. Just as the apostasy of an individual Christian happens, so also the apostasy of entire congregations and entire portions of the Church happen, as it is already documented in the New Testament.

No, it is not self-evident that the Church should be preserved. He who speaks in our Gospel knew that. It is Jesus Christ, the Lord, in the night that he was betrayed. What he said to his disciples on the night of farewell, he now says once more. But he does not say it to men. He says it to his heavenly Father. The last concern that moves him is worry for his Church. His work on earth is completed. "I have manifested your name to the people whom you gave me out of the world." "I have given them the words that you gave me." "I have given them your word." And this Word was not without fruit. "They have kept your word." "They have received them and have come to know in truth that I came from you; and they have believed that you sent me." And they have remained in this faith. "While I was

---

(St. Louis: CPH, 2012), pp. 776–77, for an example of the significance of Luther's "rainshower" remark in the history of the LCMS. MH
[204] AE 45.352; WA 15.32.11f. MH

with them, I kept them in your name, which you have given me. I have guarded them, and not one of them has been lost except the son of destruction, that the Scripture might be fulfilled." "While I was with them," so long as that is the case, there is no concern for the future of the Gospel. "And I am no longer in the world, but they are in the world, and I am coming to you" [John 17].

Now they would no longer hear his beloved voice. They would no longer see him with their eyes. What would become of them now? Never in humanity's history has one been given the kind of task the Lord gave the apostles in his farewell. This small crowd of eleven had a responsibility that had never been imposed on other men. "As you sent me into the world, so I have sent them into the world" [John 17:18]. What would become of the Gospel if they failed? And were they really the right kind of men for this task? "Then all the disciples left him and fled" (Matt. 26:56). "I do not know the man," so said Simon Peter (Matt. 26:72). This was the same Simon that Jesus praised because he had been blessed to be the first to confess him (Matt. 16:17). And this great work was entrusted to these men Jesus leaves behind: "As the Father has sent me, even so I am sending you" (John 20:21).

Yes, he sent these weak men, men who were no greater than any of us. Men who did not possess any of the natural spiritual gifts that have belonged to so many others who wanted to win over the world spiritually. And he sent them into the world that did not want to know of them and their message. "And I am no longer in the world, but they are in the world" [John 17:11]. "And the world has hated them because they are not of the world, just as I am not of the world" [John 17:14]. Oh, this world wants to be done with them already! If the world nailed him to the cross, how could they not be finished with this group of men?

He saw all that very clearly. How could he carry any illusions concerning his disciples, especially at this hour? There is only one thing for him to do. He prays for them. "I am praying for them. I am not praying for the world but for those whom you have given me, for they are yours" [John 17:9]. "Holy Father, keep them in your name, which you have given me, that they may be one, even as we are one" [v. 11]. "I do not ask that you take them out of the world, but that you keep them from the evil one" [v. 15]. "Sanctify them in the truth; your word is truth . . . that they also may be sanctified in truth" [vv. 17, 19]. He prayed for them. The farewell speech to the disciples is given in a farewell prayer. Now he speaks no more with men, but with his heavenly Father. Yes, this extraordinary chapter of the Gospel of John is then the greatest of prayers. It is not a man who prays here. No mere man can repeat it. The God-man prays here. Here prays the Eternal Son. All other prayers are the prayers of men to God, the prayers of the creatures to their Creator. There is one prayer that the Eternal Son prayed to his Father. He, the High Priest, prayed it for his Church. He whose way leads to Golgotha prayed, "I consecrate myself, that they also may be sanctified in truth" [v. 19]. And he doesn't just think about his disciples. But he looks past all the far-flung days of

Church history, past all the generations, past all the centuries to the end of the world: "I do not ask for these only, but also for those who will believe in me through their word" [v. 20]. He prays for the preservation of the Church. And this prayer is heard, that is the mystery of the preservation of the Church.

We would understand it better if we ponder what this intercession means for our lives, or what it should mean. There is nothing that keeps and bears our children like the prayers we pray for them. There is also nothing that unites parents and their children more deeply. There are fewer things to worry about concerning our children, when all our worries about them are laid in the fatherly heart of God. There is no bond that so unites and helps a married couple than to bear each other's burdens through the intercession they make for one another. So in the Church there is nothing that binds her members together like intercession. As the apostle Paul sat in prison and left his mission congregations defenseless and helpless in the world, there was still one thing that he could do for them: "For this reason I bow my knees before the Father, from whom every family in heaven and on earth is named" (Eph. 3:14–15) This prayer escapes the walls of the prison and unites him with his congregations.

Therefore, we make intercession in the church for our people and their authorities, for all who are in distress and the throes of *Anfechtung*,[205] for the sick and the dying, for

---

[205] This nearly untranslatable word was a favorite of Luther. It means a spiritual attack. MH

the Church of God throughout the world. We think of our brothers in the Diaspora. We think of the Lutheran Church in Brazil, who are bound so tightly with our Martin Luther Bund and our Franconian Church. We think of our German brothers in Australia, who remain such true friends of the old homeland, because they have preserved the German language in the Lutheran Church through the Bible, the catechism, the hymnal, and the liturgy. We think of the lonely Germans who bow their knees with us today while in Kyrgyzstan villages or in the forests of Siberia.[206] We think of all our fellow believers and of the imprisoned missionaries. And today, when we are not merely separated from them by land and sea, when we can no longer manage to give them any material help, today, we know what kind of power intercession is.

But if that is so concerning the intercessions we men on earth make for one another, how much more does it apply to the intercessions that the Head of the Church makes for her members. This prayer is truly and certainly heard. He prays for us. "But I have prayed for you that your faith may not fail. And when you have turned again, strengthen your brothers" (Luke 22:32). That saved Peter. "I do not ask for these only, but also for those who will believe in me through their word" [John 17:20]. This means us, you and me and every Christian, whose very faith rests in Jesus as his Savior. He prays for us—and his prayer is heard. This is

---

[206] The Russians carried on a program of ethnic dispersion of German populations in Soviet-controlled areas, sending many thousands upon thousands to far-flung places, while murdering Lutheran clergy. MH

why the liturgy has us sing, "The Lord be with you, and with your spirit" right before the collect. Now the Lord is with you, when you pray. He is with your spirit, when you give word to our prayer. Jesus Christ prays with us. The Church prays together with her Head. And this prayer is heard "through Jesus Christ, our Lord." He prays for us. He prays for his Church on earth—that is the miracle of the preservation of the Church. As Luther said, "For after all, we are not the ones who can preserve the church, nor were our forefathers able to do so. Nor will our successors have this power. No, it was, is, and will be he who says, 'I am with you always, to the close of the age.' As it says in Hebrews 13 [:8], 'Jesus Christ is the same yesterday, and today, and forever,' and in Revelation 1 [:8], 'He who is and who was and who is to come.' This is his name and no one else's; nor may anyone else be called by that name."[207]

Oh, who can have that faith! Oh, that we could learn something from this great childlike faith of Luther's. How much smaller would this make our worries concerning the Church if we could learn to throw all our worries on him who reserves concern about his Church for himself. How completely different would we then do what he demands we do to preserve his Church!

Only if we have this great faith in him, who wonderfully preserves his Church, only then will we know how the Church is preserved. How is the Church on earth preserved? "Sanctify them in the truth; your word is truth" [John 17:17]. "Through the word, the church is born, so

---

[207] AE 47.118; WA 50.476. MH

through the word, she is preserved," Luther once said.[208] Just as the church was founded on the word, "For I have given them the words that you gave me" [John 17:8], so Christ preserves the church through his Word. Not through the sparkling human organization, not the glorious cultus, not the wisest men, not by the most glorious church building does he preserve the church, but through the Word alone, the simple word of the Gospel, the holy message of the forgiveness of sins. "Fruitful ethics, we also find in Confucianism, shining hierarchies by the Dali Lahma, academic theology in the Synagogue, the fight against alcohol with the Turk, youth movements in Moscow, but the forgiveness of sins is found in Jesus Christ alone."[209]

The word of forgiveness only Jesus Christ can speak, because he has borne the sin of the world, so that following his departure, his Church could speak it. That is the Gospel. And it is also this word that creates the unity of the Church, the unity of all children of God: "Where this single article remains pure, Christendom will remain pure, in beautiful harmony, and without any schisms. But where it does not remain pure, it is impossible to repel any error or heretical spirit."[210] So be careful that this is so! This is what we have learned in our care for those in the diaspora. It comes through the Word, through the pure proclamation of the Gospel. That is the great service of the preservation of the Church. How they used to mock and fight with Father

---

[208] This reference could not be located. MH
[209] This reference could not be located. MH
[210] F.C. S.D. III, 6. BKS 916. WA 31.255.5–10.

Loehe as he began his great work for the diaspora, instructing the messengers with pure teaching. The congregations that he founded in America have remained guardians of the Gospel to this day. So we are in the great communion of the Church of all times, with the Fathers, who have confessed before us, with the teachers of the Church, with the apostles: "that they may be one even as we are one, I in them and you in me" [John 17:22–23].

Where a man knows that, there he knows something of the Church. The time will come when the Third Article will be understood. The question of the Church is one of the very great questions of the future. What a blessed mystery this article of faith hides, what a miracle of God the Church is. This is only known by him who belongs to those for whom Jesus Christ has prayed. "Holy Father, keep them in your name, which you have given me . . . Sanctify them in the truth; your word is the truth" [John 17:11, 17].

But we pray to him: Lord Jesus Christ, have mercy on us, you are the Savior of your Church, you the Savior of your Body. Amen.

Church's Day of Repentance
Reformation Festival
October 31, 1943[211]
Hebrews 13:7–9

Remember your leaders, those who spoke to you the word of God. Consider the outcome of their way of life, and imitate their faith. Jesus Christ is the same yesterday and today and forever. Do not be led away by diverse and strange teachings, for it is good for the heart to be strengthened by grace, not by foods, which have not benefited those devoted to them. (Heb. 13:7–9)

Shortly before the outbreak of the Thirty Years' War, on the 31st of October 1617, the whole church of Evangelical Germany united for the first time to celebrate the Reformation. In many churches the sermon text was our Epistle lesson today, the thirteenth chapter of Hebrews. One can't help but to read the old reports of this festival, and the later festivals of the seventeenth century concerning how our fathers understood and celebrated Reformation Day with anything but deep emotion. It was not, as it so often became in the eighteenth and nineteenth centuries, a festival of human admiration. They did not celebrate Reformation Day as the work of a human, but as the work of God. When they thought of Luther, they did not think of him as a hero of the nation, or a brilliant personality, but as the instrument of God, as the true slave through whose

---

[211] *Predigt: (31 Okt 1943) "Reformationsfest – Busstag der Kirche."* Feuerhahn no. 245a. MH

service God returned the Holy Gospel to Christendom. And because they did not honor the man but gave the glory to God, this festival was a day of thanks and praise—and therefore, the seventeenth century, the most difficult in German history, became the century of great songs of praise and thanks.

But Reformation Day was also something of a day of repentance for the Church. The greatest praise and thanks is always closely tied together with repentance and with the forgiveness of sins. A "festival of repentance," as a confessional theologian of the time called it, "where we should acknowledge, repent, and confess, that we with our heaped sins crying to heaven, along with our misery, tribulation, wretchedness, distress, torment, and persecution have caused the cross to hang over this Church." This was expressed even better in the old festival prayers for Reformation Day, how unthankful we have been for the Gospel, how we have grumbled at the word of truth, "that when you have fully dealt with us according to our sins, and repaid us according to our misdeeds, you have had just cause, to take away the light of your living word a full thousand times from our state." So they prayed for two and three centuries on Reformation Day. And without the serious tone of true repentance, the 31st of October was not a festival of the Church, in which the first of Luther's Ninety-five Theses was written deep in the heart: "When our Lord and Master Jesus Christ said, 'Repent,' he meant for the whole life of faith to be one of repentance."[212]

We, today, also hear this call to repentance in our Epistle lesson. The Church of Christ on earth was born of a powerful call to repentance. Her triumphal march through the ancient world and through the peoples of later centuries is the history of a great call to repentance. Every epoch of her history has begun with a call to repentance. Even the Reformation was, in its deepest essence, nothing more than the great repentance of the Church. And when God again grants an awakening to the Christianity of the western lands and the Christianity of Germany, then this awakening too will be nothing more than the great repentance of the Church in our century.

To such repentance, our Epistle already called the Christianity of the first century. We do not know who wrote Hebrews. Neither do we know the people to whom he originally wrote it. Though, there is much evidence indicating that it was directed to first-century Rome. But one comes out of the letter certain that there was already then a wane in churchly life, a reduction in church attendance, a tiredness in the life of faith. Yes, there was already at that time that which one refers to today as the exodus from the Church, there was a mild indifference to and, finally, a complete apostasy from Christ. Against this, the Letter to the Hebrews turns to a comprehensive warning to be true, to stand fast in the fight, to stand tall in the hour of temptation.

Among the numerous warnings also belongs the first of

---

[212] WA 1.229. MH

the three sentences on which our text builds: "Remember your leaders, those who spoke to you the word of God. Consider the outcome of their way of life, and imitate their faith" [13:7]. Remember your leaders—the word that Luther had translated "teachers" has a much more vague meaning in the Greek. It describes in Rome, and in many other congregations of the East, thereby, the responsible leaders of the congregations, their offices, their management, their standing among the presbytery, and oldest members. When Luther translated the text "teacher," he threw one aspect of their office to the front, the aspect that was most important. This is what the teacher of the Gospel passed on to the congregation—what Christ had entrusted to the apostles, the preaching of the Gospel, that the apostles had passed on to them, and they then passed it on to the congregation to whom they had been entrusted as shepherd. Now this generation was the first to pass on the faith. Many among them had kept true to their Lord Jesus Christ and paid for it with death, a martyr's death: "Consider the outcome of their way of life" [Heb. 13:7b]. They had been faithful to the end in the midst of fearful temptation: "Follow their example."

And so we have already in the beginning of the Church the truth that belongs to the essence of the Church: There is a part of the Church that is already completed, and a part of the Church that is incomplete, a Church in the fatherland and a Church in a foreign land, as the Eastern Church still says today. A part of the Church is still on pilgrimage here in the foreign land as guests and strangers, like the ancient people of God who had to wander in the desert before they came to the Promised Land. This is directed to them: "For here we have no lasting city, but we seek the city that is to come" (Heb. 13:14). But another part of the Church has already made it home, in the peace of the eternal Sunday: "So then, there remains a Sabbath rest for the people of God" (Heb. 4:9). And these two parts of the Church belong together. They are bound together in the communion of saints, to which all who belong to Christ are bound, the living and the dead, and those not yet born.

Yes, in the Church of God we belong together not only with those who confess the faith rightly today, but also with those who have confessed the faith before us, and with those not yet born who will confess him after us. This is the communion of the saints that we confess in the Creed. It is the communion of saints we are made aware of on All Saints' Day, the 1st of November, when this is understood evangelically. And it is only understood rightly when it is understood in light of what happened on the Eve of All Hallows [Halloween][213] 1517. There is no stronger motive to stand in the faith, in the true confession, than to remember the generations that believed and confessed before us, "Remember your leaders, those who spoke to you the word of God" [Hebrews 13:7a].

So the innumerable crowd that confessed the Christian faith and was faithful unto death steps before our soul. And

---

[213] Halloween, properly understood, means the eve of All Saints' Day; the literal translation of the German. Halloween is a Christian holy day and should be celebrated as such.

we remember the leaders who spoke the Word of God to the German people for over a thousand years, the famous and the nameless, the known and the unknown. We all know what it means that true teachers once spoke the Word of God to us. We know that it is the crown of the teaching position, of pedagogy, when a teacher teaches his students the Word of God. It is a sign of barbarism descending upon us when a people no longer want such teachers. It is a sign of the decline of our spiritual life when German Universities, or what is left of them, shame their greatest teachers, those who once taught and explained the Word of God from the rostrum. But just as the German people forget in unthankfulness or deny out of cowardice those who spoke the Word of God to them, there is one the German people cannot forget, their greatest teacher, Dr. Martin Luther. The results that followed him do not allow them to explain him away as the spiritual *Führer* of the nation in his time or the representative of a race. Because then we would not be able to understand how the results spread out not only throughout Germany, but all of Europe. Therefore they only allow for one explanation, that Luther had spoken the Word of God so deeply and clearly as to surpass all other teachers in our history. Therefore, the language of his Bible translation became the mother language of all Germans, as it always means a new epoch in the history of every language when they are given the instrument of the divine Word.

This is what Catholic theologians of our day have found in their study of the history of the liturgy to be the greatest meaning Luther has for Germany and the Christian West. They have made the remarkable observation that Luther gave the German people that which had been withheld from them since the day of Boniface [d. June 5, 754], that which Wulfila [310–383] gave the Goths, and Methodius [815–April 6, 885] and Cyril [ca 826–Feb. 14, 869] gave the Slavs: the Bible and the Divine Service in their mother tongue. One of the Catholic theologians studying Luther's German Mass [*Deutsche Messe*][214] called it the first serious attempt to create a German liturgy of the people with unique linguistic and musical means. He named Luther's festival songs the absolute unequalled model of a German church song, and explained the triumphal march of the Reformation as the power of the old evangelical Divine Service that would even move a seriously deaf spectator and listener in the church.

To understand the intent Luther had, one only needs to remember one fact. The Lord's Supper had already been celebrated in Germany for eight hundred years, yet the congregation had never heard the words of institution in the church because the Roman mass was read silently in Latin. Now, for the first time, our Lord Jesus Christ's testament rang loud and clear in Luther's German Mass [*Deutsche Messe*] every Sunday during the Divine Service in the old evangelical church: "Our Lord Jesus Christ on the night when he was betrayed . . ." Yes, "remember your teachers [*Lehrer*], those who spoke to you the word of God" [Heb. 13:7, author's translation]. And when Germany shames

---

[214] AE 53.53–90; WA 19:72–113. MH

itself today, the day of Luther's Reformation, because one attempts to undo his confessionalism in the official history and to silence the fact that he was Germany's and Christendom's greatest teacher because he spoke to us the Word of God and nothing else, we will not be ashamed of the faith he confessed and did not deny before the world. And when the Evangelical Lutheran Church becomes a small church among our people, the strong and confrontational voice of the great teacher of our church will still ring in her with exhortation and warning. "Remember your teachers, those who spoke to you the word of God. Consider the outcome of their way of life, and imitate their faith" [Heb. 13:7, author's translation].

But why is Martin Luther the greatest in the long line of teachers in the Church, who have spoken the Word of God from generation to generation? Because, no other man had understood the Word so profoundly. Because God's Word is something so completely different than all the words of men. Any man's word rings once, as it is with the words of great poets. There will come a time when no one knows Homer [800–701 BC] or Shakespeare [1564–1616] or Goethe [1749–1832], but the Lord's Word remains forever. Words of men have great uncompromising effect. The command of a lord or an army commander can uncompromisingly alter the destiny of whole peoples. But the power of a man's word always comes to an end. Every word of man kicks up against another word that is its boundary. No word of man is almighty, but God's Word remains living and powerful because it is the Word of the eternal Almighty. It is the Word through which all things are made. It is the Word of the one who judges all the living. It is the Word of the forgiveness of sins, the Word that brings redemption. That is something no human word can do. It is the Word that has become flesh in Jesus Christ, as John said [John 1:14].

He himself is the eternal Word of God. "The name," so says the Revelation of John, "by which he is called The Word of God" (19:13). The Word of God proclaimed is Jesus Christ proclaimed. "To him all the prophets bear witness" (Acts 10:43). "But we preach Christ," said Paul of the sermons of the apostles (1 Cor. 1:23). He, Jesus Christ, is the content of the sermon of the Church. He is the Redeemer, the Lord, and that is the proclamation of the teachers of the Church at its beginning. That is the message that is handed down from one generation to another. The proclamation comes and goes, but the proclamation always remains the same. "Jesus Christ is the same yesterday and today and forever" [Heb. 13:8]. This, this and nothing else, is the content of the Christian religion. This is what Luther had called the Church to remember always, a Church that had forgotten the Word of God among so many words of men, the words of human religions and human philosophies.

Luther is among the great "Christologians," the great witnesses of Christ in the Church. Like the great theologians of the Ancient Church such as Irenaeus [d. ca. 202] and Athanasius [296–May 2, 373], so he had stood still in deep, deep respect before the great mystery of the revelation of God. "The Word became flesh" (John 1:14). "Great indeed, we confess, is the mystery of godliness: He was manifested in the flesh" (1 Tim. 3:16). He sat still in worship his whole life before the mystery of the person Jesus Christ, a mystery inaccessible to all human reason, "where God and humanity are united in one, and appeared in all perfected fullness." What the Fathers of the Greek Church in the fourth and fifth centuries had worked out in deep examination of the Holy Scriptures in reverent, prayerful, reflection over the Word of God, what the Church of the ancients in the ecumenical council[215] faithfully confessed and defended against the rationale of philosophy, that Jesus is true God, God of God, Light from Light, very God of very God, being of one substance with the Father, and yet true man—these deep truths Luther had not only kept together with the doctrine of Holy Communion in his theology, but also thought through anew and rethought. In so doing he also expressed them so simply and clearly that the simplest Christian, yes, even a child, was able to report, "Whom all the world could not enwrap, lieth He in Mary's lap; A little child he now is grown, Who everything upholds alone."[216] That is the dogma of [The Council of] Nicaea [325]. Or we think about how he expressed the dogma of [The Council of] Chalcedon [Oct. 8–Nov. 1, 451], the teaching of the two natures of Christ, in his catechism: "I believe that Jesus

---

[215] The Nicene Creed was adopted by the Council of Niceae in AD 325 and revised by the Council of Constantinople in AD 381. MH
[216] AE 53.241; WA 35.434. MH

Christ, begotten of the Father from all eternity, and also true man, born of the Virgin Mary, is my Lord."[217] This explanation of the Second Article has been called the most beautiful sentence in the German language, and it is the most beautiful sentence of our language, not only because of the form, which only a very great master of the language and a greater master of prayer could shape, but because of its contents. Because therein, the eternal Word of God is expressed, the eternal Gospel: "Jesus Christ is the same yesterday and today and forever" [Heb. 13:8].

"Remember your leaders, those who spoke to you the word of God" [Heb. 13:7]. Luther spoke the Word of God to our people, and even more, to the Christendom of the world as no other, because he, like no other, had proclaimed that God's eternal Word in person is "Jesus Christ . . . the same yesterday and today and forever." But what qualified him to understand Jesus Christ more deeply than other teachers of the Church? What had equipped him with such power to witness to the world? Allow me to tell you about an experience. As a young pastor I was still working on my sermon late on a Saturday night. When I finished, I opened the window and looked out into the dark autumn night. There I heard a bloodcurdling cry: "Help! Help!" A cry as I had only heard on the battlefield, a cry a man shouts in the angst of death. It happened that it was a man who, while drunk, had fallen in the river that runs through the city and was drowning. No one could find him in the darkness. And these screams that I will never forget

---

[217] SC, Creed II.

made it clear to me what the Gospel is, what the preaching of the Gospel in the Church ought to be. It ought to be the answer to the last question of men, the question that is nothing other than the desperate cry for a Savior from men sinking in death. Not the theoretical answer, "There is a Savior," but more. Because the Gospel is the call of the Savior himself. "I am he, fear not. I am coming, to seek and bless, that means to save what is lost. I am the bread of life. I am the way, and the truth, and the life. I am the resurrection and the life. Come to me all, your sins are forgiven" [see John 6:35; 14:6; 11:25; and elsewhere]. So he says in the Gospel.

From this one can understand to what extent Luther understood the Lord Christ even more deeply than the great teachers of the Church in the ancient world and Middle Ages. The theologians of the Church of the East had bowed low before the mystery of the incarnation: "who for us men and for our salvation came down from heaven and was incarnate by the Holy Spirit, born of the Virgin Mary and was made man." So they expressed it in the Nicene Creed. And then came the theologians of the West, the teachers of the Latin Church, and asked, *Cur Deus Homo?*[218] Why would God become man? What does it mean for us men and for our salvation? A thousand years and longer have passed since Augustine [Nov. 13, 354–Aug. 28, 430], the great teacher of the Western Church thought over and searched in the Scriptures. "What does it mean, for us? Why must God become man? Why can't men save

---

[218] Book written by Anselm of Canterbury (1033–April 21, 1109).

themselves? Why does he need grace? What is grace? Does grace alone save? Or can and must the man also do something?" That was the theme of the Western Church. It was not just a theoretical question for the theologians, but a practical question for all men, those who went into the cloisters to earn God's grace, the men of the Middle Ages who sought salvation in the sacrament of penance. And to these questions, Luther gave the answer:

> With thee counts nothing but thy grace
> To cover all our failings.
> The best life cannot win the race,
> Good works are unavailing.
> Before thee no one glory can,
> And so must tremble every man,
> And live by thy grace alone.[219]

And live by thy grace, thy grace alone. Because it is all, all for naught what we men can do. Luther had experienced this in the difficult fight during his years in the cloister where he, the monk of the Western Church, yet again had to fight the spiritual fight that dominated a millennium in the Church's history. Where he recognized the deep sickness of death in man, which our reason does not recognize, but is revealed only in God's living and powerful Word when it as a two-edged sword, as our Epistle to the Hebrews (4:12) once called it, uncovers our heart of hearts, and he as our judge tests the thoughts and desires of our hearts.

Natural man thinks of himself as good or reasonably

---

[219] AE 53.224. WA 35.492. See also *LSB* 607, "From Depths of Woe." MH

good. Yet in reality he is evil in heart and mind from youth. He calls himself pious, religious, faithful to God, or a God seeker, but in reality he is an enemy of God, an emperor against God, and his empire hides behind the mask of piousness. He is sick, deathly sick, but the worst of his disease is that he does not notice it himself. His sin, Luther once said, "Is so deep a corruption of nature that reason cannot understand it. It must be believed because of the revelation in the Scriptures."[220] So had Luther understood the deep distress of man. Every worry that man seeks to hide by all means, the means of reason, the means of philosophy, the means of art, even the means, when needed, of arguing with the Bible and persecuting the Church.

Luther uncovered therein, man in his deepest distress. There among all the masks of peace, certainty, self-assurance, and pride is nothing more than the lost, a creature of God trembling before eternal death, pleading before the judge: "In the midst of utter woe, When our sins oppress us, Where shall we for refuge go, Where for grace to bless us?"[221] Do you know this cry, O children of men? Or do you avoid overhearing it in the deepest depths of your soul, where your very own cry for help screams? Perhaps you won't hear him? Perhaps you calm yourself with the sleeping pills that the devil so easily gives Christendom today with such beneficial results? The

---

[220] SA III, I, 3; BKS 434..
[221] Martin Luther, "In the Very Midst of Life," WA 35.515; AE 53.274; *LSB* 755. MH

essential claim that the question of a gracious God is a question of the sixteenth century. Today there are completely different questions shouting for debate, for example the question of whether there is a god at all. No, the question of a gracious God is the essential question of all men even today. Then, where the question of a god is taken seriously, it is always a question of the judge. "Whither shall we flee away, Where a rest is waiting?"

Allow me a moment to pause! How has our Evangelical Church in Germany become so weak? Why does her proclamation no longer make the impression on men that she made in the sixteenth century? Why is that which she has to say to all of Christendom not taken seriously by other confessions? Is it because all of us, all who confess the church of the Lutheran Reformation, no longer take very seriously the deepest and last distress of our soul in our own lives? How will we awaken the recognition of sin in the masses when we ourselves do not recognize it? When we have forgotten that all of us, even faithful Christians, remain in death, Adam's children, emperors against God, sinners who daily and richly need the forgiveness of sins? When we no longer hear the voice of our heart of hearts crying daily, "In the midst of utter woe, When our sins oppress us, Where shall we for refuge go, Where for grace to bless us?" Only when we do that will our sermons be credible.

Because of this, Martin Luther found faith in the sixteenth century. For this reason, he has found understanding in India, China, and Japan today. Because one feels it in him: He is one who has gone through the deepest distress of man, who understands the deepest distress of all men: "Where shall we for refuge go, Where for grace to bless us?" Oh friends, when our soldiers return home from the hell of the Russian war, where all the illusions of the greatness and gloriousness of alleged good men is destroyed, where they have seen man in his complete misery, where they themselves have experienced what it means to be helpless creatures before the omnipotence of death, then they might help us in Germany understand again what it means to ask, "Where shall we for refuge go, Where for grace to bless us?" and then cause the day to come for many, many men of our day when they will once again understand what Luther continues to sing in his hymn.

> To thee, Lord Christ, thee only.
> Outpoured is thy precious blood,
> For our sins sufficing good.
> Holy and righteous God,
> Holy and mighty God,
> Holy and loving gracious Savior,
> Everlasting God,
> Let from thee us fall not
> From the comfort of thy faith.
> Kyrie Eleison.[222]

Then may the day come when the great song of the Reformation with which the German people once sang Luther's doctrine of justification in their hearts, "Dear

---

[222] AE 53. 276; WA 35.515. See also "In the Very Midst of Life," *LSB* 755. MH

Christians, Let Us Now Rejoice." The hymn we sang before the sermon, not as a song of the German people, but the song of the Church of Christians in Germany. A song about the living faith, about that which alone is our salvation, our life, our justification, our blessedness, because Jesus took all that is ours on himself, all our distress, our sin, the wrath of God against our sin, all our distress over death, and as our brother he has given us all that is his: eternal justification, guiltlessness, and blessedness. As Luther's song sings,

> He said to me: "Hold thou by me,
> Thy matters I will settle;
> I give myself all up for thee,
> And I will fight thy battle.
> For I am thine, and thou art mine,
> And my place also shall be thine;
> The enemy shall not part us.
> "He will as water shed my blood,
> My life he from me reave will;
> All this I suffer for thy good—
> To that with firm faith cleave well.
> My life from death the day shall win,
> My innocence shall bear thy sin,
> So art thou blest forever.[223]

"So art thou blest forever," beloved congregation, that is grace. The sermon of Jesus Christ is the sermon of grace. We need this grace more than ever today.

Because we live in a world without grace, in a world that no longer thinks it needs grace and that now sees

---

[223] AE 53.220; WA 35.493. See also *LSB* 556, "Dear Christians, One and All Rejoice."

where they end up without grace, because grace exists in Jesus Christ alone and nowhere else in the world. This is what the man taught us, the man we remember today as the Reformer of the Church. "Remember your leaders, those who spoke to you the word of God. Consider the outcome of their way of life, and imitate their faith. Jesus Christ is the same yesterday and today and forever. Do not be led away by diverse and strange teachings, for it is good for the heart to be strengthened by grace" [Heb. 13:7–9]. Only grace and faith in grace gives man a strengthened heart. And what do we need at this time more than a strengthened heart! It is not received from the philosophy that would extol itself as a substitute for the Christian faith today, a so-called strong, manly, heroic, and tragic worldview, the strong heart staying positive toward fate when it comes, which, when one looks close is only the fateful faith of the unconscious. It deadens the inner voice of the heart of hearts, the scream of distress, "Where shall we for refuge go, Where for grace to bless us?"

Between the blind, hopeless belief in fate and the strong faith in the Savior, Jesus Christ, we all have to choose. And the choice and the fight between both would be the theme of the future. There, each of us must choose, beloved Christians, you and I, all of us. Perhaps the number of those who would choose faith in the Savior, Jesus Christ, would be modest. And perhaps we worry ourselves thinking about the future of our church. But the worries about the Church the Lord Christ has reserved for himself. He has his people even today. Yes, it is not we who choose for ourselves, but he who has chosen for us. "You did not choose me, but I chose you" (John 15:16). Then how does Luther say it? "We are not the ones who can preserve the church, nor were our forefathers able to do so. Nor will our successors have this power. No, it was, is, and will be he who says, 'I am with you always, to the close of the age' [Matt. 28:20]. As it is written in Hebrews 13, 'Jesus Christ is the same yesterday, and today, and forever' [v. 8], and in Revelation 1, 'He who is and who was and who is to come.' [v. 4] This is his name and no one else's; nor may anyone else be called by that name."[224] Yes, no one else's name, praise be to Jesus Christ in eternity. Amen.

---

[224] AE 47.118; WA 50.476.35f. MH

The Mystery of the Last Things
Matthew 25:1–13[225]

Then the kingdom of heaven will be like ten virgins who took their lamps and went to meet the bridegroom. Five of them were foolish, and five were wise. For when the foolish took their lamps, they took no oil with them, but the wise took flasks of oil with their lamps. As the bridegroom was delayed, they all became drowsy and slept. But at midnight there was a cry, "Here is the bridegroom! Come out to meet him." Then all those virgins rose and trimmed their lamps. And the foolish said to the wise, "Give us some of your oil, for our lamps are going out." But the wise answered, saying, "Since there will not be enough for us and for you, go rather to the dealers and buy for yourselves." And while they were going to buy, the bridegroom came, and those who were ready went in with him to the marriage feast, and the door was shut. Afterward the other virgins came also, saying, "Lord, lord, open to us." But he answered, "Truly, I say to you, I do not know you." Watch therefore, for you know neither the day nor the hour. (Matt. 25:1–13)

"It is absolutely horrible." These words are used over and over again to describe the impression this Gospel gives to those who have witnessed the words and actions of Christ with their eyes and ears. We who have just heard this parable of the ten virgins, which the Church reads as the last Gospel of the Church Year, have felt something of this horror deep within our frightened hearts. There lies a deep mystery within this parable, as in all the parables Jesus

---

[225] *Predigt: Letzter Sonntag im Kirchenjahr (20 Nov 1938) "Das Geheimnis der Letzten Dinge."* Feuerhahn no. 216a. MH

gave concerning the kingdom of heaven, the unfathomable mystery of the last things. Therefore, no one can truly explain such a parable so that the picture that we have noticed here, which is so often depicted in art, is clear. The picture is of a rural wedding in Palestine with the virgins burning lamps waiting for the bridegroom, whom they will escort to the wedding hall.

But the behavior of the people in this story is inexplicable and completely incomprehensible. The utter foolishness of the five virgins, who thought the oil in their lamps would last, is incomprehensible. The harshness of the others who refused to share their oil with them is also incomprehensible. "There will not be enough for us and for you" [Matt. 25:9]. Was there no other way to share the existing oil? We ask this question from a human point of view. And if, finally, they all escorted the bridegroom with weak light or dark lamps, would they not have spared him the embarrassment this had brought? But the behavior of the bridegroom is completely incomprehensible. It is, after all, a wedding and everyone is supposed to be joyous! Why does he answer so unmercifully? "Truly, I say to you, I do not know you" [v. 12], when he heard them request, "Lord, Lord let us in" [v. 11].

We are not to understand this story as one that truly portrays men. Men invited to an earthly wedding do not behave so foolishly. Earthly wedding guests are not so foolish and so unhelpful. An earthly bridegroom is not so relentlessly harsh and strict. No one here would like to be invited to an earthly wedding like this.

Only those who have a feeling for this strangeness, for the incomprehensibleness of our Gospel, only those who are horrified by the riddle in this parable are capable of hearing what Jesus has to say to us here. He will not impart human wisdom to us. This is not some picture book or fable with a moral lesson to be told to children. He doesn't speak to us of things we know, but things we do not know of, a very frightening thing that our reason finds incomprehensible, that which we call the last things. He speaks about the last things that have not yet come to be, but will be, about the great Judgment Day to which the New Testament shows the history of the world running with great strides.

"*Then* the kingdom of heaven would be like ten virgins who took their lamps and went to meet the bridegroom" [Matt. 25:1, emphasis added]. *Then* this parable will be fulfilled. *Then* the foolishness of the foolish and the wisdom of the wise will be revealed to you. *Then* it will not be of any help to men. *Then* divine patience will end. *Then* the door of the kingdom of heaven will open for the one and be closed for the other irrevocably, relentlessly forever. *Then* he himself who told us this parable will speak the words that sound so harshly inhuman to us because they are the words of divine justice! "Truly, I say to you, I do not know you" [Matt. 25:12]. *Then*, yes then, this parable will be fulfilled. No, he who has told us will fulfill it himself. He who is holy and true, he who the Revelation of St. John calls the One "who opens and no one will shut, who shuts and no one opens" [3:7].

He "who shuts and no one opens" is the one who speaks to us in this Gospel. It is he of whom we confess corporately every Sunday that it is really true. And this we have confessed of him before with our hearts and mouth: "Who sits at the right hand of God the Father Almighty, from thence he will come to judge the living and the dead." Do we take this confession seriously? Do we understand what it means? We must be clear about this, dear congregation. Millions of our people that belong to the Church outwardly no longer know of a divine judgment and a judge of the world. The thought that there exists a court of judgment to which every man and every person goes is extinguished in the souls of men. This is perhaps the deepest revolution that the Christian West, and with them also the German people, has gone through in the last two hundred years. In any case, it signifies a deeper revolution than the alteration of the worldview given to us by the natural sciences, with which we had nothing to do.

One used to portray the picture so well, that the men of the Bible and the men of the Middle Ages and the Reformation had a childish and primitive view of the world: the earth in the center of the universe, over which were the heavens as the dwelling of God, and under which was hell. This worldview was destroyed by the discoveries of Copernicus [1473–1543], so men say. For us the earth is no longer the center of the universe, and the immense space of the universe has taken the place of the old heavens. Where would there be a place in this universe for him who is coming on the clouds of heaven to judge the world?

Where is there room for a heaven as the place for the saints, and for hell as the place for the damned?

But to this we must accordingly reply, "This so-called childish and naïve worldview with its three tiers is not the worldview of the Bible." There is certainly a picture in the Bible of a wholly divided world between heaven, earth, and hell, of this side and the other side. Paul and John do not give the same picture of the world, but already in the Bible people knew that you could only speak of these things in pictures because they are far above the powers of our imagination. When they spoke of the throne of God, they knew it was not proper to think it was actually like a human king's throne. When they spoke of God's dwelling in the heavens, they didn't forget what the Old Testament says. "Heaven and the highest heaven cannot contain you" (1 Kings 8:27). And when the New Testament tells us that he ascended into heaven and sits at the right hand of God [Acts 2:33], that means, Christ shares in the omnipresence, the omnipotence, and the eternity of God equally, and that he is with us to the end of the earth (Matt. 28:20).

All the greatest teachers of the Church, from the days of the apostles to the time of the old Evangelical Church in the sixteenth and seventeenth centuries fully understood this. They were not foolish children. They thought just as deeply and astutely as modern teachers. Just as the great truth of creation and the fall into sin, the incarnation and the resurrection of Christ, the reconciliation and the consummation is completely independent of our natural scientific worldview, so the truth remains among all conceivable future worldviews that the Holy Scriptures speak of, with the old picture in the Book of Daniel (7:13–14): "Behold, he is coming with the clouds, and every eye will see him, even those who have pierced him, and all tribes of the earth" (Rev. 1:7). And the Creed says to the Church, "from thence He will come to judge the living and the dead."

No, that was not the actual revolution in the spiritual life of the Christian West, that our world and our picture of heaven have been confused. Such revolutions have already happened often. The revolution is that the men of this generation have stopped talking about the Lord Christ as the judge of the world and have abolished the world's judge. It was in the eighteenth century that Christian Europe, also our German people, were restrained by thought of a divine judgment in which every man and every person in every race on earth must account for themselves—a judgment in which all would be revealed, even hidden sins. Every act of violence and every violation of the Law, every lie and every act devoid of love, all guiltiness would be found out.

This faith was not only the assumption for the history of the Western Church, but also for the whole history of Western Civilization. Who will understand anything of the Middle Ages without understanding the violence of *Dies Irae*,[226] which rang through each century as the song of the angry Judgment Day? Who will then understand the

---

[226] *Dies Irae* are the beginning words of a song by Thomas von Celano (ca 1190–1255), "Day of wrath, day of mourning."

political history of the Reformation when they do not know how the question of the gracious God and of the justification of sinners can deeply move an entire people. That ended in the eighteenth and nineteenth centuries. Then the time came in which Claus Harms [1778–1855], in his thesis for the Reformation Jubilee of 1817, said, "The forgiveness of sins at least cost something in the sixteenth century. In the nineteenth it's completely free, and men freely reward themselves with it. At that time they stood higher than us, they were nearer to God."[227] It was at that time the great Goethe said, "How can one live when one does not daily give absolution to himself and others." That was what became of the daily and rich forgiveness of sins that Luther spoke about in his catechism: The forgiveness of sins which men give themselves. He who forgives himself his sins is his own god. And so it is wholly consistent that the modern man has reversed the comparison between God and man.

In the Bible, and in the confession of the Church, God sits in the judge's seat and man sits in the defendant's seat. Modern men sit themselves in the judge's seat and place God in the defendant's seat. For Luther the theological theme was the justification of sinners. Ever since [Gottfried Wilhelm von] Leibniz's [1646–1716] theological writing, the chief theological theme has been the justification and

---

[227] Claus Harms, *Beleuchtung der fünf und neunzig reformatorischen Streitsätze, welche Herr Claus Harms gegen allerhand vermeintliches 'Irr- und Wirrwissen' dieser Zeit herausgegeben hat. Leipzig, 1818, bei Johann Ambrosius Barth*, p. 21. MH

defense of God. If God created the world, why is it so full of sorrow and injustice? Can you still face the world with faith in God? If God is love, how can you speak of the wrath of God? If we men already forgive each other, why does God require a terrible and bloody sacrifice to be brought forward before he will forgive? If God reveals himself in history, if he wills to choose a particular people, why did he choose the people of Israel? Why not a people of a different race? And with all these questions and accusations we modern men put the living God before the tribunal of our reason's demands.

That is the actual revolution that Christendom has gone through in the last century. It is one of fundamental foolish indignation. How can men dismiss him to whom all authority on heaven and earth is given? How can men abolish Judgment Day, which the whole world's history and the life of all men rush toward? We men who have changed places with God on the divine judgment seat may as well dismiss death since both are bound so irreconcilably together. "It is appointed for men to die once, and after that comes the judgment" (Heb. 9:27). And still death remains what he is, even though philosophers search to prove that there actually is no death; like the transient, the features of all earthly creation remain even when men are eternally enlightened! Our earth remains what she is, a monstrous mass grave in which all the living must go, in which all men and all people in all kingdoms and all cultures of this earth find their earthly end. So the judgment of God and the end of all human history remains. And he also remains, who sets the goal and the boundaries for all the earth: "the holy one, the true one, . . . who shuts and no one opens" [Rev. 3:7].

That is the truth that the world, that is the Christian West, has forgotten during the last century. And it is a very serious question on which the Church of today is judged: Are we still capable of proclaiming this truth to the world anew? The Gospel for this last Sunday of the Church Year speaks to us. It lays a serious question before us: Is the Church of the twentieth century not like the foolish virgins? We confess truly with the mouth our faith in him, he who comes to judge the living and the dead. But do we take this faith seriously? Is the foolishness of the foolish virgins perhaps not our foolishness? Have we not become tired and sleepy in the light of the Christian faith? Have we not let the lamps of hope, with which we would escort the coming Christ, go out? Do we not hear the powerful cry of this parable, "Wake up"? Will we wake up before it is too late? Before we must hear from his mouth the words of judgment, "Truly, I say to you, I do not know you" [Matt. 25:12]. Will we listen to what he says in this parable about his Gospel, the complete and deep comfort, the unspeakable pleasure that he promises, the unshakable faith in him, without tiring from the wait for his return?

Then there is the deepest comfort in this Gospel. He who closes and no one opens is the same as he who opens and no one closes [Rev. 3:7], and this is his true office. He who is coming to judge the living and the dead is he who says, "Whoever believes in me, though he die, yet shall he live" (John 11:25). He who asked of his heavenly Father, "Father, I desire that they also, whom you have given me, may be with me where I am, to see my glory" (John 17:24), intercedes for all who believe in him. The judge of the world is the reconciler of the world, who with his holy unbreakable Word said to us that no one who believes in him will be lost, and that is his true office—"[He] who opens and no one will shut" [Rev. 3:7].

What a feeling of comfort, what depth of salvation is enclosed in this truth that the Christian Church has experienced throughout time. Perhaps she has never experienced it as she did in the time of the sixteenth and seventeenth centuries, when the Reformation rediscovered the complete depth of the Gospel, a living witness of which is the great eternal song that we sang today, Philip Nicolai's [1556–1608] powerful "Wake, Awake, for Night Is Flying,"[228] and the faithfully practical song, "Jerusalem, O City Fair and High,"[229] that Johann Meyfart [1590–1642] wrote during the days of the Thirty Years' War [1618–1648]. When we spoke of this before, what it means for a people when they do not know any longer of a judgment and of a judge of the world, so we must now speak of how inwardly poor a people must become to lose their faith, when for many centuries they held to the Christian faith of the resurrection and eternal life.

But our people are well advanced on their way to this poverty. They are on the way to losing heaven. How clear

---

[228] *Wachet Auf; LSB* 516.
[229] *Jerusalem, Du Hochgebaute Stadt; LSB* 674.

the heavenly light of biblical prophecy shined over Germany in the seventeenth century! How rich our people were because of it! It was not poetical fantasy. But because the sun of Christ shined upon them, they strived after "the things that are above, where Christ is" (Col. 3:1). Then the sun went under, yet the stars shined. God, freedom, immortality, these contained little of the soul which they replaced, but the stars shined. Now it was dark. Now there are only earthly lights. It is night. This also means homelessness. Those who no longer had a home in heaven loved the earth so much more, but it was homelessness. Still we speak of eternity, of the resurrection, of immortality, but that is no substitute.

There is One who speaks to us in this distress. And when you think today about the dead, when you go over to a cemetery today and step on a grave, or in spirit step on a distant grave, then hear the voice that speaks here: "Whoever believes in me, though he die, yet shall he live" (John 11:25). Hear the prophecy, "I saw a new heaven and a new earth" (Rev. 21:1). "I am the Alpha and the Omega [the beginning and the end] . . . who is and who was and who is to come" (Rev. 1:8). "The holy one, the true one, . . . who opens and no one will shut, who shuts and no one opens" [Rev. 3:7]. Amen.

The Lord's Supper in the Life of the Church[230]
Week of the Church in Nürnberg
January 5, 1939

It is with the reality of the Church, as it is with all the realities of the faith, that children can comprehend her, and yet no one can understand her completely. Martin Luther says in the Smalcald Articles, "For, thank God, a seven-year-old child knows what the church is, namely, holy believers and sheep who hear the voice of their Shepherd. So children pray, 'I believe in one Holy Christian Church.' "[231] And yet, the complete depths of this confession cannot be fathomed by even the longest Christian life, not even a life as rich in faith and experience as Luther's life. Yes, it is perhaps so that only when Christendom comes to the end of the age and looks back on all the centuries of her history will she understand the total size and gloriousness of what she confesses with these words: I believe in one holy and catholic Church.

During these hours, we will ponder the miracle of the Church as we speak of the Lord's Supper, because the Church and the Sacrament of the Altar belong together in a completely different manner. There are three marks by which the teachings of our confessions recognize the Church: the *Gospel*, *Baptism* and the *Lord's Supper*.

---

[230] *Das heilige Abendmahl im Leben der Kirche (5 Jan. 1939) in Tagungsbericht: Kirchliche Woche Nürnberg vom 1. Bis 5. Januar 1939, Nürnberg: Verlag des Evang. Gemeindesblattes, 1939*, pp. 188–200. Feuerhahn no. 218. MH

[231] SA 3, XII, 2–3; BKS 459. MH

Everything else that the Church may have can be done without in time of need, but these three things must be wherever Christ's Church wishes to be. The Church *must* proclaim the Gospel. It *must* baptize in the name of the triune God. And it *must* celebrate the Lord's Supper. And these three things are only found in the Church. There are many heart-rending spiritual messages in the world, but there is only one Gospel. Because the Gospel is the only grace-filled message of the forgiveness of sins according to Christ's will. According to Christ's will! It is the glory of Jesus Christ and the nature of his office as the Redeemer of the world that there is forgiveness of sins in him and his will alone. It is not found anywhere else in the world. "That is, in Christ, God was reconciling the world to himself, not counting their trespasses against them, and entrusting to us the message of reconciliation. Therefore, we are ambassadors for Christ, God making his appeal through us. We implore you on behalf of Christ, be reconciled to God. For our sake he made him to be sin who knew no sin so that in him we might become the righteousness of God" (2 Cor. 5:19–21). That is the Gospel and nothing else. With this Gospel, the Church has come to the people of the world. We should ponder for a moment the possibility of her coming to the world without the Sacrament, as for example the so-called Christian Quaker churches did. Can the Church call to men and cultures with the word of the Gospel alone? The answer is a definite: No! Without the *Sacraments,* the call of the Gospel would die, as a voice dies in the wind. Perhaps, it would echo softly for a while, but it would die. Therefore, *the Sacraments must accompany the preached Word.* This is shown by example at Pentecost where the first missionary sermon of the apostles was followed by the first missionary Baptism! "So those who received his word were baptized, and there were added that day about three thousand souls" (Acts 2:41). So a congregation was instituted, and there was a Church in the world. If one only preached on the mission field, and did not baptize, no Christian congregation would ever be instituted, but merely an institution for the care and support of a new worldview. If a congregation of baptized Christians abandons the celebration of the Lord's Supper, she will soon lack an understanding of Baptism. She would then become a religious organization that could not be distinguished from any other human institution.

How is the meaning of the Sacraments to be understood? We Christians of the twentieth century must once again begin to think the way the men of the Bible and the Reformers obviously thought. That is, we belong to God in *soul* and *body*, that Christ is not only the Redeemer of our soul but also the Savior, "who will transform our lowly body to be like his glorious body, by the power that enables him even to subject all things to himself." "Mighty in deed and word" (Luke 24:19). That was the impression that Jesus made on the people who believed in him. The *miracles* that Jesus did were not as it seems to the modern Enlightenment, more or less superfluous if not doubtful illustrations of his Word. Rather they were an important, essential aspect of his salvific work. "The blind receive

263

their sight and the lame walk, lepers are cleansed and the deaf hear, and the dead are raised up, and the poor have good news preached to them" (Matt. 11:5). That is the beginning of the kingdom of God. The miracles of Jesus are the dawn that precedes the full ascent of the sun. In him the redemption, which will be complete when the dead arise and God creates a new heaven and a new earth, was already secure. As now, the Church's proclamation of the Word when she preaches the glorious Gospel is none other than the continuation of the proclamation of Jesus, so the administration of the Sacraments, when done in accordance with their institution, is a work of salvation. In every Baptism and in every celebration of the Lord's Supper Christ performs the miracle today, which is an anticipation of that which will happen to us "until it is fulfilled in the kingdom of God" [Luke 22:16]. Therefore, *the proclamation of the Word and the administration of the Sacraments, and in the Sacraments again the Word and the outer elements belong inseparably together.* In this sense Luther said in the Large Catechism about Baptism: "This is the reason why these two things are done in Baptism: the body has water poured over it, though it cannot receive anything but the water, and meanwhile the Word is spoken so that the soul may grasp it. Since the water and the Word together constitute one Baptism, body and soul shall be saved and live forever: the soul through the Word in which it believes, the body because it is united with the soul and apprehends Baptism in the only way it can. No greater jewel, therefore, can adorn our body and soul than Baptism for through it we obtain perfect holiness and salvation, which no other kind of life, and no work on earth can acquire."[232] That is the truth which our Reformation fathers knew and which we have to learn again. Perhaps it is a consequence of the fact that modern Christendom has lost its understanding of the Bible that there have been so many more false teachings of men about the body circulating during this last century. Not only our soul but also our body will be redeemed. It is not only our soul that belongs to Christ but also our body. "Or do you not know that your body is a temple of the Holy Spirit within you, whom you have from God? You are not your own" (1 Cor. 6:19). "Do you not know that your bodies are members of Christ?" (1 Cor. 6:15). The Christian belongs to the Church not only in soul, but also in body. The Church is not only a spiritual congregation, like a school of philosophy, a society for the cultivation of a worldview, or what is called a "think tank" today, but it is a spirit-body congregation. Because that is so, the Church does not hover high above the lives of men like a Platonic or Hegelian School. Rather, it dwells deep within the real lives of men and cultures. Christ gave the Sacraments to the Church because she is one such spirit-body congregation that the whole of man belongs to completely. These Sacraments, Baptism and the Lord's Supper, are not merely metaphors or symbols of what God does for us; God actually works on us in them. They are not mere illustrations of the Gospel, visible representations of Christ's Word and deposits of his promise, *but they are*

---

[232] LC IV, 45–46; BKS 700. MH

particular acts of God in which his *Word* is served by an earthly *element* through which the whole man, body and soul, is redeemed. These Sacraments are as completely incomprehensible to the world as the Church to which they belong as her essential characteristics. They are as incomprehensible to the world as Jesus Christ and the miracles that tell of him. But we who believe in Christ cannot endeavor seriously enough to understand them in faith. And perhaps the right understanding of the Sacraments is an issue of life and death for our Church today in a way that most Evangelical Christians can no longer understand.

This will be made clear for us when we ask what *Holy Communion* means for the life of the *Church*. A look at the New Testament points us to the noteworthy fact that the authors of Scripture very seldom spoke about the Lord's Supper directly, but it permeates throughout in the background of the written historical accounts and apostolic letters. For example the Book of Acts hints at the great meaning "the breaking of bread" [e.g., Acts 2;42] had for the Early Church, but it does not tell the reader what the celebration actually was or the process in which it was done. The Christian reader knew that already, and the others didn't need to know. Had not Paul once been compelled by the quarrels and abuses of the Church in Corinth to write about the Lord's Supper explicitly in 1 Corinthians, then we would have no account of when and how the Lord's Supper was celebrated in Paul's congregation or what the apostles taught about it. The oldest text of Luke (which, like the Book of Acts, was written for Gentiles) has only the brief words of institution in the narration of the Lord's Supper [Luke 22:19–20.]. The Lord's Supper is missing altogether from the Gospel of John, even though he handles the Lord's farewell with particular detail [John 17]. The Early Church considered the Sacrament *of the Lord's Supper to be a mystery*, which should not be betrayed to the world. The words of institution, the process of the celebration, the earliest liturgies of the Lord's Supper have incidentally been retained from the remaining remnants of the New Testament. For example in the end of 1 Corinthians (16:22) they are warned not to share this with the non-Christian. Why not? One reason for this is that there would then be a false understanding. If anything of this leaked out to the public, it would then further this false understanding. "Truly, truly, I say to you, unless you eat the flesh of the Son of Man and drink his blood, you have no life in you" (John 6:53). Is it any wonder that when such words were heard by Gentile ears they gave substance to the rumor that Christians secretly ate the flesh and drank the blood of men behind closed doors? This stubborn rumor that played so great a role in the Christian trials is not an unimportant hint of the fact that the Early Church must have had a very realistic understanding of Lord's Supper. How could one take offence at Christian Communion in a world that was full of sacrificial meals and celebrations of communion if it was only a meal of commemoration or thought of as a mere spiritual communion? How would the Western Church explain it to those who didn't believe in Christ? They knew what the Sacrament meant because they believed in the incarnate Son of God; because they understood his death as the death of the Lamb of God, who bore the sins of the world; because they knew that he rose from the dead in his body as the first of them who sleep and that he ascended to the right hand of God and shares his omnipotence and omnipresence; because they knew that his yet-hidden glory would be visible to all men on the day of his return. Only on the basis of these articles of faith is it possible to understand the Lord's Supper properly.

Thus the Early Church, and with her the true Church of all ages, knew that Jesus did not just host an impressive farewell dinner with his disciples and command them to keep this celebration in his memory. They also knew that this meal was not just a mere anticipation of the feast he will celebrate with the redeemed in the kingdom of God. Certainly these both belong to the Sacrament, but they do not give an exhaustive description of the Sacrament's nature.

No, the nature of the Lord's Supper as the Church of the New Testament understood it was not in *remembrance* or in *hope*. The Lord of the Supper is not only he who once ate and drank this feast with his disciples. He is not only the one who we will eat and drink with when we see him in heaven. He is the present one who gave his Church something that would bridge the many centuries between his earthly life and the day of his return with this institution. Every attentive reader of the Bible knows what kind of deep disappointment filled the first generation of Christians because the day of his return remained so far off. "They will say, 'Where is the promise of his coming? For ever since the fathers fell asleep, all things are continuing as they were from the beginning of creation' " (2 Pet. 3:4). So people began to ask. It must be made very clear that this question is very serious for our nearly two-thousand-year-old Church. Where else is there a hope in this world that has remained unchanged even though century after century passes by without any visible fulfillment of it? Maranatha! "Come, Lord Jesus!" [Rev. 22:20]. For nineteen centuries the Church has prayed this prayer. This prayer, which is written at the end of the New Testament, already belonged to the Communion liturgy in Saul's days. How could she do that without flagging, literally "without omission"? She could only do it because it is fulfilled already in every celebration of Communion, because Jesus Christ is really present in any Communion celebration that is held according to his institution.[233] This is why the *Benedictus* is sung. This is why people already sang the *Sanctus* as part of the Communion liturgy in the first century. "Holy, holy, holy is the Lord." This is the heavenly Divine Service of the cherubim found in Isaiah 6. So we read in a letter from Rome to the Corinthians around AD 96: "Let us consider how the whole multitude of His angels stand by and serve His will. For Scripture says, 'ten thousand times ten thousand stood beside Him, and thousands of thousands served Him, and they cried, "Holy, holy, holy is the Lord of

---

[233] See FC SD VII.32. BKS 982. MH

Hosts, all creation is full of His glory" ' Let us too, therefore, gathered together in conscious harmony, cry to Him earnestly as with one voice."[234] Here we find the very same thought that is found in the Revelation of St. John (4:10–11; 5:8–14) that in the Divine Service, and this always means the Divine Service of the Lord's Supper, the sanctuary widens and heaven and earth become one. This is how our fathers understood it when they would pray, "May your Communion be my heaven on earth, until I am in heaven." As the Lord's Supper bridges the enormous time gap between the time of this world and time in the kingdom of God, so this Sacrament bridges the chasm between heaven and earth. Therefore it is *cibus viatorium*, the food of sojourners, who will not remain here in this state but look to the future. As Israel found manna in the desert [Exod. 16:31] and the water out of the rock [Num. 20:11], so God's people of the new covenant find the Lord's Table prepared for them as they journey out of Egypt, the here and now, to the promised land, through this world's comfortless desert. So they can continue on their way as Elijah "through the power of the same food." He is truly heavenly food, bread from heaven as the Bible calls the manna (Pss. 78:24; 105:40) and also calls the food of the Lord's Supper (John 6),[235] and not only in a symbolic sense. Wherever heaven is found, there "Christ is, seated at

---

[234] "The First Letter of Clement," *The Apostolic Fathers and American Translation.* Edgar J. Goodspeed (New York: Harper and Brothers Publishers, 1950), p. 66.

[235] See more of Sasse's views on John 6 in "Church and Lord's Supper" in *The Lonely Way I*, pp. 412ff. MH

the right hand of God" (Col. 3:1). So the Lord's Supper is truly our heaven on earth until we are in heaven, because the presence of Jesus Christ in the Sacrament of the Altar is yet another presence than that in which we believe he is everywhere, where two or three are gathered in his name. From the very beginning, the Church has found the mystery of the presence to be in the words that the Lord spoke over the bread and over the cup: "This is my body," "This is my blood of the New Testament," and not in the command to keep this celebration, "in remembrance of me" or in the anticipation of the promise, "until it is fulfilled in the kingdom of God." The deepest nature of the Sacrament is revealed solely in the words about the *body* and *blood* of the Lord. They are not metaphors. If they were mere metaphors, Jesus would have interpreted them that way himself or made it so obvious that this was the sense in which they should be interpreted so that there would be no possibility for doubt or dispute about it. The attempt to interpret the words of institution as metaphors and the institution of the Sacrament as a symbolic action in the sense of the prophetic and allegoric actions of the Bible has always led to contradictory results. If one will not accept that Jesus was speaking with dark riddles or that one can't trust him in this very hour, then the only thing that remains is the *literal* understanding. But then it is clear that the Eternal Son of God also took on flesh and blood for our sakes. The merciful *High Priest*, who at the same time is *the Lamb of God* that bore the sins of the world [John 1:29], consecrated himself (John 17:19) as the sacrifice for the sins of the world. He, who is the *Passover Lamb*, held the Passover with His disciples! So Jesus understood his own death. He, who is the one "priest forever" (Heb. 7:3) and at the same time is "the Lamb who was slain" [Rev. 13:8], gave himself as the one eternal, all-sufficient sacrifice. And as Israel ate the Passover when they were redeemed from slavery in Egypt and ate it again and again in remembrance of God's miraculous action, so the twelve ate the Passover of the New Covenant as the representatives of the new Israel (Luke 22:30), and the Church repeats this celebration continually, "in remembrance of me." As Israel ate the Passover Lamb, so ate the disciples, and so the Church eats the body of the Crucified, *because the Passover Lamb must be eaten* [Exod. 12:46]! Whoever takes offense at this must then also take offense at the sacrificial death of Christ. Since it is a miracle, our reason cannot comprehend that we are redeemed, "with the precious blood of Christ, like that of a lamb without blemish or spot" (1 Pet. 1:19). So it is also an incomprehensible miracle that we receive the true body and blood of the sacrificed Son of God in the Sacrament of the Altar, the crucified body that is at the same time the transfigured body. That is the teaching of the Holy Scriptures. This teaching presupposes that the work of redemption, as with the work of creation, effects the whole man, body and soul; that the Redeemer took on the nature of a true man; that the work of redemption must be completed through the sacrifice of his body and blood; that the redeemed belong to him in body and soul, and that we as members of the Church, "baptized into one body" (1 Cor. 12:13), who partake of the blessed bread and the blessed cup which is the Communion of the body and the blood of Christ (1 Cor. 10:16ff.), are members of his Body.

From this position it is to be understood that partaking of Holy Communion is essential to the life of the Church of the New Testament. It is the central focus of the Divine Service. In fact, it actually *is* the Divine Service. A Lord's Day without the Lord's Supper was completely inconceivable to the Early Church. Yes, even the old Lutheran Church of the seventeenth century found it hard to conceive of a Sunday without Holy Communion. Our liturgy is the result of the Lord's Supper. The ancient and beautiful name "Eucharist" reminds us still, therefore, that the Church's great praise and prayer of thanks originated in the Lord's Supper, because "Eucharist" means "prayer of thanks." And all the prayers and thanks of the Church are continuations of the prayer that Jesus Christ prayed to his heavenly Father when "he took bread, and when he had *given thanks*, he broke it" [Luke 22:19]. It is certainly no accident that the time of the great praise and thanksgiving songs of the Church is also the time in which the Church stands in awe of the Lord's Supper. It would take too long to show how each individual expression of the Church's life, from *diakonia* to the Church's self-understanding, is connected to and grows out of the Lord's Supper. However, if the deepest nature of the Church is that she is the Body of Christ, the connections are obvious. It is by the celebration of the Lord's Supper that the Church of all ages has come to understand its very being.

There is in the history of the Church no theologian who understood this connection as deeply as Martin Luther. The seriousness in which he dealt with the question of the Sacrament of the Altar is well-known, though it is often severely judged, and, in truth, no longer understood today even in Lutheran circles. This seriousness, however, is explained by Luther's deep insight into the inner unity between the *Gospel and the Lord's Supper*. There is no Lord's Supper without the Gospel. If a church, such as the Roman Catholic Church with its far-reaching events, forgets or adulterates the Gospel, there still remains a remnant of the Gospel in the Lord's Supper: "given and shed for you for the forgiveness of sins." And there is no Gospel without the Lord's Supper. If a church, as so often happens in Protestant movements, lets the Lord's Supper lapse, then the preaching of that church fades into a proclamation of human theories, and the Gospel of the Lamb of God who bore the sins of the world dies. This explains Luther's powerful double-fronted war for the *purity* of the Sacrament of the Altar against adulteration of the Roman sacrifice of the Mass, and for the *preservation* of the Sacrament of the Altar against the destruction of the Protestants, who because of their fight against the unbiblical teaching of the sacrifice of the Mass and transubstantiation also rejected the biblical teaching of the true presence of the body and blood of Christ under the forms of bread and wine.

Luther's view of the insoluble connection between the

Gospel and the Lord's Supper, and recognized by the written confessions of our Reformation, explains the dedicated faithfulness with which the Evangelical Church protected the Sacrament of the Altar. It could be said that in Germany the Lord's Supper has never had such meaning for the life of men as it had in the church of the Lutheran Confession during the sixteenth and seventeenth centuries. Yet, no one can say that at that time the *sermon*, which has the chief place in the Evangelical Divine Service, was too short. That century was also the greatest period of evangelical preaching the Church has known. The Church at that time understood well why she prayed: "May we keep your Word and Sacrament pure, until our end!"[236]

It was first in the eighteenth century that the process, which can hardly be called anything but the *Death of the Sacrament*, started. This is made most clear with a discussion of the statistics surrounding the Lord's Supper. At the beginning of this century there was still a record of Communion attendance in Lutheran Germany. We can draw a clear picture for ourselves from these records. As it happens, there would be on one festival day, for example the Reformation Festival of 1717, as many as 1,000 communicants in the Church of the Cross at Dresden. On one Sunday in the year 1701 there were 35,950 communicants in a single church in Breslau. In 1800 there were only 9,500. Communion attendance began to sink in

---

[236] *Ach Bleib Bei Uns*; Lord Jesus Christ with Us Abide, st. 2, by Nicolaus Selnecker, a favorite verse of Sasse, often quoted. See also *LSB* 585:5. MH

the middle of the eighteenth century. There was one period of increased attendance that accompanied the revival of the territorial churches, but ever since then there has only been a decline that continues through the nineteenth and twentieth centuries to our time. There are of course huge differences that remain between the individual state churches and congregations, but even so the following figures give an approximate picture of the development. Only 40 out of a 100 evangelicals went to Communion in the course of the year in 1904. Since 1920 the number has plummeted to less than 30. The official attendance records for the state churches in 1936 are as follows: Bavaria 54.88/100; Shaumburg-Lippe 53.50/100; Kurhesees-Waldeck 48.11/100; Baden 38.50/100; Württemburg 35.17/100 Nassau-Hessen 33.93/100; Hannover-Luth 33.50/100; Pfalz 32.55/100; Lippe 25.53/100; Sachsen 23.34/100; Altpreussen 20.45/100 (Grenzmark 43.20/100; Schlesien 31.37/100; Pommern 26.09/100; Westfalen 22.47/100; Ostpreussen 21.12/100; Brandenburg 21.03/100; Sachsen 17.79/100; Rheinprovinz 17.35/100; Berlin 9.84/100); Thüringen 18.90/100; Anhalt 16.38/100; Mecklenburg 14.70/100; Braunschweig 14.24/100; Hannover-Ref.13.42/100; Schleswig Holstein 9.82/100; Lübeck 9.37/100; Oldenburg 8.93/100; Eutin 8.75/100; Bremen 6.92/100; Hamburg 6.68/100. The average count for the regions of the German Evangelical Church in the year 1936 was 24.21/100. The hopelessness of these numbers is obvious, if one considers that in the same year (1936) 100 Catholics communed 1,396 times (in 1931 the number was 1,124). During this time twenty-four out of one hundred Evangelicals took Communion once, while each Catholic went to communion an average of fourteen times a year. Even if one thinks that these numbers can't be compared to each other without further details, they still point to something with irrefutable clarity: the Evangelical Church in Germany is in practice on the way to losing the Lord's Supper. The Sacrament of the Altar is becoming an individual prerogative of the Roman Catholic Church. If in Hamburg among 912,000 Evangelicals only 60,933 communicants were counted, which includes 14,608 confirmands and the families, it certainly cannot be asserted that the Sacrament, through which the Lord desires to preserve his Church on earth, still means much practically for this territorial church. It may well be asked what Luther would think of his Evangelical Church that is well on the way to losing the Lord's Supper. He would probably judge it as harshly as he judged the church of the Sacrifice of the Mass. *A church without the Lord's Supper must die!*[237]

So the question of the Lord's Supper and its meaning for the life of the Church leads to the recognition of the very deep distress in which the Evangelical Church of Germany finds itself today. But by looking this distress in the eyes we understand that it is not the result of external powers that oppose the Church but of our own deterioration. Our fall from the whole Gospel, the pure teaching, and the entire message of the Reformation has

---

[237] See *The Lonely Way I*, p. 422. MH

caused this. But this recognition, the painful recognition of our own guilt is the prerequisite for the renewal of the Church. For, just as there is no other way to salvation for the individual Christian than that of repentance, so there is also no other way for the Church. However, if we take this path in faith, realizing the depth of our defection from God and his Word, then we will know that at the end of this path is forgiveness, salvation, and the blessed Christ, our Lord, whose promise to us is true. He will also be the doctor of his Church, "its beloved Savior."

The Message of the Reformation in These Changing Times
November 19, 1942[238]

On the 31st of October 1942, twenty-five years will have passed since the Evangelical Christendom of Germany began the celebration of the four hundredth anniversary of the Reformation [1917]. There was no greater celebration than this even during times of peace.[239] I still remember the cloudy, foggy autumn morning in northern Germany, the Divine Service in the field and the celebration of Holy Communion that was the last for many of us. Immediately after the celebration, we were backed into one of the bloodiest of battles.[240] Even in the home, this day was anything but a brilliant holiday. And yet this jubilee had attained particular meaning, because with this celebration Evangelical Christendom began to have a new

---

[238] *"Der Höhepunkt der Reformation in der Zeitenwende."* In *Zeugnisse,* pp. 205–24. Feuerhahn no. 241. MH

[239] The Allies signed an armistice with Germany on November 11, 1918. MH

[240] "The resistance of the German Fourth Army, unusually wet weather, the onset of winter and the diversion of British and French resources to Italy, following the Austro-German victory at the Battle of Caporetto (Oct. 24–Nov. 19) allowed the Germans to avoid a general withdrawal, which had seemed inevitable to them in October." "Paschendaele," Wikipedia. Sasse wrote H. Kadai on August 29, 1965, when notified about an honorary doctorate. He quipped, "Yesterday I received the copy of the *Springfielder* with your congratulatory article. At first sight I felt a little as I felt when, coming down with five men out of 120 from Pachendale on the 7th on November 1917 (the day of the Bolshewist [sic] Revolution in Prussia), my sergeant major greeted me with the words, 'But we have buried you yesterday with military honors.' " Sasse-Junkuntz Correspondence, Ft. Wayne. *Letters to Lutheran Pastors* (St Louis: CPH, 2012), p. lv. MH

sense of the deepest essence of the Reformation. It is as if, with the all-encompassing grey of war, the notable encounter with death and the experience of the divine judgment that accompanies it, that modern men learned to understand the message of the Reformation anew, the message of the justification of sinners through faith alone.

Twenty-five years have passed since then, and what years! The council of history has rolled on with frightening speed. Revolutions of the earth have been completed to which a full century's worth of history belong. A few days after this Reformation festival, the Bolsheviks came into power in Russia. What have the people of the East experienced since then! Streams of blood and tears have flown. An old political and social world has been sunk, and a new one has risen up and has now been challenged in the supreme court of God. What kind of a change of destiny have the great peoples of the West experienced, who once stood at the height of world power! How the face of the earth has changed! People who had no state of their own before have grown to a stately existence and today their states have already been extinguished again. And if there seemed to be a hidden corner of the world somewhere that was shielded from all these upheavals, it has now been drawn into these world events by this second of the great world wars. When we think of our own people and the fate of Germany in these last twenty-five years, what changes in their spiritual and secular lives have occurred during this time when everything has been revolutionized? We live in a time of change without comparison.

What does the message of the Reformation mean in such a time of change? If twenty-five years ago it seemed for many people that the Reformation gave an answer to the ultimate questions of life, perhaps then it was only a conclusion to the great Christian era in the history of the German peoples? Are our people today not standing before a completely different era of man? And has not, so we are asked, the hour come in which for us and for all the world the message of the Reformation has been conclusively lost in its present meaning? How modest is the number of men who still understand it today? How narrow is the area of the Church in which they still play a roll! The men have been dead for four hundred years, they sacrificed body and soul, all they had, so that this message would remain and be preserved for them and their children. Today we are told men die for a completely different teaching. Today the world fights over things completely different than the doctrine of the justification of sinners and the Sacrament of Christ. How could it be otherwise! We no longer conduct our wars with the forces of the sixteenth century. We no longer regulate state societies and economy with the principles and methods of that time. How then should the teachings of the sixteenth century worldview still be the answer to the great questions of men in our time?

It is good and noteworthy that we take this question of the world in all seriousness and think about it in depth. Fourteen days ago we celebrated the Reformation. Today [Nov. 10] we remember the birthday of Martin Luther. Such days become days of remembrance in the Church for only one reason, that they will lead us to a deeper consciousness of that which Christendom was once given during the Reformation. Yes, it could be that the Reformation was only a significant event for the German people in Western history, and its message is merely one of the many messages that come to the surface to have great effect on the spiritual life of humanity but then pass away to make room for other messages to take their place.[241] What gives us the right, as the Evangelical Lutheran Church today, still to stand before our German people, before the Christendom of the world, and in world mission before all of humanity with this request: "Take this message. It is not merely a message of the sixteenth century. It has meaning for humanity even in these changing times!"

Yes, what gives us the right? What was it that once gave Luther the right to proclaim the message of the Reformation, the blessed message of the justification of sinners through faith alone? Because it simply is not the case that this message was a self-evident truth for the men of the sixteenth century or that it was something easier for them to comprehend at that time than it is today. Just the opposite! The men of that time were just as inclined to reject the message as they are in our time. There was the great church of that time in the West. For over a thousand years pious hearts and penetrating spirits came to her with

---

[241] For Sasse's magisterial treatment of the various "views" of what the Reformation was see *Here We Stand: Nature and Character of the Lutheran Faith* (New York & London: Harper & Bros., 1938). MH

the question of how sinners could be justified before God. And this church rejected Luther's answer to this question with all her spiritual and secular authority. And the same fact is true of the other great spiritual powers of the sixteenth century. There were the world powers of the humanistic education embodied in the great Erasmus [1466–1536], the Goethe [1749–1832] of that time. Through the mouths of these great and learned men, they said "no" to Luther's message of the justification of the sinner by faith alone. There were also the world powers of the modern religiosity that were born at that time. It was the piousness of these who broke with the institutions of the church, who would have no pope, but also no *"paper pope"* as they called the Bible. They would not believe, as Luther taught, that the Holy Spirit was given through the material means of grace in the Word and the Sacraments. They did not want an old but a new revelation; they wanted to experience God immediately and not base their religion on what past generations had experienced. So already in the name of the modern world then dawning they rejected Luther's doctrine of justification.

And so one could travel throughout the world of the sixteenth century and he would encounter this contradiction among the men of that time opposing the message of the Reformation everywhere. There is no objection to Luther's doctrine raised today that was not already raised then with the same intensity. Today he is reproached because national concerns were not of the last and highest value for him. Of course, this was already the reason the great national movement of the sixteenth century abandoned him. Over and against the nation, Luther dared to apply this word: "We should fear, love, and trust in God above all things." And the socialists of the nineteenth and the twentieth centuries have never forgiven him for the fact that something stood higher and more important to him than everything that we men understand as social justice, a completely different justice, a justice that men cannot create but that God gives us, the righteousness that comes through faith in Christ, the righteousness which avails before God.

No, the message of the Reformation was actually as strange in the sixteenth century as it is in the twentieth. The contemporaries of Luther found it just as difficult to believe as our own contemporaries. But then why was this faith found everywhere? How did it come to pass that this strange message, which the great spiritual powers of that time so decisively rejected and fought, still won the hearts of man? There is only one answer. The power this message claimed for itself was that it was nothing but the Gospel itself, the Gospel that applies to all men in every century. It came as a strange message to all men, to all peoples, and to all centuries to which it has come. It comes as a strange message because it is quite literally not of this world. But at the same time it comes as the message of God that will save men in their deepest distress, and for this reason, it is the final answer to the final question of every man.

The Gospel once came to the world as a strange message. And what we said before about the sixteenth century and how they already raised the objections then that are raised against the Gospel today, this is true of the first century also. A Jewish teaching, an invention of the Jew, Paul, they call the message of the justification of the sinner by grace alone today. There is no other teaching that has from the very beginning met with as much opposition from Judaism. "Go and learn what this means, 'I desire mercy, and not sacrifice.' For I came not to call the righteous, but sinners" (Matt. 9:13). The Jewish contemporaries of Jesus could not bear that. "This man receives sinners" (Luke 15:2). For this they nailed him to the cross. Then "who can forgive sins but God alone?" [Luke 5:21]. That a sinner can be closer to God than a righteous man, that the prodigal son comes away better off than his older brother in the parable [Luke 15:11–32], that the workers in the vineyard all received the same payment whether they worked an hour or the whole day [Matt. 20:1–16], that the thief on the cross was still unconditionally pardoned [Luke 23:39–43.], such high thoughts concerning grace looked like the end of all morals to the Jews. And it is the end of what the natural man understands about morals. And the claim that we men need grace, that we are sinners who cannot save ourselves, wasn't this claim the first to arouse the objections of our era?

No, those were the same objections the Greeks raised concerning the sermons of the apostles. And just as Friedrich Nietzsche [1844–1900] and his disciples are outraged by the contemptible, slavish morality of the Christian doctrine of sin, just as Luther's profound doctrine of sin encountered passionate opposition from the educated minds of the sixteenth century, so too did the great opponents of the Church in ancient times. Celsus [second century], Porphyry [234–305], and Julian [The Apostate, 331–363] took offense to the Christian proclamation of man's sin and God's grace because it destroyed the dignity of people. Neither is it anything new today when one protests against the idea that a unique historical event, the death and resurrection of Jesus Christ, should bring our redemption. That the historical man Jesus of Nazareth is the Son of the eternal God in the flesh, that he is "the Lamb of God who takes away the sin of the world" [John 1:29], and that he will finally come again to judge the living and the dead—those sentences stopped any understanding of Christianity among even the most benevolent of the philosophically educated in antiquity. That is shown in the seventeenth chapter of Acts.

No, the Gospel as the sanctifying message of the forgiveness of sins for Christ's sake, of the justification of the sinner alone through the faith, was no more accessible in the early centuries than in our time. It has struck men of all ages as a foreign message incomprehensible to reason. But it also strikes as the message of God that gives an answer to the final question and the deepest distress of all men. Then the final question of man is the question of whether he, the fallen, guilt-laden creature of God can stand before his Maker and Lord. As the moving song of the Middle Ages was sung concerning Judgment Day: *Quid sum miser tunc dicturus, Quem patronum?* "What shall I, frail man, be pleading? Who for me be interceding?"[242] The natural man does not want to know this kind of angst. He denies it, and yet it is still there determining the hidden life of all men. This angst concerning divine judgment is visible in the angst of men concerning death because death and judgment belong together. "And just as it is appointed for man to die once, and after that comes judgment" (Heb. 9:27). Yes, the death of men is something quite different than the death of animals. It is more than the extinguishing of life, more than a sinking into nothingness, because it is judgment at the same time.

An inkling of this judgment lives in all earnest religions of the Gentiles. It is there in the earliest Hellenism at the dawn of the greatest culture in antiquity. And again it settled back into the evening shadows of these cultured men in the late Greek and Roman world, as the grave inscriptions and the redemption mysteries in the days of the Roman Caesar show. In between, the days of light in the classic, ancient world are where the glorious art and the great science of men appeared amidst angst before the judgment to come. For the spirit of man allows no means to be free of this angst to go untried. He dreams in his religion of a god who is no longer a judge. He dreams up an ethical system in which a man is no longer a sinner, but an incomplete person that is still basically good. He thinks up a philosophy of death in which essentially there is no

---

[242] Seventh stanza of the Medieval Latin hymn, *Dies irea!* "Day of Wrath!" It was used for centuries in the Roman Requiem Mass, used especially on All Saints. Written by Orsini or Thomas of Celano in the thirteenth century. MH

longer any death, nor judgment, but only the apparently harmless passing to a higher life or the gentle extinguishment into a blessed unconsciousness. This is what the ancient Greeks did. Thus all mankind has undertaken this dream together. So it has been done in a very admirable manner in the modern world for the last 250 years.

One has to visualize this atrocious past if one wants to understand our times. About the year 1700, the confessional still stood in the churches of the West, even in the Lutheran churches, and a man could hardly picture a life without confession, without repentance, without forgiveness because everyone then living saw the Day of Judgment dawning on the horizon of his life. He knew that he was on the way to judgment. The primal question of the Christian West that had moved so many generations was still the question of these men: the question of a gracious God. When the ancient world was disintegrating, it was this question that led men into church under the influence of Christian sermons concerning repentance. For many, many centuries it led men into cloisters. It also led Luther into a cloister during the difficult spiritual struggle concerning the salvation of his soul. It also governed those who stayed in the world. [Holy Roman] Emperor Henry IV [1050–1106] had to obtain Absolution in Canossa, he could not live without it as either emperor or as man.[243] Can a man picture

---

[243] The famous "Investiture Controversy" where for deposing pope Gregory VII (Hildebrand) Henry himself (when the tables turned) stood outside the castle gates of Canossa for days (January 25–27, 1077)

one of the great German Kaisers, the mightiest dukes, or the poets and master builders, the sailors of the Hanseatic League, the great businessmen, the artisans, and the farmers without the Sacrament of repentance, and without Absolution? It is impossible.

And so it was in the century of the Reformation, the only difference being that the question of a gracious God, and peace, and forgiveness was taken much more seriously than in the centuries before. If one tries to understand the Reformation as a protest of the Germanic spirit against the Church of Rome, he has not yet scratched the surface of that history. He does not yet know how serious the question of a gracious God was taken. The Reformation occurred because of the forgiveness of sins. How do I get a gracious God? What does it mean that the eternal Son of God came down from heaven and became man for us men and for our salvation? That was the question that the Reformation revolved around. All other questions were secondary, and because this was taken so seriously, Luther's answer was also taken seriously. Therefore his doctrine of justification of the sinner by faith alone was not a theory for theologians as is thought today, but a delightful truth that the people of every class sang about from deep in the heart in the great hymns of the Reformation, and above all else in Luther's great Reformation hymn "Dear Christians, One and All Rejoice."[244]

---

begging for the pope to lift his excommunication. MH

[244] *Nun Freut Euch, lieben Christen gmein;* WA 35.422–25, *LSB* 556. MH

There probably never have been so many German hearts that have experienced the sensation of such deep bliss as when it was learned what it means concerning the Lord Christ: "That he has born all my sins, that he atoned for all the sins of man on his cross, that therefore there is forgiveness in him and him alone, that this forgiveness is offered to us completely free; that we only need to flee to him in faith; that we have no standing of our own in the court of God, we have nothing to show, no performance, no piety or justification of our own. We only have him, as it is confessed in this simple verse: 'Jesus, Thy blood and righteousness, My beauty are, my glorious dress; 'Midst flaming worlds, in these arrayed, With joy shall I lift up my head.' "[245] Everyone could understand this and experience this profound truth because the question of a gracious God was the question above all questions. And this was true in the following generations up till the time just before 1700 in all of Christian Europe, and not just among the Lutherans, but also among the Catholics and Reformed.

But then the great revolution that we call the *Enlightenment* came. Its essence was that natural human reason is the final judge of what is true and false, and man is also the judge of the Word of God. Naturally, concerning the truths of the biblical revelation, this reason could only allow that to remain which it was able to comprehend, and that did not leave much. The living God of the Bible and of the old Christian faith dwindled in the consciousness of

---

[245] Nicolaus Ludwig von Zinzendorf (1700–1760); An English translation by John Wesley, also in *LSB* 563. MH

humanity, and in his place stepped the bare idea of a god. In the place of the Holy Trinity, of the Father, the Son, and the Holy Ghost stepped every insipid trinity of the eighteenth and nineteenth centuries: the good, the true, the beautiful; god, virtue, immortality; god, freedom, fatherland as they were called. The reality of God dwindled therein and an insipid thought of a god stepped into its place. "For our God is a consuming fire" (Heb. 12:29). So spoke the Christians of the New Testament. It was just this reality that was experienced anew in the Reformation. When the god of Aristotle [384–322 BC] returned again to the New Testament, everything would be different. For Kant [1724–1804], Schleiermacher [1768–1834], and Hegel [1770–1831], God was no longer a consuming fire, but a comforting thought. If God is truly God, I am a forsaken sinner. Luther knew this. If god exists, then I am fine from here on out, then he is the guarantor of my immortality; he guarantees me that my virtuous life will find a rich reward; that is the very great expression of Kant's thought concerning god. "In the midst of hell would sin, drive us to despair;"[246] So the old Evangelical Church sang with Luther. Hardly anyone understands that now. But when reason is the judge of what is and is not credible in the biblical revelation, then yes, man has become the judge of God. So it happened in the events of the eighteenth century.

One of the profound works of the early German

---

[246] Martin Luther, *Mitten wir im Leben sind,* "In the Very Midst of Life"; WA 53.515–16; *LSB* 755. MH

enlightenment is the *Théodicée* by Gottfried Wilhelm Leibniz [1646–1716].[247] *Théodicée* means the justification of God. The Reformation was about the justification of men. The modern Enlightenment came to be about the justification of God. Is there a God? Can I believe in a God who permits what, according to my thoughts, a God of love would not allow, disease and death, pestilence and famine, war and bloodshed?! Why does God allow that? In the Reformation, man stood as a defendant before the judgment seat of God. Now in the age of the *Théodicée*, man has set himself in the judgment seat and put God in the defendant's seat. How can God, who is completely perfect allow both suffering and evil in the world? Leibniz sought to show in his book that our world is the best conceivable world. He apologized, so to say, for God and made a defense for him against the accusations of men. Others have not done this. And so the modern spiritual life has become a process in which the people wage war against the living God of the Bible and Christianity, whether this process is now guided by means of an esoteric philosophy or on the rough arms of the great revolutions of modern times from the French Revolution to Russian Bolshevism.

So the modern world has become a world in which man no longer fears the judgment of God. And why should he? In the moment that I make my reason to be the judge in all spiritual matters, the innermost importance of the

---

247 Leibniz, Gottfried Wilhelm, and Johann Christoph Gottsched. *Theodicee: das ist, Versuch von der Güte Gottes, Freyheit des Menschen, und vom Ursprunge des Bösen, bey dieser vierten Ausgabe durchgehends verbessert. Hannover: Förster. 1744.*

recognition that I am a sinner vanishes. Luther once said that the original sin that sticks to men is so deep and such an evil corruption of human nature that reason cannot understand it, but it must be believed from God's Word.[248] That means it belongs to the nature of human sin that a man can no longer recognize that he is a sinner and rebels against God by means of his reason. So the knowledge of sin in modern humanity is extinguished, and therewith also the sense that men need the forgiveness of sins. "The forgiveness of sin," as Claus Harms [1778–1855] in one of the most famous theses from the 1817 Reformation Jubilee would say, "still cost money in the sixteenth century, in the nineteenth it is completely free, and everyone freely rewards himself with it."[249] Yes, one rewards himself with it. "How can one live," Goethe once asked, "if one doesn't daily absolve himself and others?" As a child Goethe still had to learn from the catechism, "In this Christian Church he daily and richly forgives me and all believers." And so this became the daily forgiveness of sins of which it was said, "one rewards himself with it."[250] "If the trumpets of Judgment Day were to sound," wrote [Jean Jacques] Rousseau [1712–1778], the spiritual father of the French

---

[248] SA III.1.2; BKS 434. MH
[249] Claus Harms, *Beleuchtung der fünf und neunzig reformatorischen Streitsätze, welche Herr Claus Harms gegen allerhand vermeintliches 'Irr- und Wirrwissen' dieser Zeit herausgegeben hat. Leipzig, 1818, bei Johann Ambrosius Barth*, p. 21. MH
[250] Spoken on December 6, 1825, to one "Müller." Goethe, Johann W, Franz Deibel, and Friedrich Gundolf. *Goethe Im Gespraech. Leipzig, 1907*, p. 249. MH

Revolution, at the beginning of his *Confessions*,[251] "I would stand before the world and judge myself with this book in my hand. I would say loudly, Here it is, what I have done, what I thought, and what I am. . . . gather around me, you absolute being in the innumerable crowd of my co-creators. Let them hear my confession. . . . And who dares to say to you: I was better than these other men."[252]

One has to compare Rousseau's hypocritical and vain *Confessions* [pub. 1782] with the *Confessions*[253] of Augustine, Rousseau's defense of himself with Augustine's accusation of himself, if he wants to understand the magnitude of this spiritual revolution. Modern man looks forward to the judgment of God with an unshakeable peace of the soul. Or more correctly, he does not allow the thought of the divine judgment to disturb his peace, because he no longer thinks of any divine judgment. Even when he still speaks about God, he still basically believes in himself, in humanity and his glory, greatness, and power. "With might of ours can not be done, soon were our loss effected, the best and holiest deeds must fail, To break sin's dread oppression."[254] So Luther sang, and on the last bit of paper he wrote before dying, "We are all beggars, *hoc est verum*."[255] We are all beggars, that is true! No, modern man does not believe that anymore. He only knows the terrible

---

[251] Finished in 1771, but published posthumously. MH
[252] *Confessions*, Book I. MH
[253] Written in AD 397/98. MH
[254] Martin Luther, "A Mighty Fortress Is Our God." WA 35.455; *LW* 298.
[255] WA 85, TR V.317–18. MH

self-importance of man, the praise of the one great, powerful, and divine: "Mine is the kingdom, mine is the power, mine is the glory. Did you not accomplish everything yourself, my sacredly glowing heart,"[256] as Goethe's Prometheus said.[257]

Truly, it is a frightening revolution in the spiritual life of the West that has been accomplished here, frightening in that on the one hand the progress of modern culture rests on it, and on the other hand that it must go with it. It is frightening that the European man of the last 250 years is convinced that he has been the first to recognize the reality of the world and of man, when he has forsaken the great reality of life. He believes that the God of the Bible, as the judge of the entire world, that the wrath of God, the last judgment, and that eternal damnation is a figment of the imagination. He comes as the man who actually cleaned up these fantasies. He does not notice that he actually exchanged living reality for a paper theory. He thinks the great realities of life, the living God, the sin of man, and the divine judgment are mere theories. And he thinks his theories, his made-up god that does not create or judge, and, what is more, his idea of a man who is no longer a

---

[256] Quoted from "Great Poems of the Romantic Era," Stanley Appelbaum (New York: Dover Publications, 1995), p. 7.

[257] " 'Prometheus' is a poem by Johann Wolfgang von Goethe, in which the character of the mythic Prometheus addresses God (as Zeus) in misotheist accusation and defiance. The poem was written between 1772 and 1774 and first published in 1789 after an anonymous and unauthorized publication in 1785 by Friedrich Heinrich Jacobi. It is an important work of the Sturm und Drang movement." Wikipedia "Prometheus (Goethe)." MH

sinner and does not need grace is reality. Goethe anticipated this strange event, the exchange of life's realities for theories about life, and he pointed to it with the penetrating word: "We have studied ourselves out of life." That is the deep, intellectual, spiritual distress of the modern world. They have exchanged the great reality to which the biblical revelation points for paper theories. In reality, the men of our time, so proud of their sense of reality, live in an illusion.

But now the time has come when God will smash this illusion. That is the deepest sense of the spiritual change the West has experienced in the midst of the world historical events of our time. The era that began 250 years ago with a powerful protest against the Christian tradition of progress has come to an end. "Man is free!" "Man is good!" "Human reason is capable of exploring the mysteries of the world and of man!" "The earth is no vale of tears!" "We can make it a state of happiness and perfection." What has become of this hopefulness?

> "How fair, O Man, do you, your palm
> branch holding
> Stand at the century's unfolding
> In proud and noble manhood's prime with
> faculties revealed,
> With spirits fullness full earnest mild, in
> action-wealthy stillness,
> the ripest son of time. . . ."[258]

So sang Schiller in the year 1789. The French Revolution

---

[258] "The Artists," by Friedrich Schiller, translation by Marianna Wertz (www.schillerinstitute.org).

broke out a few months later, and the "ripest son of time," man, who was by nature good and noble, raced as an arsonist through the world.

What has become of human freedom? What of the powerful new knowledge of nature? Where does this technology end that has changed the face of the earth? In the hell of Stalingrad where one of the most modern industrial cities of the world, a triumph of the spirit and will of man has sunk into a terrible state![259] Where do the powerful poems and philosophies of our classical time end? These who believed that they had discovered greatness of men and their reason! How is it that many of the most meaningful poets and thinkers of this epoch have been destroyed by meaningless suffering, profound earthly pain, and boundless despair? One thinks of the deeply unhappy and solitary life of [Christian Friedrich] Hebbel [1813–1863], of the suicide of [Heinrich von] Kleist [1777–1811], of those who perished in the night of insanity like [Nikolaus] Lenau [1802–1850], [Friedrich] Hölderin [1770–1843], and [Friedrich] Nietzche [1844–1900]. And then one thinks of the corresponding countless human fates of the mass of our people, particularly in the great cities. He who looks into their souls and sees the emptiness, the naked despair that they hide behind the mask of the "joy of life," he knows that men have lost the boundless faithfulness that comes from God to their own undoing.

---

[259] The battle of Stalingrad (Germans verses the Russians) August 23, 1942 to February 2, 1943, was one of the most bloody military engagements in all history with two million casualties. MH

But where one is not yet awakened from this illusion, from this faith in men, there the violent events of our time should awaken them from their slumber. So the World War addressed us as it did so many young theologians of that time. At that time we were awakened from the sweet dream that "man is good"! Amidst the barrages we forgot how to say with Goethe: "Your eyes were the happiest to ever see her, as she was, she was so beautiful."[260] And our soldiers, who fight for life and death today on the endless battlefields in the Russian winter, they have an even starker experience. They learn from terrible scenes what happens when men trade faith in God for faith in themselves. They learn how it ends for men and peoples who do not believe in a divine judgment but set themselves up as the judge of God. They perish in the judgment of divine wrath because he who today does not recognize the judgment of God upon men and peoples, upon small and great nations, upon all the earth, yes, he who even today does not recognize that God's judgment is real, he is afflicted with an incurable blindness.

But the more God himself destroys the illusions that the proud men of the modern world have made, so much stronger will the backlash be where faith in man has long been in vogue.. A philosopher of our day who was brought up in a strict Catholic home, who as a younger man was estranged from the Christian faith and in the years after the world war returned to the faith and his church, described this backlash at the beginning of the present war as he lay

---

[260] Goethe, *Faust II, Vers 11300 ff. Lynkeus der Türmer.*

dying of an incurable disease. He wrote a farewell to his students in full view of the face of death during the Advent of 1939. Therein he wrote, "*Metanoeite*. Repent!" That has been the call since the days of Napoleon [1769–1821]. It calls even louder to the European intelligencia. *Metanoeite*—the call has rung throughout the nineteenth century and reinforced itself in the twentieth century with the cannon thunder of both great wars. It will be with great astonishment that some will look back on the last 150 years and see how at first it was but a small spiritual movement, but then larger sections of the intelligencia of the West began to see at last that the age without Christ has not brought the freedom so many others had promised. A certain unholiness began to announce itself by the power of the intelligencia, and what this unholiness exposed is wrapped up in the profound words of St. Augustine, who from his own experience recorded in his "Confessions" what he had once preached: *Jussisti enim Deus, ut sibi ipsa sit sua poenea omnis inordinatus animus.*—"For thou has appointed it, and so it proves, every man's inordinate affection shall be his own affliction."[261] Yes, he who has investigated a little into the spiritual life of the modern peoples of the West, notices how the backlash grows ever stronger against pure faith in man and culture. The judgment of God that is seen on earth today opens the eyes of many men to the reality of God and the reality of men. It opens the hearts of many men anew to the blessed message of the Reformation, the message of the justification of

---

[261] *Confessions* I, ch. 12.

sinners.

This should not be understood as if masses of men will suddenly find their way to church. There is no question. God's judgment never works in such a way that it only awakens repentance and faith. It also works obstinacy, and for many men of our day the way will not lead to the cultivation of their faith, but will end in despair. It is just as hard for the natural man today to believe in the Gospel as it was at any other time. But something else has happened. There are today more men than in the last two generations who once again know that there is a judgment from God. They know that it is not God who has to be justified before us, but we who need to be justified before him. And there are more men than we realize who have acknowledged the powerlessness, the complete helplessness, and the forlornness as deeply as it is possible for the human spirit to acknowledge of itself. In all these men, who are clueless, helpless, and standing on the edge of despair, it may be that without their even knowing it the primeval question of man, the question of a gracious God, has become the one great question of their lives. These men are asking for the Gospel even if they have no idea at all what the Gospel is. They, who are estranged from the Church and her proclamation, knock on the door of the Church and ask.

Oh what a great hour for the church of the Lutheran Reformation that would be! Because they ask for that which God entrusted to our church during the Reformation. They ask for the message of the Reformation, because the message of the Reformation is none other than the Gospel of the New Testament, the sanctifying news of the salvation of forlorn men. Nowhere would the deepest essence, the real state of man be so clear, so unsparingly, so starkly uncovered as in the New Testament. "For the word of God is living and active, sharper than any two-edged sword, piercing to the division of soul and of spirit, of joints and of marrow, and discerning the thoughts and intentions of the heart" (Heb. 4:12). Yes, this word uncovers men so mercilessly that even within Christendom one can hardly bear to think of it. One has ever again attempted to protect men from it and allow a little good to remain in him. When Luther came, the stark recognition of men and their sin as the Bible teaches was renewed.

> "Fast bound in Satan's chains I lay,
> Death brooded darkly o'er me,
> Sin was my torment night and day,
> In sin my mother bore me;
> Yea, deep and deeper still I fell,
> Life had become a living hell,
> So firmly sin possessed me.
>
> My own good works availed me naught,
> No merit they attaining;
> Free will against God's judgment fought,
> Dead to all good remaining.
> My fears increased till sheer despair
> Left naught but death to be my share;
> The pangs of hell I suffered. [262]

Only where one knows this deep forlornness of men does one understand the deep divine miracle of the

---

[262] http://www.musicanet.org/robokopp/hymn/dearchri.html; see also *LSB* 556:3–4.

salvation of the forlorn, there the comfort of the Gospel is understood completely:

> With thee counts nothing but thy grace
> To cover all our failing.
> The best life cannot win the race,
> Good works are unavailing.
> Before thee no one glory can,
> And so must tremble every man,
> And live by thy grace only.[263]

Only there does one understand the Lord Christ completely. Because there the understanding of Jesus Christ as Redeemer is what Luther's doctrine of justification is about. I am nothing. I can do nothing. I know nothing. I have nothing. If I relied on myself then my life would be for all eternity forlorn and lost. But I have a Savior "who became to us wisdom from God, righteousness and sanctification and redemption" (1 Cor. 1:30). I would never even exist of my own power. I have nothing to bring before God. I will never have a righteousness of my own, never be able to save myself. But I have a Savior. Luther was concerned with nothing else than the glory of Jesus Christ as the Savior of sinners. That is the sense of his doctrine of justification. It is the glory of Jesus Christ that he is the Savior of the forlorn, the Savior of sinners, he and he alone.

That was the message of the Reformation. It is nothing other than the pure Gospel itself. It is the message that God has entrusted to our Church. It is the message that we have

---

[263] http://www.bach-cantatas.com/Texts/Chorale085-Eng3.html; AE 53.224; WA 35.492. See also *LSB* 607, "From Depths of Woe." MH

to speak at this time to all men, the questioning, the doubting, the despairing that knock at the door of the Church. The focus of this message is the great task of the Church in these changing times, and this task has been entrusted to us alone. Therefore we are all responsible, the whole congregation, every one of us. So we will ask in this hour: Am I a living witness of this in my life so that a person could see the Gospel as it was newly discovered in the Lutheran Reformation? Do we undergo the great and hard times in which God, the Lord, forms us as though we are made happy and comforted by the Gospel? Are we, during these tremendously difficult times of war, bearers of the peace of God about which the apostle said, "Therefore, since we have been justified by faith, we have peace with God through our Lord Jesus Christ" (Rom. 5:1)? Is our house still a church in miniature, as the houses of our forefathers were, within which the catechism still is learned and prayed? Is our congregation a true evangelical congregation, a congregation of justified sinners? Or are we perhaps in our lives a hindrance to the great message that we have to speak to men during these changing times? In any case we should know the message of the Reformation remains even when we have forgotten it and unlearned it, because it is the Gospel itself. And the Gospel, the living and powerful Word of God, makes its way through the world even when we ourselves deny it.

In the first year of this war, the early summer of 1940, in one week I received two letters from the Far East, the one came from Hanhan, from the Church of the

Righteousness of Faith, as our church is called in China. These Chinese Christians who in the midst of the Great War had to fight the Japanese for their land maintained their church with terrible sacrifice during that time. They prayed therein that more would be done from Germany, that soon beneficial letters would be received in China presenting the Lutheran faith. The other letter came out of Japan, from a Lutheran congregation in Tokyo, and it contained a very similar prayer. These Evangelical Lutheran Japanese, who belong to the leading classes of their people, would like to translate Luther documents and writings concerning the Lutheran Reformation into Japanese, and asked for counsel and help from the motherland of the Lutheran Reformation. The man who wrote the letter had completed all the training there was in Eastern Buddhism and then became an evangelical [Lutheran] pastor. He discussed why Japan needs the Lutheran Reformation, because they understand Jesus Christ as the Savior of sinners, and not only as a teacher. Teachers of wisdom and of morals, the Far East has in superabundance, but they need a Savior. There in the Far East, on this side and that side of the Oriental Sea is the front of a harsh war in which the nations have turned against each other for years, and both ask for the message of the Reformation because they want Jesus Christ. Through all the peoples of the earth, during the time of the great wars, during these changing times in which we live, kings ask for Christ and his Gospel, for the message of the Reformation. In them we hear this call, look to him who is the Savior of all men and all people, and say to him,

> In the river of time we are your people,
> Thou master of all time.
> We are your people in eternity,
> For you are king of all.
> You are our Alpha and Omega,
> the beginning and the end.
> There stands the Cross of Golgotha
> Upon which all time wends.[264]

---

[264] *"Wir sind ein Volk im Strom der Zeit,"* sts. 5–7, by Hugo Reich (1854–1935). MH

Luther's Faith in the One Holy Church
Augsburg High Peace Festival[265]
August 8, 1943[266]

For three hundred years the Evangelical Church of the Augsburg Confession has been celebrating the Festival of the Peace of Augsburg, in good and in evil times, in carefree years of peace and in hard times of war. For three hundred years the right that the Evangelical faith won in this city has been of self-evident value. Will it remain so forever? What isn't questioned today? It is not self-evident, but it is a miracle of divine mercy and divine patience that the towering houses of God in this city have not yet been razed to soot and ashes like the ancient churches of West Germany. And it is just as much a miracle of God that our Evangelical Lutheran Church has not yet been taken from us. It is not self-evident that it will remain. Therefore, we must be clear that a great deal of the churchly life of evangelical Germany is built upon the loyalty, and the spirit of sacrifice, the faith and love of our fathers. But one cannot live on the inheritance of the fathers alone. In the coming spiritual war that will follow this great world war, we will not stand if we cannot find the same faith, the same loyalty, and the same willingness to sacrifice as our fathers of the sixteenth and seventeenth centuries had.

---

[265] The festival was founded to celebrate the Peace of Westphalia in 1648. MH

[266] *Vortrag [Lecture]: Augsburg, Hohes Friedensfest (8 Aug 1943) "Luthers Glaube an die Eine Heilige Kirche."* Feuerhahn no. 246a. MH

In the coming fight, the question of what the Church is will be a great one. As in all times in which congregational life is shaken to the very foundations, the question of the Church of God is already heard today by perceiving ears, the question of the congregation, and the promise is heard within it, that "the gates of hell will not prevail against it" [Matt. 16:18]. Does this Church exist? What is this mystery? What is the one Holy Church, of which the confession of the Christian faith speaks? Today, the world judges us with this question. The other confessions judge Lutheranism with this question. Let us think about this during this celebratory hour of the Festival of the Peace of Augsburg. Let us think about what we as Lutheran Christians have for an answer. This we will do by remembering Luther's strong faith in the one Holy Church.

There is no harsher reproach raised against Martin Luther than the allegation that he has destroyed the unity of the Church. Yes, even more, that he is one of the great destroyers of the Church. Naturally, this reproach also sits in judgment of us who confess the faith of the Lutheran Reformation and our Church that is called the Evangelical Lutheran Church. This is why the Evangelicals in old Augsburg had to endure so much suffering until they were allowed to celebrate their first Festival of Peace in 1650. It was then still not only human malice that drove their Catholic compatriots and the Catholic clergy to fight against the Evangelical cause, even if the suffering and sin of humanity also played a very great role in this fight. No, even in the fight that the Jesuits led against the Reformation in Augsburg, great concern for the Church would be revealed because the Church, her unity, yes, her existence, seemed to be threatened by Luther and the Reformation. Only those who share this great concern, who understand how people on both sides of Christendom were willing to fight for the preservation of the Church, they alone are able to understand that era, its significance and its misery.

The poet Gertrude von Le Fort [1876–1971] gave a moving account that described the destruction of Magdeburg in the year 1631. In the end it describes how the evangelical cathedral preacher said farewell standing before his beloved towering cathedral for the last time. "Inside, the imperial host celebrated their idolatrous mass, and outside the burning ruins spread out before him. The city Magdeburg was like the ruined city of Jerusalem in the Gospel of the Tenth Sunday after Trinity. A wet wind assaulted his face with the smell of the charred rubble, and still another carried a stench from the buried cellars where the many, many dead lay, who fled down there only to die a miserable death of suffocation. Then he stepped into the entrance and heard the confession of faith from the altar: *'Credo in unum Deum Patrem omnipotentum factorem coeli et terrae, visibilium omnium et invisibilium.'* 'I believe in one God, Father Almighty, maker of heaven and earth, of things visible and invisible.' He listened. 'This was the old confession of faith, the same one that he himself had spoken with deep respect so many times in this towering cathedral, the rich confession of his fathers, and if God willed, of all his children and grandchildren would speak it too! It seized him with complete wonderment that he would hear this confession one last time in his beloved cathedral at this moment of farewell . . . for a moment he completely forgot that it was the papists who had begun it . . . and he listened a bit longer, 'and in one lord Jesus Christ, the only begotten Son of God . . . God of God, Light of Light, very God of very God' and then sentence after sentence to the end of the Second Article: 'and will come again in glory to judge the living and the dead.' There in spirit he saw [into the future] as the destroyed city cellars trembled once again with the resurrection of the twenty thousand dead. And now, Christendom, responsible for the twenty thousand dead and buried in the ruins of Magdeburg and gathered together there for the judgment of the world, must be prepared to fall at the feet of grace, the all-embracing grace of Jesus Christ, whose kingdom shall have no end. That was the pardon of Christendom, absolution for a broken love, his kingdom will have no end, and the kingdom of his love would overcome all separation. And now his spirit looked upon the completion of the kingdom of Christ, the New Jerusalem, there from the interior of the cathedral a new voice penetrated his ear: '*Et unam Sanctum catholicam et apostolicam ecclesiam.*—I believe one holy, catholic, and apostolic Church.' And then he joined in the confession saying: 'I believe in one Baptism for the forgiveness of sins.' "

To me, this pious poet's description is the most beautiful expression of the deep tragedy that hangs over the fight between confessions and over the confessional splitting of Christendom in all times. Faith in the one Holy Church of God, this was the prerequisite for the deep earnestness of that discussion. Our Fathers saw that the one holy catholic Church of God was in decline amongst the papists. So they held fast with strong loyalty and unspeakable sacrifice for the Gospel as it was understood by the Reformation. The Catholics thought that the Reformation threatened the unity and existence of the Church. So they fought each other. Both sides of the Church fought for the one holy, catholic Church of God.

Only when one understands that can one take seriously the reproach that was heaved against Luther and the Lutheran Church. Even today, when at least in German Catholicism a better and deeper understanding of Luther has been awakened, and one truly believes that Luther threw his protest against a decaying hierarchy and secularized church out of his inner Christian conviction and faith, even today there remains this one great reproach, that Luther went too far, that he set his own judgment over and against the judgment of the whole church and the highest teaching office. That he is the founder of modern subjectivism and individualism, and so, even if against his will, he is the destroyer of the Church and her unity.

This reproach seems to be confirmed by that which the Protestants themselves have said. Has not modern Protantism celebrated Luther since the beginning of the Enlightenment as the liberator of the individual from the prison of the Church? "The solitude of the soul with its God," that is the Protestant sense of religion. So I was taught as a student by my dogmatics professor, who would treat everything philosophically.[267] Protestantism no longer spoke of one Church of Christ, of one communion of saints. "Protestantism can do without church," or so [Adolf von] Harnack [1851–1930], the great church historian tirelessly imprinted upon us students.[268] He then preferred to abolish the misleading use of the word "church," just like the philosophical *Führer* of modern Protestantism, the great son of this city, Ernst Troeltsch [1865–1923]. But this was not only done to the learned, but also to simple members of the congregation.

Yes, if they are still members of a congregation in any sense at all, these individual men who come to church for their own private edification, to which church the minister goes to satisfy his own private needs, here today and there tomorrow, individually, and alone. They no longer know what it means to confess: "I believe in one Holy Church, I

---

[267] "My great teacher in Systematic Theology was Heinrich Scholz who later as colleague and friend of Karl Barth in Münster taught Philosophy and helped as one the great polyhistors of our time, to lay the philosophical foundations of modern mathematics and physics." Sasse, *Reminiscences of an Elderly Student*. Heinrich Scholz (1884–1956) was at Berlin 1910 to 1917. See Scholz's main systematics work, *Religionsphilosophie von D. Dr. Heinrich Scholz*. (Berlin: Verlag Von Reuther & Reichard, 1921). The copy of this book in Walther Memorial Library (Concordia Theological Seminary) is from Sasse's library. Almost the entire book is underlined with marginal notations in Sasse's hand. MH

[268] Dr. George Beto wrote to A. R. Suelflow on Dec. 18, 1989, "I recall in one of his lectures he [Sasse] quoted Adolph Harnack and almost emotionally referred to him as 'my great teacher.'" This occurred in 1961 to 62, when Sasse guest lectured at Concordia Theological Seminary, Springfield, during Beto's presidency. MH

believe in the communion of saints!" Let's be honest, the Evangelical Church in Germany in many areas is already dead because of this individualism. Other areas lie dying, seized by an apparently incurable disease. From where does this disease come? Has it infected our body from elsewhere? Or was it there in our blood from the beginning as our fellow Catholic Christians claim, as one consequence of the Reformation that was in its very essence the dissolution of the Church?

When we answer this reproach, we will not take the matter lightly. Yes, we can ask the counter question: What was the unity of the Church's condition before the Reformation? A half a millennium previous a pope placed a bull on the chief altar of the *Hagia Sophia* [Church] in Constantinople, the great shrine of the Greek Church in which dreadful anathemas abolished the communion between the Eastern and Western churches. This split remains still today. So Luther cannot be to blame. Around 1400 there was strife in Western Christendom between two and at times three papacies that accused and excommunicated one another themselves. Neither can Luther be to blame for this. But the reproach is not answered by this. One can never lose his own blame merely by putting the blame on another. It must be asked: What did Luther believe concerning the Church? How did he understand the Church? Yes, it could be that he had a much deeper understanding of the Church than his opponents. He understood her so well because he did not understand her deepest essence on the basis of human theories. For even the most venerable theories were still human theories, but he understood her on the basis of God's Word. And it just might be that the truth about the Church, which Luther found, waits for the day when all of Christendom will find it also. The truth knocks on the door of the Roman Church even today and waits to see if anyone is prepared to let her in.

In any case anyone who knows Luther and has studied his writings will have to admit that if there was ever a theologian that immersed himself in the deepest mysteries of God and the Church, it was Luther. And even more: If there was ever a Christian man who lived in the reality of the Church and the communion of saints, then one would have to say that it was our Reformer. He who experienced the deepest loneliness truly knew what the loneliness of the soul with its God is: God and the soul, the soul and its God. But he also knew that no one came to the faith on his own. "I believe, that I cannot by my own reason or strength believe in Jesus Christ, my Lord, or come to him, but the Holy Ghost has called me through the Gospel, enlightened me with his gifts, sanctifies and keeps me in the true faith, just as he calls, gathers, and enlightens the whole Christian Church on earth and keeps her with Jesus Christ in the one true faith."[269] The faith of an individual Christian is never without the faith of the whole Church because it is the same Holy Spirit that wakens the individual to faith in Jesus Christ that also gathers all into the Church as the people of God. And he gives all his goods and gifts in this

---

[269] SC, Creed III. MH

community: "In this Christian Church he daily and richly forgives me and all believers all our sins." Because Luther lived in this reality of the Church of God, he was able speak about her so simply and plainly. Yes, in general it is a characteristic of the great teachers of the Church that they are able to speak of the great mysteries of God so that even the simplest member of the congregation can understand them.

Against all the learned speculation concerning the Church, Luther posed the thesis: "A seven-year-old child knows what the church is, namely, holy believers and sheep who hear the voice of their Shepherd."[270] In order to avoid the possibility of a false understanding of the Church arising, he used the un-German word *Church*. The people, and so also Luther meant by the word "church" a building made of wood and stone. But in reality Church meant the "holy Christian people on earth, in whom Christ lives, works, and rules"[271] This people of God, this Christendom, as he named it, is "the noblest work of God from whose will all is made, therein the great miracle happens daily and sin is forgiven, death taken away, righteousness and eternal life are given, which no one sees except through faith."

No one sees except by faith the miracle of God that happens daily in the Church. Faith alone sees the reality of the Church. On this point, the contrast with what Rome understands about the Church begins to emerge. What Luther reproached his Roman opponents for is that they did

---

[270] SA 3, XII, 2; BKS 459 (see note 8; also WA 51.524 note. 6). MH
[271] AE 41.144; WA 50.625. MH

not take this article of faith seriously: "I believe in one holy, catholic and apostolic Church." For him the Church is no visible article, the Church is an article of faith. Were the Church, as the great Jesuit theologian [Robert] Bellarmine, [1542–1621] an opponent of the reformers maintained, as visible as the kingdom of France and the Republic of Venice, then it would not belong to the confession of faith.[272] I cannot see the Church, the people of God, the Body of Christ, or the temple of the Holy Ghost, as the realities of this world are seen. If I stand outside the Church of St. Peter in Rome and see and hear as the pope faces the crowds of people and celebrates and gives the blessing *"urbi et orbi,"*[273] then I still have still not seen the Church.

So did Luther only know of one invisible church? Of one ideal that is not yet reached here on earth, a Platonic state, as the opponents mockingly accuse? Is he also a representative of the doctrine that there are two churches, a visible and invisible church, the visible to which all the baptized belong, and the invisible to which all elect belong? *No*! This doctrine, as some of the Reformed churches

---

[272] "The one true Church is the community of humans brought together by profession of the true faith and communion in the same sacraments, under the rule of recognized pastors and especially of the sole vicar of Christ on earth, the Roman Pontiff. . . . The Church is indeed a community [coetus] of humans, as visible and palpable as the community of the Roman people, or the kingdom of France, or the Republic of Venice." *Disputationes de Controversiis Christianae Fidei adversus huius Temporis Haereticus* (1586–1593) (Venice, 1721), 53; quoted in Bernard P. Prusak, *The Church Unfinished: Ecclesiology through the Centuries* (Paulist Press, 2004), p. 278. MH

[273] "To the city and to the world" refers to the papal blessing given at public addresses by the pope in Rome. MH

would express it, is not Luther's doctrine. Truthfully, he did occasionally speak of the Invisible Church. On occasion He also spoke of a twofold Christendom: "The first, which is natural, basic, essential, and true, we shall call 'spiritual, internal Christendom.' The second, which is man-made and external, we shall call 'physical, external Christendom.'"[274] But immediately following he said this, "Not that we want to separate them from each other; rather, it is just as if I were talking about a man and called him 'spiritual' according to his soul, and 'physical' according to his body."[275] For Luther, there are not two churches, one visible and one invisible, but only one Church with a visible and an invisible side.

When from the balcony I look at this church on Sunday and out into the congregation gathered for Divine Service, my eyes cannot distinguish this gathering from a worldly gathering or of the gathering of any other religious cooperative of the world. And yet I know: In, with, and under the outer gathering there is the Church of God. I know it certainly enough, because the means of grace are there: the Holy Gospel, Holy Baptism, and the Sacrament of the Altar. Where the Gospel of the grace of God is proclaimed, the justification of sinners, completely free, without works of the Law but by faith alone, there Christ is present in his Word. There he forgives sin. Where a child of man is baptized, there Christ is present. There he, who is the true Father of all, speaks what the children in heaven

---

[274] AE 39.70; WA 6.296. MH
[275] AE 39.70; WA 6.297. MH

and on earth call his great word of grace: "I have called you by name, you are mine" [Isa. 43:1]. Whatever becomes of these children of men, if they remain with Christ the Lord or leave him, if his way leads to eternal life or to eternal death, what was said to him there in the hour of Baptism remains valid as God's offer and is meant seriously. As deep as a baptized soul may fall, as far as he may flee from God, the fatherly arms of God remain open for him, as long as this life remains. And the forgiveness that the Lord Christ has acquired for him is certain when he returns to his Baptism with sincere repentance. And where a congregation celebrates the Lord's Supper according to his institution, there Jesus Christ is truly present according to his divine and human natures. He serves the sinners with that which he gave up and shed for them on Golgotha; with his true body and blood, and with these he incorporates them all into one, he incorporates them anew as members of his Body.

Where the means of grace, the Gospel, Baptism, and the Lord's Supper are, there Jesus Christ is really present. Our eyes don't see him. Yet he is there, so real, so near, as only he is in his own. And in the inconspicuous means of the Word, Baptism, and the   Lord's Supper he performs the great miracle of his saving mercy. A miracle is not merely such a thing as the resurrection of Jairus's daughter [Mark 5:22–24, 35–43] or the stilling of the storm [Luke 8:24]. A miracle is the forgiveness of sins, which he speaks to us. A miracle is the rebirth of Baptism. A miracle is the eating of his body and blood in the Sacrament of the Altar. These great things are hidden under the inconspicuous means of grace. The world does not see this and cannot see it. Our natural eyes perceive nothing of it, and yet the real presence of the Lord is there, the reality of his miracle, the reality of his Church.

That is the deepest essence of the Church as Luther understood it. The Church that Luther believed was the Church of the real presence. He believed in the Church because he believed in the real presence. Perhaps there are many among us who have wondered about that and perhaps have taken offence that Luther remained so stubborn in the strife over the Lord's Supper concerning the meaning of the words of institution: "This is my body." That is not his obstinate nature, but his great worry that the Church of the Reformation would lose that upon which the Church has always lived, faith in the real presence of Christ. If Christ is in a heavenly location far from this world, where he has only left behind authority, orders, and commands; if we confuse him with our fantasy, and must visualize him with our faith; if he is only present according to his divine nature, and not also according to his human nature as the God-man, who has taken on our poor flesh and blood, and is present with us according to his humanity, as he is present with the Father according to his divinity, then we are a lost little band in this world. Because, we have to admit that without him we are nothing, that without him and his presence, the Church is a helpless, poor, despairing band of men.

I believe in a Holy Church, that means: I believe that in

his means of grace Christ is present. Because it is so, because Christ gathers the Church around his living and present self, therefore it is a Church of the poor, the wretched, and the mean. The reign of Christ, the kingdom of Christ is, as Luther and his followers in the confession of our Church said, *cruce tectum*, hidden under the cross.[276] That Christ is Lord, that the world will finally see, namely, when he at the end of all things manifests his glory, and every knee bows before him, and ever tongue in heaven and on earth and under the earth confess that Jesus Christ is Lord to the glory of God the Father [Phil. 2:11]. But until then his glory is hidden to the eyes of the world, *cruce tectum*. And therefore the poor, the distressed, the persecuted, the misjudged, and the abused belong to the Church throughout the world until the very end of the Church.

As the true Christ is only the Christ who bears the wounds from suffering the cross, so the only true Church of Christ is the Church that is not a church of glory, but a Church of the cross. Where the church appears gleaming in glory, and accepts the power and honor of this world, something isn't right. A church before which the world powers bow is certainly a false church. A church to which the powers of the world pay homage, give their sympathy, and are subjugated to is no longer the church that the powers of this world have beaten on the cross. In 1539 Luther made the remark in his great "Letter on Councils and the Church" of how one could differentiate between the

---

[276] Ap VII.18; BKS 237.

one true Church and the false vainglorious imitation. There he says, "Seventh, the holy Christian people are externally recognized by the holy possession of the sacred cross. They must endure every misfortune and persecution, all kinds of trials and evil from the devil, the world, and the flesh (as the Lord's Prayer indicates) by inward sadness, timidity, fear, outward poverty, contempt, illness, and weakness, in order to become like their head, Christ. And the only reason they must suffer is that they steadfastly adhere to Christ and God's word, enduring this for the sake of Christ, Matthew 5 [:11], 'Blessed are you when men persecute you on my account.' They must be pious, quiet, obedient, and prepared to serve the government and everybody with life and goods, doing no one any harm. No people on earth have to endure such bitter hate; they must be accounted worse than Jews, heathen, and Turks. In summary, they must be called heretics, knaves, and devils, the most pernicious people on earth, to the point where those who hang, drown, murder, torture, banish, and plague them to death are rendering God a service. No one has compassion on them; they are given myrrh and gall to drink when they thirst. And all of this is done not because they are adulterers, murderers, thieves, or rogues, but because they want to have none but Christ, and no other God. Wherever you see or hear this, you may know that the holy Christian church is there, as Christ says in Matthew 5 [:11–12], 'Blessed are you when men revile you and utter all kinds of evil against you on my account. Rejoice and be glad, for your reward is great in heaven.' This too is a holy possession whereby the Holy Spirit not only sanctifies his people, but also blesses them."[277]

Ubi Christus, ibi ecclesia.[278] Where Christ is, there is the Church. In this word one the oldest fathers of the Church [Ignatius of Antioch; d. ca. 112] has expressed the mystery of the Church. It also expresses Luther's faith in the Church. *Ubi Christus, ibi ecclesia.* We men do not build the Church, not with the power of our faith, not with the holiness of our lives. Because if the Church is called a holy people, a communion of saints, that is not to be understood as it is ever more understood in Church history: The Church shall be a holy people, so we are concerned that only saints belong to her. Out with everyone who is not holy. The glory of Christ demands that. So, let us at least throw out the worst sinners! Then one begins to start classifying the sinners that must be excluded from the Church. How often has this been attempted in old and new times? How impressive is the highly moral Early Church or the newer communions that the one holy, one pure Church has produced. Or which, as the Donatists of the ancient world commanded, that the clergy at least be free of deadly sins. But just as often as it has been attempted to produce this ideal, has bitter disappointment been experienced. The communion of saints becomes the congregation of Pharisees.

Luther drew a thick line through all these endeavors. He pointed out, and this is one of the great benefits of his

---

[277] AE 41.164–65; WA 50.642. MH

[278] "Where Christ is, there is the church." Ignatius, Letter to the Smyrneans VIII. MH

thoughts concerning the Church, that a completely false understanding of the glory of Christ was operating here. Because if the actual office of Christ is that of Savior, then it is not his glory that he lives among the pure but among sinners. In a letter of spiritual counsel to his Brother Georg Spenlein [ca. 1486–1563],[279] the young Luther had on the April 8, 1516, once written the word of absolution to the man who wrote to [Luther] the curate of souls: "Learn Christ and him crucified. Learn to praise him and, despairing of yourself, say, 'Lord Jesus, you are my righteousness, just as I am your sin. You have taken upon yourself what is mine and have given to me what is yours. You have taken upon yourself what you were not and have given to me what I was not.' Beware of aspiring to such purity that you will not wish to be looked upon as a sinner, or to be one, for Christ dwells only in sinners. On this account he descended from heaven, where he dwelt among the righteous, to dwell among sinners."[280]

It was a turning point in Church history when this word was written because now for the first time it would be acknowledged what it means that the Church is the communion of saints: not a congregation that is more or less sinless, but a congregation of faithful sinners. It is the congregation that knows that our own doing is nothing even in the best life! It is the congregation that knows: I am nothing. I know nothing. I can do nothing. I have nothing to

---

[279] 1486–1563. - 1512 Universität Wittenberg, 1520 Augustinian Monk, 1520 Universität Erfurt, 1529 Pastor in Creuzburg, 1544 Pfarrer in Arnstadt, 1553 Pastor in Wüllersleben. MH
[280] AE 48.12–13; WA Br 1.35–36. MH

bring before God other than a cudgeled and smashed heart. I have no holiness or righteousness of my own and never will. But I have that which God has made our certainty and righteousness, justification, and redemption. Now, Luther could confess with a blessed certainty: "I believe in one Holy Church. Because this church is your people, and you alone are holy." The righteousness and the holiness of the Church is not a righteousness and holiness of men. It is the righteousness and holiness of Christ. The Church, which Luther believed, is the Church of justification and therefore the Church not of the Law, but of the Gospel.

I believe in one Holy Church. One Holy Church. When Luther passed through a graveyard, he felt the comforting nearness of blessed eternity. Because he knew here in this graveyard the saints would be resurrected on Judgment Day. I do not know who these saints are. But I know the dead that lie here have heard the Gospel once in their lives, they have believed in him, and those who believe in their Redeemer are holy.

And as Luther believed in the holiness of the Church, so he also believed in her unity and he saw this unity in time and space. The Church passes through the centuries from the earthly days of Christ to the day of his return, from the days of the apostles to the beloved Day of Judgment. Because it is not only the living that belong to the Church of God. In the Church of God we are bound with those who have believed in Christ before and with those not yet born who will have this faith and die a blessed death. This Church is always there, even in the darkest times of the church's decay. Church history did not end with the New Testament and then begin again in 1517 or 1530. No even in the centuries of the papal church, in the Middle Ages, our fathers belonged to the Church of God: "Yet, by means of his power and miracles, God has seen to it that under the pope there has nevertheless remained the church: first, Holy Baptism; second, [the reading of] the text of the Holy Gospel from the pulpit in everyone's native language; third, the holy forgiveness of sins and absolution, both in the confessional and publicly; fourth, the Holy Sacrament of the Altar, which has been offered to Christians at Easter and also during the year, even though they have robbed it of one of its forms; fifth, the calling or ordaining to the parish ministry, the preaching office, or the care of souls, to bind and to loose, and to comfort at the time of death and at other times; for many have retained the custom of holding the crucifix before the dying and of reminding them of the sufferings of Christ in which they should trust, etc.; finally, also prayer such as the Psalter, the Lord's Prayer, the Creed, and the Ten Commandments; also, many good hymns and canticles, both in Latin and German. Now where such articles have remained, there surely the church and a number of saints have remained, for they are all the ordinances and fruits of Christ with the exception of the robbery of the one form [of the Lord's Supper]. For that reason Christ has surely been here among his own with his Holy Spirit and has preserved the Christian faith in them."[281]

---

[281] AE 38.177–78; WA 38.221. MH

And as the Church passes through time, as she is there even when one thinks she has disappeared, so is she over all the earth wherever men call on the name of Christ. We also know how seriously the Evangelical Lutheran Church has taken church boundaries, with the boundaries of the Confessions. They refused and still refuse today to recognize a false understanding of the Gospel, an unbiblical baptism, or a sacrament of the altar that does not agree with the Gospel of Jesus. But they know that the Holy Church of God is not only contained in the Church of the Augsburg Confession, but throughout the world. Yes, even as the Roman Church itself does not refuse to recognize the Church of God among the church communions from which the Church of Rome is separated. Our confessions express the ecumenicity and catholicity of the Church of Christ in Luther's sense in the beautiful statement, "the article of the Catholic or common church, which is gathered together from all nations under the sun, is completely comforting and highly noteworthy, because the crowd of the godless is much greater, even innumerable, who bitterly hate the word and persecute it externally, as there are Turks, Mohammed, and other tyrants, and heretics, etc. Therefore true doctrine and the Church are often so completely suppressed and forsaken, as happened under the papacy, that there would be no Church and often seemed as if it disappeared completely. Therefore, that we may be certain and not doubt that a Christian Church lives on earth and is that which Christ brought into existence, even though the godless crowd is more numerous and greater, that even the

Lord Christ is here on earth in the assembly called the Church and daily works forgiveness of sins, daily hears the Law, daily brings abundant, steadfast comfort to the afflicted and refreshes them, so it is a comforting article of faith: I believe in a Catholic, common, Christian church. Therefore no one thinks it is possible that the church is just one more external police force to which this or that land is bound, as the Pope of Rome will say. But it certainly remains true that assembly of men is the true church who hear and though in the world truly believe in Christ, who have *one* gospel, *one* Christ, *one* baptism and Sacrament [of the Altar], who are guided by *one* Holy Spirit, even if they have completely different ceremonies."[282]

That is Luther's belief in the one Holy Church. That is the faith that our Evangelical Lutheran Church has confessed since the days of the Reformation. That is the faith in the Church that your fathers have confessed when here in Augsburg they gathered for one year in the house of St. Anna-College for Divine Service because their church building had been taken. That is the faith that they confessed as they in endless joy and with thankful hearts celebrated the first Festival of the Peace of Augsburg.

That is the faith in the one Holy Church that we confess. Today on the 8th of August 1943, four years into the Great War, do we know what this faith means? I believe in the one Holy Church, that means faith in a sense of world history in which God the Lord gathers his people out of the people of the world, out of all generations of history,

---

[282] Ap. VII.9, German; BKS 235

that is the sense of all history, that God gathers his people even from the German people, that he not only judges and punishes with his almighty Word, but he also saves and rescues in this time through which we now pass. We believe him because we believe in his Holy Church. We believe in the Church of God, the hidden kingdom of Christ in this world, that means to believe in them even in the midst of one of the greatest wars of all times, amidst rage and hate that disunites humanity from all men, because in this Church and Kingdom there is peace for all people. He alone is peace, because he alone has the full authority to say, "Peace I leave with you; my peace I give to you. Not as the world gives do I give to you. Let not your hearts be troubled, neither let them be afraid" (John 14:27).

And what the world is, we now know. What the world is we see in the destroyed cities of Germany, in the destroyed cathedrals of the Rhine that were houses of God for a thousand years, in the smoke-blackened ruins of the old churches of Hamburg, Lubeck, and Rostock. But through the meaningless misery of this time, through the distress of death and the deepest human despair, we hear this voice that speaks to the congregations there, "Peace I leave with you; my peace I give to you." And we speak with the apostles, "He himself is our peace" [Eph. 2:14]. And we pray with the Church of all times, "Amen. Come, Lord Jesus" [Rev. 22:20]! And we confess with heart and mouth, with the whole of Christendom: "I believe in the Holy Ghost, one Holy Christian Church, the communion of saints. Amen."

CPSIA information can be obtained at www.ICGtesting.com
Printed in the USA
LVOW08*2302041013

355438LV00004B/16/P

9 780982 158654